BUILDING
DEMOCRACY
ON SAND

ADVANCE PRAISE FOR

Building Democracy on Sand: Israel without a Constitution

"Arye Carmon's *Building Democracy on Sand* is a deeply personal, intellectually rich, and historically precise illumination of Israeli democracy, the institutions that undergird it, and the complex contours of the Zionist movement that animated its creation and have shaped its history. Marshaling decades of experience as a political analyst and president of the Israeli Democracy Institute, Carmon enables us to see clearly the forces that today imperil the state of Israel as well as how they might be mitigated. This book is urgent reading for all those who care about the future of liberal democracy, not only in Israel but around the world."

—**Ronald J. Daniels**, President, Johns Hopkins University

"For three decades, Arye Carmon has been one of Israel's most forthright and impassioned advocates for a permanent constitution to root the country's fragile democratic principles in deeper liberal foundations. In this poignant and incisive work—part personal memoir, part political history—Carmon traces the unfulfilled mission to fashion a secular, pluralistic, and inclusive democracy as it has confronted an escalating hegemonic campaign to reshape the state around rigid, orthodox religious values. The 'deepening crisis' of contending identities, he warns, must somehow be resolved consensually if Israeli democracy is to thrive and endure."

—**Larry Diamond**, Senior Fellow, Center on Democracy, Development and the Rule of Law, Freeman Spogli Institute for International Studies, and Bass University Fellow in Undergraduate Education, Stanford University

"Arye Carmon's book, part autobiography and part a deep analysis of Israel's secular-religious divide and fundamental identity crisis, is a vital read for policymakers and the public interested in Israel's future. His dissection of the 'Zionist deficit' and the factors creating the chasms within Israeli society, and his prescription for change—all derived from his decades of service in support of Israel's democratic well-being—are incisive and likely to promote a healthy and overdue debate about these issues."

—**Daniel Kurtzer**, Princeton University, US Ambassador to Israel (2001–2005)

BUILDING DEMOCRACY ON SAND

Israel without a Constitution

Arye Carmon

HOOVER INSTITUTION PRESS

Stanford University | Stanford, California

www.hoover.org

Hoover Institution Press Publication No. 705

Hoover Institution at Leland Stanford Junior University,
Stanford, California 94305-6003

First printing 2019
25 24 23 22 21 20 19   7 6 5 4 3 2 1

Manufactured in the United States of America

The paper used in this publication meets the minimum Requirements of the American National Standard for Information Sciences—Permanence of Paper for Printed Library Materials, ANSI/NISO Z39.48-1992. ⊚

Cataloging-in-Publication Data is available from the Library of Congress.
ISBN: 978-0-8179-2315-0 (pbk. : alk. paper)
ISBN: 978-0-8179-2316-7 (epub)
ISBN: 978-0-8179-2317-4 (mobi)
ISBN: 978 0 8179-2318-1 (PDF)

For a better, sustainable, and stable democratic way of life
for my grandchildren and their generational peers.

Contents

Foreword by George P. Shultz ix

Author's Note to the English-Language Edition xiii

Introduction 1

Part One: The Challenges of Sovereignty

1 Between Reason and Faith: Preliminary Notes 13

2 Diasporic Nation and Territorial Nations 33

3 The Zionist Deficit 41

4 "Negation of the Exile": Stumbling Block
 to Acculturation 49

5 The Gordian Knot: Religion and Nationhood 85

6 The Transition from Sovereignty-in-the-Making
 to Sovereignty 93

7 Ben-Gurionist Statism 105

8 The Ethos of Survival 121

9 The Centrality of Death in Israel 131

Part Two: The Religious Counterrevolution

10 The Interaction between Governance and Religion 149

11 Diverse Characteristics of the Counterrevolution
 in Religious Zionism 163

12 The Counterrevolution in the Chronological Mirror 185

Finale as a Prelude	233
Acknowledgments	241
Notes	243
About the Author	253
Index	255

Foreword
by George P. Shultz

Arye Carmon is the founder and first president of the Israel Democracy Institute (IDI), a leading think tank in Israel. I served as honorary chairman of the institute since its inception twenty-seven years ago and have taken pride in its important accomplishments. I have also served as the chairman of IDI's International Advisory Committee, enabling me to participate even more closely in the institute's activities as a "think-and-do" tank.

In his book *Building Democracy on Sand*, Arye Carmon draws on deep experience to offer the reader a fascinating inside look at the workings of Israel's unusual democracy. The Israel that is revealed in this book is quite different from the one most people know. In the media, Israel is mainly portrayed as a nation focused on physical survival. It is seen by both its supporters and its critics through the prism of national security and international diplomacy. Yet, in my many years of public service and particularly during my tenure as secretary of state, I became familiar with diverse aspects of Israel's story—its military, political, and economic development, as well as the extraordinary feat of absorbing a million immigrants from the former Soviet Union. I was always amazed that a small, young nation coped so well with all of these simultaneous, interlocking challenges.

Building Democracy on Sand explores the ways in which the fabric of Israeli democracy is an essential, underlying component of all aspects of national life. A product of Carmon's work at the Hoover Institution, Stanford University, it represents an attempt to diagnose crucial drawbacks at the heart of Israeli democracy, which faces threats to the very essence of its being. The crucial issue of state and religion has never been properly handled by the nation's leaders and authorities, and today the country reaps the consequences. Indeed, this democratic fabric is susceptible to many stresses and tensions. Today, in Israel's eighth decade of existence, many feel it is more fragile than ever. Major political shifts both within and outside Israel have spurred initiatives that are challenging the foundations of democracy. In this book, the author expertly explores the roots of that susceptibility and, as a participant-observer, describes how Israel's mechanisms of governance contend with the complexities of a vulnerable and multicultural Jewish state whose citizens bring a variety of norms and traditions into the public sphere.

Certainly, other nations have faced similar challenges. More than sixty democracies have come into being just in the last few decades. Most of these, in their formative years, drafted constitutions that defined their collective national identity. But Israel, as Carmon explains, still lacks a constitution. As a result, Israeli identity remains fluid, a work in progress. In the absence of a constitution, no clear and formal guidelines exist to mediate the controversies that arise within the unique mosaic of Israeli society, which brings together ultra-Orthodox Jews, religious Zionists, Russian immigrants, secular native-born Israelis, Arabs, and others. Carmon is troubled by the vulnerability of the secular foundations of Israeli democracy and by the threat religion poses to the integrity of Israeli society and its democracy. His account incorporates an expert's experience with autobiographical anecdotes of moments that uniquely shaped his thoughts on Israel and the entwined issues of religion and democracy.

Israel is justly renowned for its miraculous success in establishing the foundations of robust statehood: impressive defense capabilities, a thriving economy, and vigorous democratic institutions. Yet an existential challenge still lies on the horizon. Israel has yet to establish a constitutional consensus to accommodate the differences in defining its collective identity. The country where the Jewish people exercise their right to self-determination, as Carmon vividly demonstrates, has yet to find an Archimedean balance between particularistic Jewish values and universal democratic values. The ongoing struggle for this balance is a hallmark of the vibrant, boisterous Israeli culture I have come to know. It would be a difficult struggle even in a benign regional context. But the unresolved status of the Israeli-Palestinian conflict and the absence of a clear border separating Israel and the West Bank make the challenge even more formidable.

Another critical dilemma facing Israel as a Jewish state is the coexistence of two sources of authority: the democratic and the divine. Ideally, the establishment of an Israeli constitution would resolve the perennial problem of religion and state, which Carmon analyzes in detail. But this tension remains unresolved throughout much of the Middle East. In the wake of the Arab Awakening, *Building Democracy on Sand* assumes an even greater urgency. Israel's neighbors, some of them newly liberated from authoritarian regimes, must also find tools to reconcile democracy and Islam.

What most distinguishes this book is the narrative voice of the author. Arye Carmon is not just a chronicler of the evolution of Israel's democracy, he is also an active player in the drama. *Building Democracy on Sand* is both the biography of a vital institution and the autobiography of its founder, a man I have to come to characterize as a "realistic optimist." As a realist, Carmon is well aware of the fragility of Israel's democracy—which is the very reason for the existence of IDI. As an optimist, he never ceases to point the way forward, toward a consensual constitution that would provide a new foundation of stability for the State of Israel.

Israel is a "start-up nation" whose material achievements are wondrous to behold. It also possesses the ability to develop a healthy, robust, and resilient democracy. Potentially, it can become the proverbial shining city on a hill, a beacon for freedom-loving people everywhere. Arye Carmon's vision for Israel would honor all sectors of its society, enabling the preservation of difference within a shared identity. Such a vision can and must be realized. For a nation like Israel, it is an existential necessity.

GEORGE P. SHULTZ,
Thomas W. and Susan B. Ford Distinguished Fellow,
Hoover Institution, Stanford University

Author's Note to the English-Language Edition

Just as non-Westerners can find themselves bewildered by certain phrases and customs in the United States and Europe, non-Israelis may be confused by concepts in this book that are almost second nature to Israelis.

Following are explanations of some of the concepts in this book, starting with *halacha*, the body of Jewish law that developed over the centuries and which continues to guide Orthodox Jews' behavior, and continuing with a glossary of important words and phrases.

Halacha is the collective body of Jewish religious laws derived from written texts and oral traditions. These laws, decrees, and regulations have accumulated throughout the centuries and include interpretations decreed and collected by rabbis. *Halacha* is based on biblical commandments, subsequent Talmudic and rabbinic law, and customs and traditions compiled in many books.

Historically, in the Jewish diaspora, *halacha* served as an enforceable avenue of law, both civil and religious. Since the period of the eighteenth-century Jewish Enlightenment (more or less parallel to Europe's Age of Enlightenment), some have come to view the *halacha* as reliant on rabbinic interpretation.

With the impact of modernity in the past couple of centuries in general and the rise of Zionism in particular, we can distinguish between two principal approaches to understanding the ramifications of the *halacha*.

According to the first, the *halacha* originated in divine revelation and by its very nature is theological, independent of time frame or historical context. The *halacha*, therefore, does not react to changes in the human condition but is authoritatively in charge of guiding the lives of Jews, whether in exile or in the State of Israel, in predetermined paths. *Halacha* teaches religious observers how to fulfill their religious requirements between themselves and God. To fulfill our role as a holy people, we imitate God's actions. The true reason for following *halacha* is because God commanded us to do so.

According to the second approach, mainly led by religious Zionists in Israel, the *halacha* does react to the founding of the State of Israel. This approach assumes that the *halacha* is a dynamic, normative system that constantly revives and reshapes itself.

The question at the heart of this book is the extent to which "a *halachic* reaction" to the founding of a secular Jewish sovereignty is possible.

I have taken as a point of departure the assumption that the inclusion of *halacha* as part of the political processes in a democracy is an unresolved issue; that there is an inherent unsettled tension between the legal laws of a sovereign-democratic state and those pertaining to statehood that emanated from texts that evolved when the Jews were scattered among many nations. A fundamental factor substantiating this assumption is the lack of significant rulings pertaining to statehood within the *halacha*.

The Jewish view of religion (church) and state differs from Islam's view, with its *sharia*, and Christianity's view, with its historical background. Islam's classic political worldview does not recognize separation between religion and politics. The Prophet Muhammad was both a political and a religious leader, as were those who succeeded him. According to this view, it is not possible to lead the Muslim community without a religious authority.

In contrast, in Christian Western nations, religion and religious sources of authority exist separately from political authority and have done so since the mid-seventeenth century, when the Peace of Westphalia established religious tolerance, among many other developments.

But, as this book explains, there has been no political history in the life of the Jewish people for two thousand years, placing them and *halacha* in a unique position. As Menachem Lorberbaum noted in *Politics and the Limits of Law: Secularizing the Political in Medieval Jewish Thought* (Stanford, CA: Stanford University Press, 2002), the *halachic* tradition minimized the treatment of political issues and by and large supported a secular approach to politics.

Ashkenazi, Sephardi/Mizrahi: Ashkenazi generally refers to Jews from Europe, including western Russia, Ukraine, and the Baltics. Sephardi generally refers to descendants of Jews who were expelled from Spain and settled in North Africa and nearby areas. Mizrahi Jews lived in the Middle East and western Asia, including Iran, Syria, Georgia, and Uzbekistan.

Conservative and Reform Judaism: Most American Jews belong to one of these strains of Judaism, which are modern and inclusive, although still upholding many Jewish traditions. In Israel, the Orthodox Jewish establishment rejects these positions and insists that people who converted to one of them, or whose fathers were Jewish but not their mothers, are not true Jews.

New Jew vs. Old Jew: The concept of the "new Jew" endorses agency over victimhood, favors strength and power over spirituality and heritage, and contrasts the fighting spirit of modern Israel with the helplessness of the exile (the Old Jew).

Hebraism: Hebraism embraces the Hebrew Bible as the inspired word of God but rejects the rabbinical traditions that underpin much of Orthodox Judaism.

Orthodox monopoly: In Israel, the Orthodox rabbinate has power over the definition of Jewishness and enforces Orthodox rules on marriage, divorce, adoption, and many other areas of life, both religious and civil.

Secular Jews: They regard themselves as ethnically and culturally Jewish but are not religious.

Zionism: This national liberation movement to create a homeland for the Jewish people culminated in the creation of the nation of Israel and continues in expressions of support for the nation.

Introduction

This account is an invitation to my Israeli compatriots to join in a common awakening. It is a wake-up call for those entrusted with the future of Israeli democracy to invest in a sincere effort to mend the country's divisions. It is a call for a historical *tikkun* (repair). I look at this treatise as my own "doctrine," an attempt to grapple with the fragile and wounded system known as Israeli democracy. This work is motivated by a feeling of partnership in a historic genesis in the creation phase of Jewish political sovereignty.

My generation has borne this feeling upon our shoulders as the dark cloud of missed opportunity has hung over us.

Near the end of the twentieth century, the first fifty years of Jewish statehood in Israel came to a close. The assassination of Israeli prime minister Yitzhak Rabin on November 4, 1995, marked an ominous start to the second half century of Israel's modern existence. Over the course of Israel's first fifty years, the momentum of the Zionist movement led to achievements that were unprecedented by any measure. These exceptional achievements were in the field of "hardware"— that is, the formal functions of the state. We established formal procedures for state agencies and institutions, including elections, in every branch of the government. We built a powerful military and a thriving economy. On the other hand, the "operating software"—the guidelines that accommodate human diversity and enable coexistence in the civilian collective—is still riddled with weaknesses and must be repaired.

The Zionist vision of bringing Jews from all corners of the earth to Zion, where the Jewish people could realize their right to self-determination, was achieved to an impressive extent. The most impressive cultural achievement is the revival of the Hebrew language, which is today the spoken language of all of the state's citizens. The State of Israel is a state of immigrants. In 2018, about 75 percent of its 8,950,000 citizens were Jews. Among them, about 70 percent were native-born, the second or third generation.[1]

Today, however, more than seven decades after the state was founded, the principle of inclusion has yet to be fulfilled vis-à-vis all of the immigrants (and their descendants) from the various Diaspora communities. Israel's Declaration of Independence, proclaimed on May 15, 1948, envisions a Jewish and democratic state that grants full equality to all of its citizens. But this vision seems to be fading over the horizon. In a concrete sense, there is no consensus on the characteristics that define Israel's identity as "Jewish and democratic." On the contrary, these characteristics are the source of deep discord within the very bonds that are supposed to help unify our fractured country and facilitate coexistence. The definition of this "Jewish" characteristic is under the control of an Orthodox Jewish monopoly and the "democratic" values of this Jewish country are threatened by the ever-growing voices of ethnocentric nationalism.

As a result, one of the prime principles of democracy—the principle of inclusion—has been challenged by a reality of exclusion. The Jewish-Orthodox monopoly over the definitions and characteristics of the state's Jewishness has promoted a problematic association between religion and politics. According to the principle of inclusion, every individual and group in a democracy should be equally included in its civil society, regardless of their sectorial affiliation, gender, ethnic background, and religious or secular worldview. Nonetheless, the representatives of Jewish Orthodoxy in Israel, whether Zionists or non-Zionists, impose exclusion by political means and preclude the possible equal presence of non-Orthodox identities.

This book is, for me, the first chapter in a long and strenuous journey of formulating a consensual mix of secular democratic and religious components. The aim is to define the place of religion and the fences required to inhibit the intrusion of religion into politics. Furthermore, this consensual formula should grant legitimacy for multicultural, multi-identity definitions of Jewishness.

In 1991, I launched the Israel Democracy Institute along with Bernard Marcus, the founder of Home Depot. Former US secretary of state George Shultz joined the management team of the nascent think tank and was fond of calling the IDI a "do tank" because of our constant mission to achieve real-world results.

The founding of the IDI was a response to a historical, primal need of the Jewish people, which just a few decades earlier had taken on the burden of political sovereignty after two thousand years of exile. Then and now, the defining characteristic of Israeli democracy—at least on the surface level—has been an especially busy agenda compared to other democracies. As a result, most of the energy of Israeli elected officials and of the architects of public policy is directed toward the here and now at the expense of the long term. Except for the Israeli military (the Israel Defense Forces), most of the country's public institutions are focused on dealing with dynamic and emergency situations which can change at a moment's notice any day of the week.

In the face of this reality, my colleagues and I at the IDI decided on our own to address the weaknesses and vulnerabilities of the constitutional infrastructure of Israeli democracy. We declared that our focus would be on the future. We have done so by researching electoral reform, by strengthening the democratic foundation of Israel, and by formulating reforms designed to streamline the functioning of the executive branch on issues of great importance, including budget allocations and the relations between the national and local governments. Our flagship project was a decade long attempt to help hammer out a constitution. The State of Israel does not have a constitution and its absence resonates in a number of ways which I describe in this work.

With all due humility, I consider the creation of the Israel Democracy Institute to have been the realization of a mission. This is because I feel that Israeli democracy is still in its formative stages, as discussed below, and we are privileged to witness firsthand the exercise of self-determination and political sovereignty by the Jewish people. Over the years, this feeling has grown as the IDI's programs developed and the institute established itself as one of the key defenders of Israeli democracy.

The vulnerabilities and weaknesses of Israeli democracy manifest themselves across many fields. Over the years, I have wondered why the sources of the secular foundations of Israeli democracy and the relationship between religion and politics in Israel are so fragile. This fragility has far-reaching implications for the functioning of Israeli institutions and worsens the ever-deepening rifts in Israeli society. This is why I have devoted so much time and effort to this mission. The publication of this book is the beginning of the realization of this mission.

Israel is a parliamentary democracy. Members of the parliament—the Knesset—are chosen in nationwide elections. There are no electoral districts as in the United States; the entire country is a single district. On Election Day, Israelis cast votes for a party list by placing a single slip of paper in an envelope in the ballot box. When the votes are tallied, the number of seats each party is awarded in the 120-seat legislature is determined based on each party's percentage of the overall vote. Israel is one of the few democracies with a unicameral legislature. This parliament is among the smallest and youngest in the world. The hectic, dynamic political agenda it is tasked with managing is unprecedented.

About three decades after founding the IDI, I passed the torch on to the next generation of leaders. For their sake, I tried to outline the implications of this early stage of Israeli democracy in terms of its structural-institutional and normative-ethical dimensions. I felt like a radiologist holding up an X-ray to find the weaknesses and fissures that could threaten Israel's democracy. When I look at this metaphorical X-ray, I feel a mix of satisfaction from IDI's achievements and contributions to Israeli society, together with a strong sense that we missed opportunities to advance the constitutional process.[2]

The State of Israel lacks a constitution to bind the workings of Israel's democracy and a bill of rights to safeguard the freedoms of its citizens and underpin the norms of its civil society. Instead, Israel has a compilation of what have been labeled "basic laws" designed to serve as a provisional constitutional framework. Nine of these basic laws define the formal procedures of Israel's democracy, including Basic Law: The Government, Basic Law: The Military, and so on. Most of these laws do not have constitutional protections that would prevent them from being altered by a simple majority. The two most recently passed basic laws—Basic Law: Human Dignity and Liberty and Basic Law: Freedom of Employment—were supposed to mark the beginning of the formulation of a bill of rights. But since the two bills were passed in 1992 the constitutional process has been halted.

The lack of a constitution has far-reaching repercussions. Unlike more substantive and developed democracies, Israel lacks the consensual underpinnings that stabilize governance and enable the inclusion of diverse outlooks and beliefs. I have long been intrigued by the question of what makes our secular democracy so vulnerable.

The role of religion in Israeli public life undoubtedly plays a major role in the weakening of the secular foundation of Israeli democracy and culture. The glaring absence of a constitution is crucial to the way religion has worked its way into public spaces, where it threatens Israel's democracy. The members of civil society in Israel have never experienced the impact of a written constitution in democratic life; a written constitution has never guided their way of life as a sovereign-national collective. In the meantime, not only do secular Israelis ignore the weaknesses of Israeli democracy, we deny that they exist.

What we are left with is tension between the Jewish religion and the State of Israel. Without a bill of rights, Israel has never resolved the issues of "freedom of and freedom from religion." What has instead emerged is a deepening crisis of identities in Israeli society, dominated by the rift between secular and religious Israelis. Over the seven decades since the founding of the State of Israel, the lack of a constitutional arrangement on the matter of separation of religion and state has led to volatility that has at times been volcanic. One of the goals of this book is to unpack the causes of this disastrous failure in order to forge a constitutional framework to deal with this issue.

Israeli society is a multicolored mosaic. It is rich, diverse—and deeply disharmonious. It is made up of a collection of heterogeneous minorities: Arabs, religious Zionists, ultra-Orthodox Jews, new immigrants, secular Jews, Ashkenazi, and Sephardi. None of these minorities are monolithic and their members run the full gamut of the political spectrum, creating a sort of disharmony that can sometimes be jarring. This mosaic—or "map of tribes," as President Reuven Rivlin termed it—is not static. As a diverse society, Israel is a patchwork of diversity. But this diversity is on a slippery slope, tumbling into divisiveness. There are signs of increasing friction and mutual demonization and enmity among the different minority groups, a reality that threatens the future of Israeli society. I believe there is a direct correlation between the deepening divisions in Israeli society and the country's weak secular foundation.

The Israeli author Haim Be'er wrote a blurb for the Hebrew edition of this book: "The centrality of the Israeli-Palestinian conflict blurs and silences a conflict that is many times more tragic, deep, and dangerous: the deep conflict between democratic-Zionist Israeliness and Orthodox-*halachic* Judaism. Arik Carmon, with profound knowledge, insight, sensitivity, involvement, and, especially, with wisdom of the heart, sets out in his book to examine whether the two can be reconciled and how this reconciliation can be accomplished."

I may be biased, but I believe that Zionism—the national liberation movement of the Jewish nation—is an extraordinary example of motivation and achievement unprecedented in the history of nations. Zionism has wrought a structural, moral, and cultural metamorphosis in one of the most ancient nations on earth: the Jewish people. This enormous accomplishment serves as the underlying context for this essay. My critique is not intended to detract from the achievements and contributions of the Zionist revolution. Readers should also note that any analysis of Israel's essence and functioning as a sovereign nation should take into account the ongoing threats to its physical existence.

My goal is to develop proposals for long-term solutions to Israel's societal ills. These proposals will be based on an attempt to understand what has caused these problems in the past and what their implications are for the present.

A Further Invitation for Discourse

"For whom do I toil?" I assume this question crosses the mind of every author as he presents his work to a publisher. I'm particularly interested to see whether second- and third-generation Israelis find my work intriguing. Is there enough here to stimulate the discourse that I hope will be sparked by my work? Also, to what extent will my book rekindle interest among young Diaspora Jews in the critical dynamic of events that have taken place in the sovereign political home of the Jewish people?

The Zionist revolution created a watershed (or fault line, depending on whom you ask) event on May 15, 1948. On one side is two thousand years of Jewish history and on the other side is the existence created by Jewish political sovereignty. On one side is a multifaceted cultural kaleidoscope, full of various languages and identities and traditions that were formed across the world over dozens of generations. On the other side is the sputtering national effort to build a single, unified people.

This fault line between the Jewish past and the Zionist present is part of the personal biography of every member of my generation born in Israel around the time of the founding of the state. It is part of our memories and our way of life. The ways my parents would joke around in Yiddish and their nonnative accent in Hebrew, or the way the parents of my Sephardi Jewish friend pronounced the guttural letters, were among the countless reminders of the proud and powerful cultural remnants they held on to. These remnants created cultural backlashes that typified life on this fault line or historical watershed between the past and present.

Above all, the fault line reminds us of the historical primacy—an era of genesis—that we are part of as Jews. This feeling has faded. I don't believe my children or my grandchildren can relate to it. The existential distance that separates my children and grandchildren from this watershed–fault line is not far. They and members of their generations are still children of the rebirth of Israel. This is a historical fact and it is part of their responsibility for the future of the state. It is a responsibility that their contemporaries in territorial countries do not share. The distance in consciousness from the same line, however, has grown significantly. This raises the question of how we can internalize the concept of genesis in the minds of these generations and instill a sense of the historical primacy of their Jewish heritage. Also, how can we foster this connection in Diaspora Jews? I don't have an answer, but of one thing I am convinced: a brave embrace of this connection may be the source for hope.

Part One

The Challenges of Sovereignty

I perceive myself to be a son of the Zionist revolution, whose roots of identity were torn from his own past.

A few months before my father died, we moved him from his home in the Beit Hakerem neighborhood of Jerusalem—where he had lived for six decades—to a nursing home not far from our home in central Israel. He was ninety-seven years old and apprehensive about the move. When he arrived at the nursing home and the back doors of the ambulance opened, I began to understand his fear. My wife Tzipa and I were waiting for him in the parking lot next to the nursing unit. We could see the bewilderment in his eyes, which had already begun to dim. His Filipina caretaker, Sarah, wheeled him down the ramp from the ambulance in his wheelchair as his eyes shifted restlessly. When we entered the unit and he saw the residents of the nursing home, he seemed to finally grasp what was going through his mind. In his home in Beit Hakerem, where he lived alone, he had forged a self-image of a youthful man who stood tall and was a great conversationalist. Now, without warning, he was suddenly surrounded by feeble men and women who needed constant medical assistance. For my father, seeing them was like looking into a disturbing image of his own fate. My father remained silent. A few minutes after the nurse showed him his room and bed, I asked him what he thought of his new surroundings. Softly, he said, "Okay"—but it was the type of "okay" you wouldn't wish upon your enemies. From then on, he observed the world from the seat of a wheelchair, as his mind slipped into a thickening cloud of dementia. There were occasional moments of lucidity, though he was disoriented and couldn't distinguish between past and present. I felt compelled to try to prod him to speak, thinking this would help him maintain his connection to the world as he gradually took leave of it. Usually, on the way to my visits, I'd string together familiar and routine topics of conversation: his daily activities, the grandchildren, the next visit, and so on. Once, on my way there, I heard myself trying to elicit a dialogue of a different sort. As I wheeled him to a corner of the garden shaded by sycamore trees, I said, "Dad, you know, you've never told me about your mother's family."

My father was only three years old when my grandfather was killed in action during World War I in an area that is today in Ukraine. Grandfather Hirsch Leib, for whom I was named (in reverse—Ari Zvi corresponds in Hebrew to Leib Hirsch), was (I assume) a forced conscript in the Austrian army. My father was an orphan and it was always evident to me that this was a powerful part of his identity. But otherwise, I knew very little about his past.

My parents belonged to the pioneering generation that founded the State of Israel. As members of the liberation movement of the Jewish people—Zionism—they also followed the principle of "negation of the exile," which severed me and my generation from our past. Only recently, while working on this book, I belatedly realized that when my parents were in their early twenties, the age of my oldest grandchild, they left their parents' home in Poland, never to return. Presumably, for five or six years they exchanged letters with the family they left behind. And then, in 1939, the connection was cut off. Poland was captured by the Nazis. My family—my grandfathers and grandmothers, uncles and aunts—were all murdered.

I picked up bits of information over the years but far more remained a mystery. I hardly knew what my paternal grandmother Henia was like or much of anything about her background. I didn't know who Hirsch Leib was or where he was killed, and most details about my father's extended family were unknown to me. When I asked my father to tell me about his mother, I was mainly looking to strike up a conversation and not necessarily trying to reveal unknown details of my family's history. My father responded, "Yes, my mother Henia had two brothers. They lived together with us [my father and his sisters] and with their families in Stojanow. [Stojanow was a small town in eastern Galicia, today Ukraine. My father didn't use the term *shtetl*, whose origins are in the Jewish Diaspora.] One was a balegule [wagoner] and the other was a greengrocer."

And then he sank back into the fog of dementia. It was clear to me that he came from a poor family. Without a breadwinner, his mother relied on her brothers, who themselves struggled to make ends meet. I parted from my father after that visit with a heavy heart. I was struck by the realization that I was in my seventies and I had never made an effort to learn about my parents' lives.

In a beautiful wooden box at my parents' home were faded, yellowing pictures of my mother's parents, her two brothers and two sisters, my father's sisters and his mother. There was also a collection of pictures from their training with friends in the Gordonia youth movement in Lvov and immigration to Palestine as pioneers at Kibbutz Hulda in the mid-1930s.

For me, those photographs embodied my entire family history. Of course, during my childhood my parents had told me about their families. I knew the names of their brothers and sisters—but nothing more. Fanka was my father's older sister; but what was the name of her husband? What was the name of her daughter who died in the Holocaust? What work did she do? Did she live in a town? What about my mother's older brother, what did he do? When did each of them move, whether from the town (Rava-Ruska) to the big city (Lvov)? After my parents died, as a single child, I was left with only the top canopy of our family tree, knowing nothing about the earlier branches and the roots that ran back generations.

Though much of my family history remains a mystery, I can understand and explain the historical perspective that shaped my views on the meaning of "Jewish and democratic" and what it symbolizes for me.

In other words, the disconnect between my family's past in the Jewish Diaspora and the role of present and future Zionism in forming the core of my identity was so deep that I forgot the names of my two uncles a moment after my father mentioned them. After our short conversation that day, I left feeling bewildered, frustrated, and on the brink of tears. I was gripped by the pain of missed opportunity, realizing I had built a biography without yesterdays, a tree without roots.

On my next visit, a few days later, my father was waiting for me on the walkway. This was out of the ordinary. I usually had to wait for him to finish his afternoon meal or nap, and only then we would head out to the garden. Not this time. Sarah, my father's doting, endlessly loyal Filipina caretaker, was already waiting with him near the parking lot and led him toward me as I got out of my car. He looked impatient and his eyes sparked with tense anticipation.

"Arinka," he greeted me, "Do you know anyone at the Polish embassy?" I was astounded. Why would he be interested in the Polish embassy?

"Dad," I asked, "Why are you asking about the Polish embassy?"

"Arinka, I thought maybe we could save Mother and my sister," he said. There are no words to describe the pain and shock of hearing him say this. I was speechless. My first thought was that my dad needed help, needed some way to pull himself out of the abyss of yesterday. "Dad," I asked, "Do you remember how old you are?"

"Ninety-seven," he responded without hesitation.

"And if your mother were still alive, how old would she be?" I asked.

"Ahh," he mumbled. Silence. He was lost in his world and I was here—picking up the pieces of my shattered soul.

But no more than a few moments passed and he asked again: "Maybe you have connections at the Polish embassy?" I asked him, in enormous pain, my voice choked with emotion: "Father, do you remember there was a Holocaust?" And he, with veiled eyes, staring, inquiring, or I don't know what, again said, "Ahh," and fell silent. I hugged him, trying to convey the warmth of love, and he languished in the wheel chair, unresponsive.

Chapter 1

Between Reason and Faith

Preliminary Notes

The 3,500-year history of the Jewish people lacks a tradition of responsibility for political sovereignty. The Jewish people have no continuous, reinforced tradition of political accountability. Thus, the State of Israel—the young state of an ancient people—is in many ways the Jewish people's first experience in bearing collective responsibility for political sovereignty.

In its eighth decade, is Israeli society in danger of losing its solidarity and cohesion? Is the widening rift between its diverse segments creating a tangible threat to its long-term existence as a political entity? What is the source of legitimacy for the secular character of the democracy and what are the threats to the strength and stability of this legitimacy? What does the future hold for the Jewish and democratic state?

These questions and others they raised have been at the bedrock of my professional career, in particular during my years leading the Israel Democracy Institute (IDI). They have guided me through decades as a scholar and have led me to several basic assumptions that serve as the foundation for the "doctrine" I seek to articulate. This doctrine aims to provide a diagnostic platform for examining the historical and contemporary circumstances that generated these questions. Based on this diagnostic platform, and in the spirit of my work at the IDI, I aim to tackle the policy challenges and propose a long-term prescription for changing the current reality.

These are my seven assumptions:

1. The Jewish people lack a solid and orderly tradition of responsibility for political sovereignty.
2. The Jewish people have a history of dispersion and diaspora which is far different from the histories of territorial nations that have a background of sovereignty and territorial control.
3. Political passivity is the most prominent characteristic of two thousand years of exile. This passivity resulted from the convergence of Jewish religion and nationhood since time immemorial.
4. The Zionist revolution to liberate the Jewish people was a secular revolution.
5. The fact that Jews stood on the sidelines of the secularization process that took place over centuries in Christian countries meant that the secular Zionist revolution—which aimed to transform the course of Jewish history—developed with an inherent deficit.
6. This "Zionist deficit" was the result of a secularization process that was revolutionary rather than evolutionary.
7. Within the secular Zionist revolution, a religious counterrevolution emerged and continues to gain strength, threatening the future of our democracy.

Since the founding of the State of Israel, particularly in recent decades, Israeli society and political culture have changed at an unprecedented pace. These changes have entailed far-reaching and dynamic developments, including changes in our normative foundations. They have brought demographic changes and have widened economic disparity between the haves and have-nots. Above all, Israel has undergone constant transformations in its political culture and conduct, which have been characterized by polarization and increasing extremism. In addition, political structures and governance capabilities have weakened—if not collapsed.

These dynamic changes are unique in comparison to other countries. For example, Israel's population numbered about 3.3 million people at the time of the Yom Kippur War in 1973. When the war started, about 53 percent of Israeli Jews were immigrants and most of the others were children of immigrants—like me. By the middle of the second decade of the twenty-first century, the population had soared to over 8.5 million. This enormous demographic change has had a major effect on all of the aspects noted above, including the socioeconomic and cultural characteristics of Israel.

I was born in the first half of the 1940s in Jerusalem to parents who arrived from Poland in the fifth aliyah (wave of immigration) and were among the founders of Kibbutz Hulda in central Israel. My identity was shaped by three components: the values of the Labor Zionist movement; the *Yiddishkeit* ("Jewishness" in Yiddish) I imbibed from my father's stories; and the ethos of the fighters who fell in the War of Independence. I was raised with the values sowed and cultivated by the founders of the State of Israel. These were the values of the labor movement, which could be defined today as social democracy. My *Yiddishkeit* came from my personal experiences with events and fragments of culture that I drew from stories at home, encounters with the ultra-Orthodox Mea Shearim neighborhood during my early childhood, and the sights and sounds of the Jerusalem of my youth. My many years of work related to the Holocaust deepened this *Yiddishkeit*. I was in high school when I first came across *Parchments of Fire*, three volumes of writings, letters, poems, and stories written by fighters who fell in the battlefields of Israel's War of Independence. The words of these fallen fighters—who in the Hebrew saying were "the silver platter on which the Jewish state was given"—helped shape my identity, instilling in me a commitment to contribute to my people and my country in the model of these "new Jews" I idolized.

Today, more than forty-five years after the Yom Kippur War, about 80 percent of Israel's Jewish population is native-born. Most are still first-generation Israelis, and Israel's fast-changing society is still primarily an immigrant society. Based on twenty-five years of observing the political processes in Israel, I contend that the collapse of political structures (mainly the political parties) and the weakening of others (such as the Supreme Court) are a direct consequence of two closely related factors: the lack of a tradition of responsibility for political sovereignty and the Zionist deficit. I use the concept of the Zionist deficit to describe a significant ideological and practical shortcoming in the Jewish national liberation movement. This deficiency is one of the factors underlying the vulnerability of the secular underpinnings of our democracy. (I will discuss this at length below.)

These two factors account for the fragile foundation on which the institutions of our democracy were built. They have hindered the creation of more solid normative foundations and underline the vulnerability of the secular underpinnings of Israeli democracy. On top of this, Israel is still engaged in a struggle for its physical survival in the face of external threats. Thus, the structural shoulders of Israeli democracy are fragile and vulnerable considering the heavy loads they must carry. In fact, there is arguably no other nation in the world with such a complex load of issues on its public agenda. Each of these issues cries out for a stable and solid foundation.

Israel in the twenty-first century lacks the consensual underpinning—a social contract in one form or another—that is essential for integrating a nation into a sovereign collective. The consensual underpinnings of developed democracies are the glue that binds different groups in a sovereign collective and enables them to coexist, with each group maintaining its own beliefs. This is usually expressed in a written constitution that plays a key role in shaping the political culture of the sovereign-national collective.

There are various narratives that permeate the political culture of Israeli Jews. The two dominant narratives reflect opposing views of the Zionist revival. Both date back to the early days of the national liberation movement of the Jewish people and have waxed and waned over the years. For the leaders of political and practical

Zionism, the revival is the result of a secular rebellion against the centrality of religion in the Jewish nation's way of life and against the expectation of messianic redemption in particular. The proponents of the second narrative, religious Zionism, added a messianic element to the secular Zionist revolution, portraying it as "the beginning of our redemption."

For various reasons, Israel has ignored the need to define and establish the place of religion in public life. This has generated a deepening conflict of identities over time. Thus, we live in a state whose identity is defined as "Jewish and democratic," but the question of who defines its Jewishness is the subject of profound disagreement. This is not a theoretical-ideological disagreement; this argument entails verbal and physical violence and bears the seeds of a Kulturkampf. The assaults on public spaces by those acting in the name of religion also reflect the institutionalized monopoly of Orthodoxy in defining the Jewishness of the State of Israel.

In recent years, the IDI's Democracy Index has addressed the question of the balance between "Jewish" and "democratic" and how Israelis view this question. The answers are critical because they reflect the weight of particularistic values versus universal values in the identity of Israelis. In addition, in light of the Orthodox monopoly over the Jewish particularistic dimension, these answers provide an indication of how Israelis will act when religious values clash with democratic values. In 2017, only 12 percent of *religious* respondents, compared to 61 percent of *secular* respondents, said that the Jewish dimension is too strong. The data were similar in 2018: 8 percent of religious respondents, compared to 61 percent of secular respondents. On the other hand, in 2017, only 8 percent of secular respondents said that the democratic dimension is too strong and 9 percent answered similarly in 2018, compared to 44 percent of religious respondents in 2017 and 46 percent in 2018. (Among Arab citizens of the State of Israel, in 2018, only 8 percent of the respondents said that the democratic dimension is too strong, compared to 80 percent who contended that the Jewish dimension is too strong.)

The two fundamental groups of factors that are supposed to define the identity of Israel as a single collective are the particular and the universal, the Jewish and the democratic. The particularistic characteristics of a nation are defined by the collective identity of the individuals and groups that comprise it. As Samuel Huntington notes, a nation is "a remembered community, a community with an imagined history, and it is defined by its historical memory of itself."[3] A nation cannot exist without a common national identity ingrained in the minds of its members as a shared memory of struggles, of victories and defeats, heroes and villains, enemies and wars. According to these criteria, Huntington continues, the United States at the beginning of the nineteenth century cannot be defined as a nation because it lacked a national history and had no *national consciousness*. The Civil War was the high price the United States paid to become a nation. The war gave birth to the American nation, whose characteristics were shaped in its wake. In the postwar years, American nationalism and patriotism were forged as Americans came to identify unconditionally with their country. Before the Civil War, Americans spoke of their country in the plural, as "these United States." After the war, they used the singular: "the United States." As President Woodrow Wilson noted in his Memorial Day address in 1915, the Civil War engendered something new: "a national consciousness."[4]

To what extent has national consciousness developed in Israel? Can it be said that Israelis share a common historical memory? One of the seminal achievements in establishing a shared national consciousness is, of course, the Hebrew language, which is a cornerstone of solidarity, an anchor for contending with the challenges of the particularistic elements in the collective identity. Still, questions like these express some of the challenges in molding Israeli society. The principal challenge in the particularistic dimension of Israeli identity is to define the role of religion in the national consciousness of Israelis. In Israeli life today, as in fact since the state's inception, an Orthodox monopoly has held sway. Thus, the main challenge lies at the heart of the divide, at the focal point of the conflict of identities. The Orthodox monopoly makes the following questions more acute: *Is this monopoly a decree of fate? How can we resolve the contradictions between different views on the role of religion in defining the nation? Is it possible to accord legitimacy to multicultural, multi-identity definitions of Jewishness?* The search for consensus in answering these questions is a necessary condition for achieving balance between the particularistic and the universal.

This dual definition of Israeli identity should also shape the way non-Jews, predominantly Muslim Arabs, belong to Israeli society as citizens with equal rights.[5] However, the existence of two clashing national narratives prevents consensus on the universal and particularistic components of Israeli identity. Although Israel is in its eighth decade of independence, it has yet to define fruitful and effective formulas for coexistence between these two components of identity. On the contrary, the concept of "Jewish and democratic" is today the subject of profound disagreement. The discontent stemming from this dispute stirred feelings of despair and doubts about the justice of the Zionist idea, as well as disbelief in its intention to offer tools for advanced Jewish-democratic life in the modern world. And it is important to reiterate that due to the nature and pace of changes in Israeli society, the days of a Zionist majority in the State of Israel are numbered.

The Zionist vision drove the magnificent project of the Jewish people's national liberation movement, which was unique in bringing a nation back from all corners of the globe to reclaim its land. As noted, it was essentially a rebellion against the Jews' *galut* (Diaspora) ways of life and a rejection of the expectation for messianic redemption. The national liberation of the Jewish people from its past and from its dependence on its two-thousand-year-old religious tradition was a secular revolution. However, from the midst of this secular revolution, a religious counterrevolution developed, strengthened, and is continuing to grow.

The dialectic process that has empowered the religious counterrevolution is at the heart of the diagnosis in my doctrine and is described in detail below. This process raises questions about the vulnerability and weaknesses of the Zionist process from the outset. What were the fundamental flaws in the Zionist process and what was the nature of these flaws? At the same time, studying the sources of these fundamental flaws enables us to characterize the sources of the weaknesses and vulnerabilities of Israeli democracy, which by definition rests upon secular foundations. In other words, I would like to assume that the weaknesses and vulnerabilities of Israeli democracy developed primarily from the fundamental flaws in the Zionist process. Those flaws have clear repercussions on the structures and normative underpinnings of our democracy and on what has prevented Israel from becoming a substantive, stable, and sustainable democracy.

Thus, from the democratic perspective, the question is: To what extent can religion and politics in Israel cohabitate? The connection between the Jewish religion and politics in the state of the Jewish people is a recurrent theme in the development of my doctrine. This leads to the question: What can be done to ensure the stability and existence of democratic politics in Israel? I cannot deny the fact that Judaism was historically a political religion in essence and substance. The history of our people includes a number of political institutions—king, prophet, high priest, and Sanhedrin, for example. There were laws covering the full range of the national collective's life—agriculture, taxes, *shmita* (the fallow year), and war. These laws applied to the public space and the entire body politic. However, in the early days of the State of Israel these laws did not become part of my historical memory or that of many others like me.

I landed in Madison, Wisconsin, for my doctoral studies at the University of Wisconsin in the winter of 1971. Our campus wasn't spared the rough-and-tumble student antiwar protests that had roiled campuses from Columbia to Cal–Berkeley, but I was too busy working on my English, summarizing lectures, and writing papers to get caught up in it.

Fresh from the eastern side of the Mediterranean, I had a new enemy to contend with—the frigid Wisconsin winters. (The locals like to say there are only three seasons in Wisconsin: winter, June, and July.) I'd been in Madison for several months and had yet to adjust to the atmosphere on campus.

The adjustment was demanding, and with it came a feeling of alienation. Luckily, the arrival of visiting professor Georges Haupt in the spring semester eased this feeling to some extent. The fact that this Parisian was a Jew never came up in the seminar he led for PhD students and he never hinted anything to me about his Jewishness during our conversations—that is, until one very special and significant moment.

Haupt sat two or three rows ahead of me during a showing of Vittorio de Sica's *The Garden of the Finzi-Continis* at a movie theater in Madison. Our eyes met for a moment just as the theater went dark. As the credits rolled at the end of the film, I saw Professor Haupt hurry out of the theater before anyone else rose from their seats. Despite the darkness, I was certain I saw him wiping away a tear.

A few days later, I invited myself to lunch with him, and as we ate he began to drift back into his past, far away from the University of Wisconsin campus.

He spoke of growing up in an assimilated Jewish family in the city of Satu Mare (now in Romania), famous for being the birthplace of the Satmar Hasidic sect. Haupt said there were two types of Jews in his hometown—followers of the Hasidic Rebbe Joel Teitelbaum and the assimilated, secular Jews who worked as smugglers on the Hungarian-Romanian border just outside town.

He said that like the rest of the assimilated smugglers, his family didn't define themselves as Jews. All that changed when the Nazis and their collaborators arrived in 1944 and burned this identity into them, figuratively and literally. As Haupt's father was forced on a cattle car to Auschwitz, Teitelbaum was smuggled out to pre-state Israel, leaving his followers back in Satu Mare to be consumed by the inferno. This fact was not lost on Professor Haupt, who cynically brought it up.

Haupt then spoke about the hostility he had developed toward Jewishness, which he said had come to symbolize to him "something steeped in negativity."

He explained that he "knew how to define what I opposed; I was unable to characterize my Jewish identity in a positive way."

I sympathized, because for years I had felt something very similar.

Years later, Professor Haupt's remarks to me at that fateful lunch inspired my idea to formulate a sort of "secular manifesto" for Israeli civil society at the IDI. Like Haupt, my colleagues and I knew how to define our secularity in terms of what we were against, what we rejected. What we lacked, though, was a positive foundation for this identity.

We invited other colleagues to join us, including historians of Zionism and several others who had worked on a "secular-Jewish bookcase," which was an attempt to distinguish secular from religious scripts. We met on two weekends in the town of Zichron Yaakov, about a dozen of us working to revamp the principles, thoughts, and ideas at the center of the works of Zionist visionaries like Theodor Herzl, Ahad Ha'am, Yosef Haim Brenner, and others. We weren't looking to reinvent the wheel, just trying to adapt these ideas to the cultural practices of Israel at the end of the twentieth century.

We outlined proposals and wrote up the minutes of our discussions, but kept running headfirst into the same wall: How do we turn these ideas into a document that can offer meaning and substance and be a rallying cry for those who don't seek their answers in liturgy or belief in a higher power?

Simply put, we failed.

There were a few reasons for our failure. For one, we didn't have a marketing plan or any resources to promote one even if we did.

Moreover, there was a lack of sufficient demand for the project. This is the same exact problem that led us to address the topic in the first place, and it left me deeply frustrated.

The failure of Israel's founders to formulate a constitution has been a source of great frustration for me as well, though the reasons for this failure trace back far longer, deep into the history of the Jewish Diaspora.

In addition to the assertions outlined above, I wish to add another premise to my doctrine: the Jewish collective did not undergo the same types of secularization processes that occurred in the predominantly Christian democracies from which the Jewish national liberation movement drew its inspiration. As I explain below, the collective's Jewishness is undergoing a different sort of secularization that is fundamentally different from its Christian counterpart. This is partly because the very evolution of the Jewish nation was so unlike that of Christian nations. The secularization that took place in Christian countries laid the foundation for their constitutional stability and led to the emergence of a free-market economy and revolutionary scientific and cultural achievements. We cannot say the same about the history of the Jewish people. In our unique case, the diasporic Jewish nation lived for two millennia as a national-religious organism that had no sovereign framework. This is part of why there was no legacy of political sovereignty to guide early Zionists in the creation of a nation-state. As a result, concepts like "state," "statehood," and "sovereignty" were never fully formed. This is why Israel's democracy did not formulate or ratify a constitution.

Democracy is the only political system capable of sustaining the Jewish nation-state because it is the only one that defines the national collective as "sovereign." As such, especially in a highly diverse society, the political process requires consensual underpinnings and a constant effort to foster compromise. This makes governance possible. Politics is the lifeblood of any democracy and the prism through which society filters all of its myriad worldviews and interests.

In Israel, the religion-state relationship and the place of religion in public life were left undefined and remain so to this very day. As in other developed democracies, religion is present in some public spheres in Israel. However, unlike other countries, the following question is often asked in Israel: Does religion pose a threat to the political system? At this stage, I have no unequivocal answer to this question. The search for an answer entails an effort to characterize the fundamental components that should define Israel as a single collective that is both particularistic and universal, Jewish and democratic. "Jewish" and "democratic" are not mutually exclusive—though balancing the two is an essential and deeply challenging part of the formation of a multicultural Jewish identity.

Leo Strauss famously pondered: What is the human problem for which the Jewish problem is the "most manifest" symbol? The answer is the conflict between universal commitments and particularistic affinities. This conflict gets more complicated when it involves a particularistic tradition like Judaism that claims a divine origin. Strauss found that achieving equilibrium between the universal and particularistic in Judaism requires overcoming the conflict between Judaism and Greek philosophy, as embodied by the archetypes of Jerusalem and Athens: the theologian and the philosopher. Both archetypes must be open to the challenges of the other. Philosophy must be subject to critical rationality as philosophers attain knowledge and their opinions evolve. Biblical faith, on the other hand, is characterized by piety and submission. It springs from the fear of God. As humans, our lives are characterized by a radical sense of dependence on God and the need for divine mercy.[6]

My doctrine stems from a specific Jewish-secular cultural platform, which forms the basis for its entire ideological structure. Secular Judaism is multifaceted. First of all, it is based on a humanistic foundation. As such, secular humanistic Judaism regards Judaism as a cultural tradition that does not depend on a divine presence. Secular Judaism emphasizes the humanistic values embodied in Jewish culture. This serves as a basis for the individual's identification with Jewish history and culture.

By taking my doctrine public, I am trying to do far more than present another viewpoint on a sensitive subject or publish an academic treatise doomed to collect dust on a university library shelf. Rather, I offer my perspective as the cornerstone of a process of rehabilitation and revitalization, as part of a search for solutions for a fragile reality.

Israel is characterized by a relatively broad range of cultural diversity. There is tension and even conflict between my cultural platform and those of other sectors of Israeli society. The secular-Jewish cultural platform of my doctrine is strongly linked to my democratic worldview, which holds that democracy, the democratic way of life, and civic behavior in a democracy are all based on consent.[7] Democracy is an ongoing saga centered on navigating a vast array of ambiguous situations. It is a murky process, and any decision made by the citizens in a democracy is ultimately, in one way or another, the result of reconciling a wide spectrum of outlooks and ideas. And although this process doesn't always lead to compromise, this recognition of differences fosters stability and is vital to democracies.[8]

Consent is not a behavioral principle of Israel's political culture.[9] This is an impediment to inclusion: consent is connected to inclusion. The principle of inclusion—accepting all of the participants in civil society as equals, despite political, ethnic, social, and other differences—can only be applied if there is a constant effort to achieve compromise, which is a prerequisite for establishing consent. Some of the discourse in Israel today widens cultural rifts far more than it builds bridges or establishes consensus. In Israel, those with opposing political views are seen as the "other" rather than merely "different."

I wish to distinguish "otherness" from "differentness." "Otherness" is the negative mode of human relationships while "differentness" reflects the positive one. The centrality of otherness in the relations between different sectors of Israeli society stifles the potential for solidarity and worsens societal tension.[10]

My premise is that the centrality of otherness in Israeli society developed in the collective consciousness of Jews living in exile, as an ongoing response to the way Jews were viewed by the non-Jewish population. The history of anti-Semitism is defined by this framing of Diaspora Jews as "the other." I assume that there is a clear link between the "otherness" that anti-Semites attach to Jews and that which we apply to ourselves. The rise of Zionism and the establishment of the State of Israel in 1948 severed the newly sovereign Jewish people from the past, which was completely bereft of anything approaching statehood. I assume that this engendered a major shift in how Jews perceived their otherness. No longer Jews in a world of non-Jews—the Jews of Israel were now a nation of their own, set apart and autonomous.

In Israel's first two generations, it was unable to form a strong tradition of responsibility for political sovereignty. In territorial nations, the tradition of political sovereignty developed in an organic, evolutionary manner. In the diasporic nation, the cutting of ties between the people and their past hindered the development of such a tradition. In addition, the ideology of negating the exile and the Jewish collective's heritage and cultural ties caused a crisis in the relations Jews in Israel had with themselves and with those they saw as "the other." In my view, this crisis is the result of how the "I am the other" approach has been duplicated from the Diaspora experience to that of present-day sovereign Israel.

Considering all this, what constitutes tolerance in a reality driven by identity conflict? In Israel today, there is a wide range of disharmonious cultural differences that exacerbate this conflict. As Francis Fukuyama writes: "If we do not agree on a minimal common culture, we cannot cooperate on shared tasks and will not regard the same institutions as legitimate . . . when a stable, shared moral horizon disappears and is replaced by a cacophony of competing value systems, the vast majority of people do not rejoice at their newfound freedom of choice. Rather they feel an intense insecurity and alienation because they do not know who their true self is."[11]

As discussed below, the Zionist horizon of "a new Jewish society" and "a new Jew" was too narrow. It was based on the worldview of pioneers from Eastern Europe and on breaking away from the cultural heritage of two millennia. This made it more difficult to lay the foundations for a shared culture. This is the source of our contemporary reality, of the disagreement and divisiveness, and of the ascendance of the element of "otherness" rather than diversity. In retrospect, the ethos of manifest destiny among the Zionist pioneers was a powerful engine that drove the miraculous revolution in Jewish life. This ethos catalyzed the development of the material infrastructure for establishing political sovereignty for the Jewish people in the Land of Israel. Certainly, the upside of the Zionist revolution is very impressive. However, from the same retrospective view, we must also assess the downside and its implications. As noted, the prototype and focus of the pioneering ethos, the manifest destiny of Zionism, was "the new Jew," whose personal traits were an antithesis to the exilic Jew. The identity components of "the new" were compressed into "Hebrewism," which became the salient cultural symbol and watchword of the rebellion against the religiousness of "the old" exilic world. The pioneering ethos and its identity components, however, were not sustainable over time. Within a few decades of the state's birth, the pioneering ethos eroded, along with the identity traits of Hebrewism. In practice, during Israel's initial decades, the Orthodox religious monopoly over the definition of Jewish identity gradually took root, replacing Hebrewism.

This monopoly emerged in the context of a disharmonious mosaic as Israeli society absorbed a wide diversity of Jews from all corners of the world. The Zionist vision was challenged by different configurations of identity, including some whose components were based on religion, nationalism, and ethnicity, unlike the identity components of the Zionist "Mayflower" elites: the Ashkenazi pioneers from Eastern

Europe, who regarded themselves as superior. Members of various groups that comprise the mosaic called civil society—ultra-Orthodox Jews, immigrants from the former Soviet Union, Arabs, national-religious Jews, Mizrahi Jews—feel that their identity is not accorded suitable respect by the outside world or by other members of the shared collective. As Fukuyama observes: "Identity grows, in the first place, out of a distinction between one's true inner self and an outer world of social rules and norms that does not adequately recognize that inner self's worth or dignity."[12]

In the preface to *Identity: The Demand for Dignity and the Politics of Resentment*, Fukuyama writes: "The rise of identity politics in modern liberal democracies is one of the chief threats that they face, and unless we can work our way back to more universal understanding of human dignity, we doom ourselves to continuing conflict."[13] In the Israeli context, I believe that the basis of agreement—the condition for achieving harmony—must come from a deeper clarification of the meaning of the words "Jewish" and "democratic" and especially a clarification of the balance between them. It is a challenge to construct a language that can bridge different cultures and identities and allow for coexistence.

In this reality, what potential is there for tolerance when there are so many conflicting identities? The Israeli cultural mosaic is made up of such a vast array of tiles that are foreign to one another that societal discord is inevitable. This reality poses a challenge for those who seek to foster harmony through dialogue and some sort of broad social consensus.

Is it possible to build new lines of communication or an entirely new discourse between secular and religious people, one that takes into account the different ways they perceive the world and the existence of a higher power? This question is by no means theoretical. A person's view on the existence of God can have a profound effect on his way of life.

One way to illustrate this dynamic is to compare the lifestyles of four Israeli men in their early twenties:

The **ultra-Orthodox man** most likely does not serve in the Israeli army, meaning he is bereft of any connection with one of the central cultural institutions in Israel. By his early twenties, he is probably already married to a woman he met in an arranged marriage and the couple probably has at least one child. A decade from now, he will be the father of 6.5 children, according to the average for men from his sector of Israeli society.

At this age, **the national-religious Jew** will still be serving in the army and will have no sexual history, even if he has a girlfriend. He will most likely start a family before the age of twenty-five and father around 4.5 children over the next ten to fifteen years.

The secular Jewish man is also in the army (or has just finished his service). He has no religious or cultural restrictions that would keep him from engaging in casual sex before marriage and his considerations for starting a family are vastly different from those of his ultra-Orthodox and national-religious counterparts. On average, he will marry in his late twenties or early thirties and father 2.3 children.

In **the Arab sector**, it is more difficult to define a prototypical male. In general, however, we know that between the ages of twenty and twenty-two, about 40 percent of Arab men in Israel are not working, studying, or engaging in any sort of civilian national service. Overall, the average number of children per Israeli Arab family is 2.9, and this number is declining.

Though none of these four groups is monolithic, the differences in their lifestyles are significant and shed some light on the tension among the various Israeli identities. When examining these tensions, we again are forced to face the question: Can Israel build a means of communication between these cultures and their various degrees of religious observance or belief in God? If so, how? In a world of many public spaces (including the dominant political one), which of them have room for God? The answers to these questions cannot be theoretical but must serve as a basis for social-cultural change.

Is there common ground for reason and faith? According to my doctrine, no other alternative is acceptable. One of the main objectives of this book is to examine the possibilities of facilitating this coexistence. There is extensive and rich literature on the possibility of bridging reason and faith, democracy and religion, the universal and the particularistic. As guidelines for crafting a proactive strategy, I present below insights from the writings of John Rawls and Jürgen Habermas. This strategy should help formulate a detailed diagnosis of the problem as it exists in Israel. And the exposition of this diagnosis is the aim of this book.

Both Habermas and Rawls struggle with the question of how to include religion in the public sphere of a pluralistic society. In an attempt to keep government secular, both philosophers distinguish between the public and private spheres and comment on the need for religious citizens to be "reasonable."[14] Each, however, assigns religious citizens different levels of responsibility in public spaces. Rawls puts the onus on religious citizens to make themselves understood by the secular. Further, when it comes to public issues, Rawls stresses that citizens' obligation to the public good must come before their loyalty to their religious beliefs. Alternatively, Habermas envisions deliberation as a mutually recognized learning process and advocates equality of deliberation between the secular and the religious.

According to Rawls, democratic citizens must be able to justify their views on public matters through the values of this public political culture. All citizens, Rawls writes, ought to "be ready to explain the basis of their actions to one another in terms each could reasonably expect that the other might endorse as consistent with their freedom and equality."[15] When a citizen's ideological worldview and political conception of justice conflict, the latter outweighs the former.

Like Rawls, Habermas acknowledges the need for citizens to be reasonable. In his essay "Religious Tolerance: The Pacemaker for Cultural Rights," Habermas distinguishes between reasonable and unreasonable religious citizens, calling on citizens to cognitively differentiate between their religious and public roles. "If conflicts of loyalty are not to simmer," Habermas writes, "the necessary role differentiation between members of one's own religious community and co-citizens of the larger society needs to be justified."[16] Habermas deems the religious citizen's understanding of his need to differentiate between his religious and public roles the "modernization of religious consciousness." Like Rawls, Habermas believes that laws must be built from a "shared political culture, [the] egalitarian standards of the community at large, [which] cultural groups are expected to adapt their internal ethos to."[17] Habermas and Rawls share the concept of public political values.

While Habermas asks the religious to adapt their internal ethos to the state, he also asks the state to adapt its culture to accommodate religion. According to Habermas, "To date, only citizens committed to religious beliefs are required to split up their identities . . . into their public and private elements. They are the ones who have to translate their religious beliefs into a secular language before their arguments have any chance of gaining majority support."[18] Here Habermas diverges from Rawls, who envisions a sharper division between private and public values. Habermas asks religious believers to accept the modern condition of pluralism and to differentiate their religious duties from those owed to the state.

Rawls's prescription for including religion in the public sphere is for citizens to draw public values from religious texts or traditions in order to build an overlapping consensus. For Rawls, the duty of civility obligates citizens to translate their faith beliefs into public political terms. Public reason is the litmus test for allowing religion to enter the public sphere. The social contract obligates reasonable citizens to abide by mutually understood laws. Rawls stresses adherence to public values as a firm bottom line. Only in doing so might the sovereignty of the state be preserved when dialogue between the secular and religious involves large groups of ultra-religious citizens.

I believe that there is no alternative but to reconcile reason and faith. This reconciliation will be built by answering a number of grand questions. For instance, is twenty-first-century Judaism ready for political-state coexistence? Furthermore, can Israel's democracy accommodate the Jewish religion? How would incorporating Judaism into Israel's democracy affect the governing of the state? What would be the implications for Israel's values when it comes to rights and personal liberty? Specifically, to what extent would the inclusion of the Jewish religion in the Israeli democracy threaten liberty and equality as fundamental principles and what would it mean for the treatment of minorities and women?

To examine these questions seriously, we must first explain the connection between how religious Zionism views statehood and the concept of a state ruled by *halacha*. Is there a place for God in public spaces in a democracy? In what areas is this inappropriate? Is there any role for rabbinic rulings in the framework of the Israeli democracy's constitutional-legal authority? In Israel today, the religious establishment is loath to recognize constitutional-legal authority that is not within the bounds of Jewish religious law.

Before I discuss my doctrine, I should emphasize that I do not view the separation of religion and state in Israel as a realistically achievable goal in the foreseeable future or even further down the road. I also assume that a secular division between religion and state is not essential for sustaining a stable democracy and I reject outright the possibility that a civil war based on the issue of religion could break out in Israel and threaten the country's democracy.

As noted, we at the IDI failed to make our secular manifesto a platform of discussion. I present this essay as a sort of alternative, a vehicle for future discourse with religious Zionists, non-Zionist Israelis, and non-Israeli Jews. It all comes back to the same goal I laid out above: to build a framework for shared political life in an Israeli society stitched together by a vast array of diverse identities.

Reason and faith—can they walk together?

Chapter 2

Diasporic Nation
and Territorial Nations

As with my father's family, most of my life I knew very little about my mother's family history. My only clear memory is of Lonek, the youngest child in a family of five, mainly because my mother would always tell me I was so similar to him. His face, peering out of family photographs, is seared into my memory to this day. My mother's oldest sister, Sabina, was born to my grandfather Ze'ev's first wife, while Sarah, Leibish, my mother, and Lonek were born to his second wife, my grandmother Henia.

Sabina and Sarah emigrated to Argentina in 1924, when my mother was twelve years old. Her sisters were among the 150,000 Jews who left Eastern Europe for Argentina through Baron de Hirsch's Jewish Colonization Association. As a youngster who grew up in an unequivocally Zionist atmosphere, I could never understand what led them to emigrate to Argentina, of all places, and not pre-state Israel. Around two decades later, the two brothers, Lonek and Leibish, were murdered in the Holocaust along with their wives, children, and parents. These were my cousins and the grandparents whom I never had the chance to know.

Released in 1979, *The Last Sea* was the second part of a documentary trilogy on the Holocaust produced by the Ghetto Fighters' House. The film focuses on the efforts of European Jews to flee annihilation by the Nazis and emigrate to Mandatory Palestine by any means necessary. As a young lecturer at Ben-Gurion University, in 1979 I was asked by Beit Hatfutsot—The Diaspora Museum in Tel Aviv—to lead a discussion following a screening of the film. We invited eleventh-graders from one of the most prestigious schools in Tel Aviv to view the film with their parents. We had no idea what would happen at the screening and were caught totally off-guard.

As planned, we stopped the film about halfway through and I invited five students and five parents (who were informed in advance) to the auditorium stage. Nonchalantly, I turned to the first parent sitting to my right and asked: "What did you feel?" To everyone's surprise, he answered: "I came to Israel on the [illegal immigrant ship] *Exodus*."[19]

Still recovering from my astonishment, I started to ask a follow-up question but he cut me off.

"My daughter is sitting there," he said, pointing toward a woman sitting in the auditorium.

"And how did she respond when you told her your story for the first time?" I asked.

"This is the first time she's hearing it," he replied.

"How could that be? Why didn't you share your story with her? What was there to hide?" I asked. I don't remember his exact words, but his reasoning was profound and completely persuasive. He had wanted to isolate her from his past in order to protect her.

Similar incidents occurred at nearly all of the half-dozen screenings held after that first discussion. Parents who arrived in Israel from Yemen as part of Operation Magic Carpet, who crossed the Arabian Desert on foot from Iraq and Jordan, who fought in the War of Independence, or who endured many other cases of trauma and perseverance to make it to Israel had concealed their pasts from their children.

One time, a girl who sat with her mother (and introduced herself as the daughter of cookbook author Ruth Sirkis) raised her hand and said (I'm relying here on my memory): "In Switzerland, children are born in the valleys of the Alps where their parents, parents' parents, and parents' parents' parents were born. With us, each person has such a unique biography."

My mother's parents had five children, who ended up in Argentina, Palestine, and the ovens of Auschwitz. My biography, including the lost chapters in my family's history, is also unique.

∾

After two thousand stateless years in the Diaspora, the Jews of Israel are grappling with their collective identity as a political entity. In its eighth decade of independence, Israel is beset by social turmoil and lacks the strong foundations needed for a stable future as a sovereign country.

One of the principal assertions of my doctrine is that the Jewish people simply lack a natural propensity for political sovereignty, being that they spent two thousand years as a stateless, wandering people adrift in exile. This has repercussions on how Jews experience their newfound political sovereignty. Israeli democracy is still under construction, with a national identity crisis supplying constant friction. These problems raise the question: To what extent do they threaten Israel's ability to ensure statehood for the Jewish people in the future?

There is extensive literature on the history and concept of sovereignty in its various forms, beginning with the works of political theorists Jean Bodin and Thomas Hobbes in the sixteenth and seventeenth centuries, respectively. For our purposes, sovereignty is the essence and manner of governmental power and the sources of its legitimacy in a particular political collective. Sovereignty distinguishes the particular political collective from other collectives and also distinguishes between the various social groupings within a collective.[20] Sovereignty reflects the spirit or the essence of the social contract of a nation. In most democratic political collectives, the sovereign entity's values and ways of governance are reflected in its constitution.

Only two generations after the founding of the State of Israel, it's still too early to say that democracy is a way of life for the young country. Israeli society is polarized and there is no social consensus on what type of country it should be. When comparing Israel to other democracies in the developed world, it becomes clear that having a tradition of responsibility for political sovereignty is crucial to maintaining strong, stable democratic institutions.

For historians and political scientists, there are three things that are considered essential to the development and nourishment of national sovereignty: a political tradition, a sense of cultural continuity, and territory. The ongoing reality of statelessness that characterized Jewish history for thousands of years in the Diaspora eliminated the possibility of integrating these three conditions into the Jewish nation.

These factors have made Israel's development as a nation-state unique. The sudden transition in 1948 from a stateless people to a sovereign nation was not organic—it did not stem from a continuous historical development, but rather from the revolutionary severance of the Jewish people from their historical continuity.

On the other hand, thousands of years of longing for territory and the Land of Israel kept the Jewish people in a mind-set and identity of exile. For seventy generations, the exile was perceived in the collective Jewish consciousness as temporary, with the Jewish people constituting a community much more than a geographic location. We could perhaps call exile "a state of mind," or as Jewish-American historian Ben Halpern noted: "The exile is not a geographic place but an existential condition."[21]

Jews survived in exile with the help of a strong, cohesive communal system. This communal system was centered on mutual assistance, reinforced by a belief in the end of days and the eventual arrival of the Messiah. For a homeless people, internal cohesion functioned as an essential aspect of daily life.

The Diaspora was never a static reality. The identity of the community and its individual members was constantly changing, reinforcing the feeling that exile was the vessel through which Jews shaped their collective identity over time. While Jews lacked territory and a political tradition, they possessed a powerful cultural continuity throughout thousands of years of exile, which compensated to some extent for the other preconditions of sovereignty which were lacking in Jewish history. This, along with Judaism, replaced territory as a source of existential meaning for Jews. In addition, voluntarism created an alternative for the element of statehood.

In the Diaspora, voluntarism reflected the high level of expectations individual Jews had from their community. This element of voluntarism was embedded deep in the DNA of the Jewish experience, compensating in part for the absence of a tradition of responsibility for political sovereignty. This helps to explain the significant philanthropic activity of Diaspora Jews, and of North American Jewry in particular, and the large number of nongovernmental organizations (NGOs) operating in the third sector in Israel.

The tightly knit nature of Jewish communities and their strong spiritual and cultural values often contributed to friction with their non-Jewish neighbors in the Diaspora. The often violent clashes between Jews and their neighbors—and violent attacks on Jews by neighboring gentiles—also served to steel their communal and national bonds through the overwhelming emphasis on survival. These clashes forced individuals to make sacrifices and to contribute their talents, their resources—sometimes even their lives—for the sake of the future of the community.

In terms of modern sociology, over the generations individual Jews in Diaspora communities were focused on the future and driven by a belief that voluntarism and self-sacrifice were key to the survival of the Jewish people.

By its very nature, volunteering is free of the restrictions that bind state institutions and preserve the infrastructure of the state. Thus, by serving as a solid foundation of Jewish communal life, volunteering prevented the development of civil consciousness. In other words, the price of developing voluntarism as an alternative to a tradition of statehood was the absence or nondevelopment of the concept and practice of Jewish civilian life. Without political sovereignty, Jews did not develop the internal discipline required of the individual in the framework of state-subject relations. This was especially true until the time of the nineteenth-century "Jewish Emancipation," during which several European nations rescinded restrictions on Jews and extended equality and citizenship rights. But even afterward, Jews in the Diaspora regarded the state's institutions as "them"—and "them" was always in tension with "us." This forged a schism between Jews whose lives were based on communal volunteering and those whose lives were anchored in the concept of civility, a concept which took on different forms and meanings over the course of history.

As an aside, it is interesting to compare the historical factors that shaped the way Jews became involved in the politics of statehood post-1948 with the factors that shaped the early pioneers in the United States. The pioneers—nearly all of whom were Puritan-Protestants—possessed certain sustainable political elements that over several decades helped to build a political consciousness. This consciousness later facilitated the framing and ratification of the American Constitution in the late eighteenth century and its subsequent development in the nineteenth century. In contrast, the dearth of these same traits in the Jews in the Diaspora may be key to understanding why they showed little interest in concepts such as the state, statehood, and sovereignty.

Jewish political passivity can be attributed to the centrality of messianic redemption in the collective consciousness of Jews. This element of messianic redemption, even when its presence was weak, is what preserved the uniqueness of Jewish nationalism. And this messianic redemption, which stemmed from Judaism operating in a vacuum of Jewish political sovereignty, constituted—and may continue to constitute—an impediment to the development of a consciousness of individual liberties, political independence, citizenship, democratic government, scientific education, and economic advancement.

"The Jewish people," Yeshayahu Leibowitz wrote, "is not defined by a territorial definition but by a historical definition. The historical Jewish people, the raison d'être for this state and the sole source of its vitality, was not defined by the same criteria, the same hallmarks, the same objective contexts that define other groups regarded as peoples." According to Leibowitz, "Human manipulation of the Torah led to the integration of the exilic reality into the Jewish religion. Jewish law [*halacha*] became accustomed to regarding the Jewish people as a public devoid of independent political-state functions and the Jewish person as a person devoid of civic obligations; Jews were not responsible for the civic roles defined by the society or government to which they were subject." Jewish religious thought and consciousness and their expressions in Jewish law were established as part of a utopian view of an end-of-days state, a state to be ruled by the Messiah King. "This state [Israel] is secular in essence and religious Judaism only has Jewish law based on the assumption of exile and foreign rule as a norm for Jewish reality," Leibowitz wrote.[22]

Chapter 3

The Zionist Deficit

I have often wondered: Is there something inherently wrong in the development of Zionism? Were the processes that weakened the secularization of the Jewish national liberation movement a matter of fate? I examine this by looking at what I term the Zionist deficit. This term describes a significant shortfall, both in theory and in practice, in the secular foundation of the Zionist revolution, a deficit that affected the developmental processes of the liberation movement of the Jewish people. Before discussing this subject, two things should be clarified up front. First, this critique should be viewed in the broad context of the historical achievements of the Zionist movement, which engendered a tectonic change in Jewish history. Second, it seems in retrospect that significant parts of the Zionist process could not have developed in any other way. Thus, in speaking about what I call the Zionist deficit, it is difficult to determine whether it reflects an inherent flaw in the Zionist process or is the result of failures that occurred along the way that weakened the movement's secular impetus.

The national movement of the Jewish people, in all of its theoretical, organizational, and operational aspects, arose and took shape in Europe in the late nineteenth century. The revolutionary spirit behind each of these aspects stemmed from a rebellion against the core element of the Jewish way of life in exile: the religion. It was a secular revolution. The flaws, or "the deficit," are thus linked to the revolutionary nature of the secularization process the Zionist movement fomented. This was unlike the secularization of Christian Europe, which was not driven by an alternative worldview that clashed with religion or that was based upon ideological principles. This secularization grew from the gradual removal of divinity from certain public spheres and the establishment of modern sovereignty based on earthly foundations. This process had many achievements, including the development of a groundswell of support for universal humanism as an alternative to the divine as a source of meaning and purpose.

Similarly, the forefathers of Zionism did not define themselves as secular. Only in retrospect do we describe their various worldviews as "secular." In exile, the dispersed Jewish nation was outside or on the margins of the secularization processes that took place organically over centuries in Europe. On the contrary, the Zionist movement was a revolutionary transformation, severing one old reality from the new one.

The Zionist revolution sought to break away from the past and forge a new Jewish future as a liberated people in a state of our own. Zionism was essentially a *secular* revolutionary movement. It sought to remove the centrality of religion from the life of the Jewish people and focus instead on their newfound existence as part of a sovereign Jewish state. This secular revolution continued for a few decades but was not powerful enough to prevent the rise of a religious counterrevolution.

Up until around the fifteenth century, God and religion were ubiquitous in the politics and culture of every sovereign Christian entity in the West. Religion did not carve out its own area of influence. Rather, it was interwoven in all matters, including the worlds of public officials. Over time, the role of God and religion in the Christian West began to gradually evolve. The end result was a reality that rejected the centrality of religion in social life and in relations between the state and its subjects. These secularization processes transpired in Christian territorial nations.

While most of these countries included Jewish communities, Jews were not part of the secularization process. For one, they were a nation divided and scattered across the Diaspora, with no territory to call their own. Also, because the Jewish people were a nation defined by a religion, they were for the most part left out of the secularization process until the nineteenth century.

There were two defining components of Jewish political identity during seventy generations of exile: acceptance of the governing law of the countries they lived in and a never-ending anticipation of redemption with the eventual coming of the Messiah.

For Diaspora Jews to preserve their unique identity they were required to adapt their way of life to the non-Jewish governments in their home countries and live at peace with them. This was a means of survival and a way to preserve Jewish cultural continuity. It also reinforced the detachment of Jews from political activity in their home countries and drew them further into their internal community life. Withdrawn from public life, they passively accepted the supremacy of the ruling government, what is known in Hebrew as *dina d'malchuta*.

This political passivity became a central characteristic of Jewish communities in the Diaspora and partially explains why the leaders of Zionism devoted so little attention in theory and practice to concepts like state, statehood, and sovereignty. This comes into sharp contrast when looking at the early chapters of the American nation, whose founding fathers were a product of the Christian secularization processes that took place in their countries of origin in Europe. The Enlightenment of the seventeenth and eighteenth centuries helped shape their political socialization and the formation of their collective identity as the founders of the United States.

For the ancient Israelites, the forty years of wandering in the desert after the exodus from Egypt was meant to help them develop a group consciousness and a readiness for sovereignty. Their journey through the wilderness was meant to forge a new identity and help them cast aside their consciousness as slaves. When the Jewish people went into exile after the Romans destroyed the Second Temple in Jerusalem in 70 CE, Jews adopted a sort of passive collective ethos, one of sitting back and waiting for the Messiah, their fate beholden to the whims of God. They saw their history and lives as divinely ordained. Their yearning for the Land of Israel was not expressed in any sort of desire for political independence or territorial sovereignty.

Zionist leaders of the late nineteenth century faced a tremendous challenge. They had to find practical and psychological ways to divorce Jews from their history of political passivity and embolden them with a revolutionary political zeal.

To some extent, this passivity was already fading in the nineteenth century due to the Emancipation and the rising industrialization and urbanization of Europe, as well as the rise of new national identities across the continent. It is difficult to assess the impact these historical processes had on Jewish history. My assumption is that even if these external processes influenced Jewish political consciousness and the historical reality in its various forms, the long lack of political sovereignty remained the dominant variable in the Jewish reality.

The Zionist movement came of age during the transition to a new era. This transition required redefining religious fundamentals and, in particular, their role in the politics of sovereign states, where "freedom of religion and freedom from religion" are embedded in a constitutional bill of rights. In Christian territorial collectives, such infrastructure had developed in a gradual process over centuries. The Zionist revolutionaries were the standard-bearers of a national liberation movement that was built upon secular ideologies. However, they lacked a sufficiently firm secular infrastructure. Consequently, the redefinition of the place of religion, and its role in politics in particular, remained outside the political-theoretical discourse before and after the establishment of political sovereignty in the State of Israel.

Before they could liberate their people, these revolutionaries first had to create a new collective consciousness. This new consciousness challenged the existing Diaspora consciousness, which was shaped by repression and the constant need to adapt to situations beyond their control. This challenge ran headfirst into what I refer to as the Zionist deficit—the fact that Jewish people had never undergone a gradual, evolutionary process of secularization.

There are many milestones in the secularization of the Western world. They are closely linked to the rise of Christian democratic nation-states and the establishment of modern sovereignty, scientific advancements, development of the free-market economy, and dramatic cultural changes, to name a few. The Westphalia treaties enhanced the principle of *cuius regio, eius religio,* whereby the religion of the head of state determines that of the sovereign entity. This became the basis for defining the relationship between religion and state. The secularization of the West also led to the development of the concept of sovereignty of the people, while the Peace of Westphalia can be counted as one of the foundations of modern diplomacy, which developed along with the rise of modern nation-states. This rising secularism can be seen also in the wars waged after the Peace of Westphalia and through the late twentieth century and early twenty-first century, which centered on national or state conflicts and not on religion.

The process of secularization paved the way for a gradual change in consciousness as religion no longer played a central role in the social order of Christian countries. The secularization process did not entirely disconnect religion from politics. Rather, it created a debate between these two worlds. Far from a radical upheaval, philosopher Charles Taylor likened the secularization process to rearranging furniture in a space whose basic components have remained unchanged.[23] The incremental change in consciousness during secularization entailed processes of cultural reproduction. In other words, the secular civil culture developed over generations and was the object of processes of internalization, acculturation, and reconstruction.[24]

It was a much different story for the founders of Zionism. The changes they wrought were revolutionary. These changes directly challenged the old way of the Jewish world, and this upheaval was by no means gradual. Zionist secularization was a product of a revolutionary act that occurred over the course of only a few decades. I describe this Zionist secularization, with all its paths and derivatives, as the Zionist deficit.

Was the Zionist deficit inevitable? Zionism was bound to the Land of Israel, which was the setting for the transformation of the Jewish people and revival of the Hebrew language. The emphasis on settling the exiles of the Diaspora in the Land of Israel and the revival of the Jewish language were revolutionary acts that were part of a struggle by Zionist leaders to eliminate Diaspora culture from the national collective consciousness. In the Land of Israel, the Zionists would forge a new society and a "new Jew" who was defined by secularism and landed innovation—the antithesis of the exile.

Zionism rescued the Jewish people from political passivity and established the sovereign home where the Jewish nation is exercising its right to self-determination. This is its great achievement. The thesis of the Zionist deficit addresses the failure to define the place of religion in the collective identity of the new Israeli nation and in the political processes of Israeli democracy. The core issue is that a cultural transformation and change in consciousness did not emerge in Israel as a natural counterpart to the Zionist revolution. The Jewish people in Israel left "the exile," but did the exile leave them? This provocative question leads to others: How prevalent are the traits of exile in the consciousness of Israelis? To what extent have the ideas and values of the secular Zionist revolution been internalized in the Israeli collective consciousness? The discussion in the next chapter assumes that due to the revolutionary nature of the Zionist movement's achievements, its foundational ideas and values could not be sustained through acculturation.

Seven decades after the founding of Israel, it is clear that one of the main drawbacks of the Zionist deficit has been the problematic relationship between Judaism and democracy in the Israeli collective consciousness. The balance between "Jewish characteristics" and universal democratic values is a controversial topic. No less controversial is the monopoly that Orthodox Judaism has on how Jewishness and Judaism are defined in Israel. This reality, a direct result of the Zionist deficit, is reflected in the conflict of identities in Israel.

In retrospect, Zionist leaders should have encouraged free and open interpretation of the Jewish cultural heritage forged during seventy generations of exile. It was a mistake to try to erase the cultural foundations of the Jewish people after thousands of years of history in exile, during which this culture was the anchor of the Jewish people's consciousness of history. The Zionists rebelled against the foundations of Judaism, when instead they should have found new ways to embrace the richness of Jewish history and civilization. They should have found a way to develop new, free interpretations of Jewish liturgy, philosophy, and texts like the *Shulhan Aruch* (the huge collection of questions and responses on Jewish law), which meant so much to the many generations of their own forefathers. This would have validated the secular nature of the Zionist revolution while also solidifying the place of the Jews as a national collective. It may have also helped establish new meaning and purpose for a generation of Jews who were severed from their own past. Instead, they focused on the motif of "negating the exile," which left no room for free interpretation of Judaism. Instead, an alternative emerged: an Orthodox monopoly on Jewish life and observance in Israel, which was followed later on by a religious counterrevolution.

In retrospect, it is easy to understand why multicultural and pluralistic interpretations of Judaism lack legitimacy in Israel. It also becomes clear why Conservative and Reform Jews—the backbone of Judaism in the United States—are the subject of formal boycotts by the religious authorities in Israel.

So what is the Zionist deficit? It is the clear, tragic failure of Zionism to build a democracy that tolerates an alternative model of Jewish life and builds a collective Jewish identity based on a democratic and humanistic foundation. This Zionist deficit is also a Zionist tragedy.

Will Zionism be able to overcome this flaw, this Zionist deficit? I am certain it can. If we respond to the wake-up call sounded at the beginning of this book, resolve to address the disagreements and rifts in Israeli society, and work to foster a sense of partnership in the genesis of political sovereignty for the Jewish people, we will be on the right track. In practical terms, if the Israeli collective can overcome the Orthodox monopoly in defining the collective's Jewishness and accord legitimacy to other ways of defining Jewishness, both religious and nonreligious, it will have taken a major step toward rectifying the Zionist deficit.

Chapter 4

"Negation of the Exile"

Stumbling Block to Acculturation

In 1949, when I was still in kindergarten, we moved from the ultra-Orthodox Mea Shearim neighborhood in Jerusalem to the center of the city.

The move from Mea Shearim to downtown was nothing short of a voyage between two cultures. Unlike today, back then there were quite a few secular Jews in north Jerusalem, in neighborhoods like Beit Yisrael, Kerem Avraham, and along Geula Street and the Mea Shearim market. These neighborhoods were diverse, but the *Haredim* (ultra-Orthodox) dominated the human mosaic of the time. As a five-year-old boy, my eyes were fixated on the men with their beards and *shtreimels* (large, circular fur hats worn by many *Haredi* men after marriage) and the women in their long dresses. Compared to this human spectacle, the sights and sounds and architecture of the city center were monotone and dull.

Our first year living in the house on Hillel Street was focused on integrating into a "different Jerusalem"—more political and urban (taxi stands and movie theaters were scattered all over), in keeping with the style and atmosphere of Jerusalem of the 1950s.

In my young eyes, our synagogue, Yeshurun, on King George Street was a beacon of "Jewishness," remarkably different from what

I observed in the years we lived in the heart of Jerusalem in Mea Shearim. The walls of the building had a slight curve and were made of lovely Jerusalem stone. The front doors were big, wide open, and didn't force you to have to shove your way in. More than anything else, it was the worshippers who were different.

There were two groups of parishioners at the synagogue: the regulars, who were observant but not *Haredi*, and the *epikorsim*, who were dyed-in-the-wool secular Jews. The second group included my father (who I believe wouldn't have considered himself a full member of this secular tribe). Most members came to *shul* in order to reconnect with memories from their parents' homes. The second group included professors, judges, and government workers. Most were Ashkenazi and lived in Rehavia, then a middle-class neighborhood that ran right along our street.

The walk from our house to the synagogue was short but the sights always captivated me and helped shape my identity as a Jerusalemite. My dad and I would pass by the old Knesset building, the Yahalom House, and the famous stationery store, Merkaz. To our left, we'd cast our gaze toward the walls of the Old City in the distance and the mountains that stretched across the horizon.

We would walk across the eastern side of King George Street, taking in the sights of the city. When we'd cross the street to the doors of the synagogue, we'd always take a glance at the Jewish Agency and Jewish National Fund buildings and then we'd duck inside, escaping the bustle of the city.

My father never hid from me the fact that during the High Holidays he was trying to strengthen my connection to my heritage and to Eastern European Jewish culture. The men gathered in the central assembly hall of the synagogue. As a young boy, I didn't realize that all of the women were huddled together in a separate women-only section upstairs.

During our first year at 3 Hillel Street, my dad took me to High Holiday services at the Yeshurun synagogue. I sat on his lap and looked at the open prayer book. I stared at the letters and words that were meaningless to me, as the prayers of the worshippers filled the air all around me. Much more meaningful for me were the stories my father told me on the way home. These stories were from his mother's house, and they are etched into my memory to this very day. Walking home from synagogue, my father and I stopped in a city park and sat down on a bench. He told me about his childhood in the *heder* (a Jewish religious school for boys) and about the candles his mother would light every Sabbath. The word he engraved in my mind was *Yiddishkeit*, that all-encompassing term for Jewishness and the things and feelings that signify to us what it means to be Jewish. From that first year at our new home until my father's last days, we kept this tradition of walking to synagogue on the High Holidays.

Years later, when I was a student at the Hebrew University High School (Leyada) in Jerusalem, my father gifted me with another *Yiddishkeit* experience. On the eve of the second day of Rosh Hashanah—the Jewish New Year—we walked to Mea Shearim and drifted through the *shtiebelekh* (small synagogues) and *kloyz* (study hall). My father felt like he had returned for a moment to his little town, Stojanov, and he told me about the *shtiebel* (in Yiddish: small house) used by the Hasidic Jews for prayer, Torah study, and as a meeting place. The *kloyz* in Mea Shearim was home to the elite of the ultra-Orthodox community and was far more elegant than what my father knew from his childhood.

When my father passed away, it saddened me that I knew only about a single branch of my family tree. This lack of knowledge of my family history reflects the duality within my own identity.

∾

Acculturation is a process in which the individual gradually internalizes the principles and values of a given culture. Professor Zvi Lamm wrote, "Through them, he will examine and assess the behaviors prevalent in his society and their norms in order to choose behaviors that match his views, beliefs, conscience, aesthetic sense, etc.—all of which derive from the culture he internalized."[25]

In other words, acculturation describes the ways of transferring a heritage of social, cultural, and political structures from one generation to the next. This is intertwined with political socialization—the process in which individuals acquire opinions, beliefs, and values related to their nation's political system and their role as a citizen. Through the principles and values of a given culture, the individuals who comprise a sovereign political collective adapt the prevailing behaviors and underlying norms of their society to their views, beliefs, conscience, and aesthetic sense, all of which stem from the internalized culture. Over generations, acculturation enables the renewal of the foundations of the collective consciousness in a given culture and the adaptation of these foundations to the changes that occur in reality. Acculturation processes are evolutionary and can be found in all nation-states.

In territorial nations, the main object of acculturation is the tradition of responsibility for political sovereignty that developed organically in evolutionary processes. In the young state of the diasporic nation, it was impossible to establish a strong tradition of responsibility for political sovereignty in two short generations of territorial political sovereignty. Israel, the new state framework of the Jewish nation, has yet to overcome the anomaly that was the principal characteristic of the diasporic nation's life in the exile. In the case of territorial nations—such as Sweden, France, and England, whose cultural roots are planted deep in their territory, where the civic culture evolved over generations—the historical narratives serve as a foundation for acculturation processes. Among these nations, the historical narratives are a significant component of the citizenry's identity, alongside an allegiance to the universalism of secular messages. In the same way, the ancient cathedrals in these nations link the past to the present by virtue of their presence and aesthetics. Generally speaking, the civil societies in these nations maintain an equilibrium between the universal normative foundations of democracy and the particularistic characteristics of each nation's specific cultural identity. In territorial nations, there is a platform for inculcating the tradition of civic culture in the education system. In Israel, the state of the diasporic nation, the topics of acculturation have yet to be fully shaped. This poses a major challenge for the State of Israel. In comparison to the "acculturating society" in territorial nations, Israeli society should be seen as a "formative" one.

The rich, timeless culture of the Jewish Diaspora was not given a home in the Jewish homeland. The founding fathers instead sought out a new culture for the nascent Jewish society of Israel and battled over the basic outlines of Jewish sovereignty in the Land of Israel.

These efforts by the founding fathers of Israel are part of a conflict of identities. They raise a number of questions: What are the physical boundaries of the Zionist project? Who defines our Jewishness? Can "Jewish" and "democratic" coexist side by side? In other national collectives, citizens are educated to accept and incorporate the tradition and civil culture of the country as their own. In Israel, what should or should not be acculturated has yet to be defined. In an established, territorial state with a tradition of statehood, the education and acculturation processes are built into the school curriculum. They are designed to instill the foundations of the civil culture, as well as the discipline required for the individual's autonomous decisions. This school curriculum facilitates the development of the skills required for political participation. In Israel, there is no such tradition. Schools must provide a political education and help formulate the meanings of sovereignty and being a citizen in civil society.

In the decades before and immediately after Israeli independence, Zionists rejected Jewish Diaspora life in order to build a "new Jew" in the state of Israel. Thus cut off from their shared cultural past, the Jews of Israel had no foundation of cultural continuity on which to build the new state. Could this have worked out differently? I like to think so. The leaders of the generation that founded Israel did not find a way to use the rich history of Diaspora Jewry as the foundation of the secular Zionist revolution or to make Jewish traditions more accessible through a process of secularization. These failures only caused the Zionist deficit to grow and planted the seeds of a religious counterrevolution that changed the face of Israel.

Indirectly, it also highlighted the lack of a state tradition. The founding generation of Zionism dismissed more than seventy generations of Jewish history and the role that myth and heroic legend played in Jewish ties to their ancestral homeland. It is not clear to what extent the architects of Zionism studied the development of nationalism in other contemporary nation-states or whether they noted that these states not only promised their people a place in the new-modern world but also emphasized a connection to a shared culture, landscape, and geography, as well as a heritage defined by heroism and mythology. The Zionists instead emphasized the physical world of the Bible, the history of Jewish sovereignty, the "eternal" Hebrew language, and the geography of the Land of Israel

The first prime minister of Israel, David Ben-Gurion, saw the biblical prophets and the Old Testament as embodying the values of the Jewish national movement. Often referred to as a sort of George Washington of Israel, Ben-Gurion further reinforced the negation of the Diaspora by helping define Israeliness and Hebrewness as the new embodiment of *Yiddishkeit*.

My childhood consisted of two distinct phases: the early years, of which I remember little, and the years from the end of the War of Independence in 1949 to 1956. The first chapters of my life took place inside two small rooms that my family shared with another family on the fourth floor of a building on Mea Shearim Street in Jerusalem. What is deeply ingrained in my memory from that time is a series of little memories from the days before and after the war.

During those years, I had the privilege (as my mom liked to emphasize) to attend the Sukenik kindergarten. It was founded in 1914 in the Zichron Moshe neighborhood in Jerusalem by Hasya Sukenlk, the wife of Professor Eleazar Lipa Sukenik, an archaeologist. The Sukeniks' son, Yigael Yadin, was the second chief of staff of the Israel Defense Forces and his brother, Yossi, was a famous theater actor.

The second phase of my childhood is full of vivid memories. In those years, we lived on the fifth floor of a building on Hillel 3. This second phase was in my eyes "normal" in every way: elementary school across the street, violin lessons twice a week, and—starting in fourth grade—regular meet-ups of my youth group.

I was a latchkey kid—on my neck I wore a cloth necklace with a key at the end—and I was a very independent child. I played soccer, read books, went to the cinema—pretty much did whatever I wanted. Our childhood home on 3 Hillel Street was surrounded by movie theaters: Orion, Orna, Ron, Tel Or, Arnon, and Eden. I loved to go to movies, sometimes with my friend Menachem Baram and often by myself. When I was nine years old, in 1952, I came home after watching a movie about pirates. I asked my dad to make me a sword out of wood and he went to the hallway and took two pieces of wood and got to work making me yet another toy that I didn't need. As he pounded the nails in the hallway of the building, we heard someone furiously climbing the stairs toward us. My dad and the stranger, who had reached our doorstep, stared at one another and their eyes began to fill with tears. The two men fell into each other's arms and I was left dumbstruck. To this day, I can hear their cries of "Moishe!" (my dad) and "Henek!" (the man in the stairwell).

My father was Henek's counselor in the Gordonia youth movement in Lvov, Poland. After my dad left for Palestine in the mid-1930s, Henek stayed behind and survived the Holocaust. In Auschwitz he met his wife, Fanka, and the two came to Israel with their children, Maya and Monek. Many years later, during the shiva (a weeklong period of mourning observed by Jews) after my mom's death, I learned far more about my parents' involvement in the rehabilitation of Henek and his family. Their story was one of unspeakable loss followed by restoration in the Land of Israel. It was a moving story of a family that rebuilt their shattered lives in a country that was too focused on defining its new identity to feel compassion for the traumatized refugees among them. The "rehabilitation" of that family in postwar Israel began at the Dell Hotel in the Nahalat Shiva neighborhood in Jerusalem. After living in the hotel, they moved to a house in the Musrara neighborhood, along what was known as the borderline of Jerusalem that divided the city. Like most of the houses in the neighborhood, it had been abandoned by its Arab owners during the War of Independence. The signs of abandonment were still visible: the wild grass that grew in the yard, the laundry lines which remained in permanent disarray.

Only a few dozen meters away from the house was a narrow alleyway that led to the barbed wire fences along the no-man's-land. From time to time, far off in that forbidden zone, an unlucky donkey would wander onto a land mine and depart the no-man's-land for good. When I think of this setting, it all seems surreal. The house where the Koren family lived, Henek and Fanka and their children Maya and Monek and their old grandmother—all of them Holocaust survivors— was only fifty meters from the entrance to the Notre Dame cathedral. Only fifty meters away was a giant cement wall blocking the pathway to east Jerusalem. Also, only about two hundred meters to the west was the Russian Quarter and nearby the studios of Kol Yisrael ("Voice of Israel") national radio station and also the offices of the Education Ministry. This was the strange mosaic of Jerusalem of the 1950s, a little microcosmos whose very existence boggles the mind.

In the second half of the 1950s, my family helped the Koren family move to an apartment in Rehavia where they would stay for the next three decades. Fanka was a counselor in the nurses' school at Hadassah Ein Kerem Hospital and Henek worked as a supervisor at the transportation authority. Maya and Monek graduated from Gymnasia Rehavia high school. During the seven-day mourning period following my mother's death, I learned a lot about the unending emotional rehabilitation process the Koren family endured, due to the fact that my parents were so deeply involved in helping the family rebuild their lives in Israel. Thanks to my parents, the Korens' struggle became part of my life story.

I often think about Maya, who was my age, and how the two of us weren't all that different from one another. We both attended great schools growing up. Both of us became professionals: Maya an instructor at the nurses' college and I an academic. And both of our mothers were Polish Jewish women who seemed to prove the old joke that there's no such thing as a Polish Jewish mother joke— they're all just reality. And then there were our fathers, who after just a few sentences in Polish revealed that they weren't nearly as Middle Eastern as they looked.

But there were tremendous differences between us. While my early childhood was spent as the son of Zionist pioneers attending an elite kindergarten, Maya was born into the inferno of Auschwitz and the nightmares she endured were cloaked in smoke and mystery. Her childhood home was constantly cloaked in trauma from a period of evil unrivaled in human history, while mine was a house full of kids' magazines, not trauma and lingering pain.

The Zionist revolution sought to create a new national identity for the Jews by negating the exile and attaching the Jewish people instead to the physical and cultural landscape of the biblical Land of Israel. This anti-Diasporaism filled an ideological and psychological need of the founding fathers of Zionism. However, this severing of Jews from their past and rebuilding of their lives on a biblical foundation in Israel eroded the basis of the secular revolution. It amplified the Jews' lack of roots in the territory of Israel and gave a strong tailwind to the religious counterrevolution.

At the same time that the Zionist forefathers were cutting Jews off from their past in exile, they were also trying to attach Jews to a different, ancient past in the Land of Israel. By building a secular-Hebrew-biblical culture to fit the landscapes of the country and through imitating the ways of indigenous Arabs, they were showing their desire to build a country based on a distant time and place. The

Zionist pioneers launched a broad cultural effort to adapt traditional religious observances to a new, secular reality in the Land of Israel. For example, secular nationalism turned the festivals of Sukkot, Passover, and Shavuot—the three "pilgrimage holidays" in Judaism—into celebrations of political liberation and the fall and spring harvests.

During my childhood, my extended family lived on three different kibbutzim. I remember as a child collecting the *hagadot* (Passover booklets) produced by the kibbutz movement. All of them were focused on two main themes: liberation and the springtime. There was no place for God in the booklets. In recent decades, the kibbutzim have largely stopped using these *hagadot* booklets and religious nuances have returned to most holidays in the kibbutz movement. It appears that the fervent effort to build a secular Hebrew culture failed to supersede the ancient Jewish culture and heritage which live within the Jews of Israel. The objects of the secular revolution rebelled against it and the sidelining of generations of history was a resounding failure.

I have devoted many years of my professional life to an effort to develop a moral approach to deal with the lessons of the Holocaust. I named the program I developed "Teaching the Holocaust as Education for Values." I tried to overturn what I coined the "macabre symmetry" between Nazi perpetrators ("Auschwitz was another planet" and the Nazis were beasts; "them versus us") and their Jewish victims ("they went like sheep to the slaughter"; "them versus us"). My basic approach was that in order to draw moral conclusions, I must, as a human being and as a Jew, look at Auschwitz as an event within human history and the murderers as human beings like me. I developed the concept of a "continuum of deteriorating evil," with a human being—myself—at one end and, on the other, an SS officer serving in a concentration camp. Regarding the actions of the Jewish victims of the Nazis, my argument is that we have no moral right to judge them. In the best case, we must contend with the moral dilemmas Jews faced while trying to survive in the hell on earth that was the Holocaust.

Israeli society has always perceived the Holocaust—a central trauma in our national consciousness—in terms of might. We looked at the physical power of Israel to stop another Holocaust from happening and the strength and courage of native-born sabras as opposed to their Diaspora kinfolk. Although this attitude has waned some since, for decades in Israel it was a matter of "us" and "them." We were the heroic sabras who defeated seven Arab armies in the 1948 War of Independence and they were the meek Jews of the Diaspora whose existence was defined by extermination. In Israel, Holocaust Memorial Day was titled "Holocaust *and* Heroism Remembrance Day." Israel not only sought to honor the sacrifice of Jews who fought the Nazis but also to paint a contrast between the fate of the Jews of Europe and those who had achieved statehood and rebirth in the Jewish state.

These concepts of "we" and the strong and sturdy "new Jew" with "golden curls" contrasted with the image of Diaspora Jews. "Holocaust and Heroism Remembrance Day" praised the fighters in the ghettos and cast Israel as a revival that contrasted with the decimation of the Holocaust. The rebirth of the Jews in Israel after the Holocaust also entailed a sort of negation of the Diaspora and the glorification of the new Jew as the antithesis of the old Jew in the exile who was a powerless victim. It was the favoring of strength and power over spirituality and heritage. Ben-Gurion was fond of saying that the founding of Israel was a "leap" and the turning of a new page in Jewish history, not an extension of the history that had ended in the Diaspora.

Professor Eyal Naveh writes that in the first years of the state of Israel, "The Holocaust was presented as the tragic end of the Diaspora and was used as a legitimate, central reason for the founding of the state. The Holocaust was seized upon as vindication of the worldview of the Zionists on two main fronts—the negation of the Diaspora and solution provided by Jewish sovereignty in the Land of Israel."

For years, I have wondered if we forsook our spiritual and moral heritage for the sake of cultivating this new, heroic Jew. When it comes to the Holocaust, our culture of "never again" does not encourage appreciation of the depth of our loss or the ramifications of having been orphaned from a rich heritage that spanned millennia. We focused on survival, not on mourning the loss of a culture.

The Eichmann trial has been a part of my life ever since that evening in May 1960 when I heard on the radio that Israeli Mossad had captured the Nazi war criminal and brought him to justice. My first personal connection with the trial was a complete coincidence, but the symbolism wasn't lost on me, even as a young man. On Monday, May 23, 1960, I was waiting with my parents to leave the house for the bus stop, where we planned to take line 12 to the Russian Compound in the city center. Jerusalemites from all over the city were heading to the compound at sunset, where there was an open call for extras to shoot a scene in *Exodus*, the classic Hollywood epic about the founding of Israel, based on the novel by Leon Uris. We had heard that the legendary Paul Newman—who played the fictional sabra pioneer hero Ari Ben-Canaan—would be there for the shoot, which was to be a depiction of a street scene in Jerusalem on the night of the declaration of independence by David Ben-Gurion.

As my dad tried to rush us out the door, and just before he was able to shut off the radio, we heard the sound of a news bulletin and suddenly the voice of Prime Minister Ben-Gurion over the airwaves:

"It is my duty to inform the Knesset that not long ago, the Israeli security services captured one of the greatest of all Nazi war criminals, Adolf Eichmann, who along with the Nazi leaders was responsible for what they termed 'the final solution to the Jewish problem,' the annihilation of six million European Jews. Adolf Eichmann is already in custody in Israel and he will soon stand trial in Israel in keeping with the Nazis and Nazi Collaborators (Punishment) Law of 1950."

About a year later, on April 11, 1961, the Eichmann trial began with a famous speech by Israeli attorney general Gideon Hausner, who would preside over the Eichmann trial. I stood on the lawn of the national library at the Hebrew University in Givat Ram and listened as the following words were chiseled into the consciousness of all Israelis:

"In this place, where I stand before you, the judges of Israel, to hold Eichmann accountable, I do not stand alone: I am one of six million accusers."

On that same day, I was a senior in high school, making the most of a long teachers' strike. In addition to the long hours of studying for my matriculation exam, I also spent no shortage of time listening to the testimony of witnesses in the Eichmann trial, which were broadcast in full on Israeli radio. During the teachers' strike, I would often cross the wadi (a dry creek bed) between the neighborhoods of Beit Hakerem and Givat Ram in order to study in the main hall of the national library. That same Tuesday, I joined hundreds of other students who crowded together to hear Hausner's opening remarks.

The testimonies that were heard from the witness stand sparked a metamorphosis in the collective consciousness of 2.2 million Israelis. A few weeks later, the radio would broadcast the witness testimony that would change my life.

This testimony was particularly shocking, and the shock lingered long after the witness left the stand. The survivor was named Dr. Leon Welichker Wells, a resident of the United States and an internationally renowned scientist. He told the horrified courthouse about the liquidation of the ghetto in Lvov—the metropolitan city outside shtetl Stoyanov—and gave a terrifying account of his time working in "Death Brigade 1005." The brigade was made up of prisoners who were forced to work as laborers for the Nazi death machine. The doctor spoke of how he and the other members of the brigade were forced to help the Nazis dispose of more than thirty thousand bodies at the Janowska extermination camp. The bodies of these helpless creatures were burned in the Nazi crematoriums and their bones ground to dust by prisoners who had no choice but to comply.

Out of sixty-seven members of his family, Dr. Welichker Wells was the only one to survive the horrors of the Holocaust.

"Prosecution: On June 15, 1943, forty people, including yourself, were taken from the Janowska camp, as you said, to pave roads."

"Welichker Wells: Yes. But it wasn't actually road work—it was the Death Brigade, Special Operations Formation 1005."

"Prosecution: What was the role of this unit?"

"Welichker Wells: Our job was to unearth the bodies of Jews who had been murdered over the previous three years. We then had to pile the bodies on top of bonfires, grind the bones that remained, and then remove any valuables from the piles of ash. Like gold teeth and rings. Finally, we had to scatter the ash into the wind so it would not be found.

"The role of the officer in charge was to make sure that not a single body remained. They had a precise list of the number of bodies that were buried in every single mass grave. There were times when we would spend hours looking for a single body that had gone missing. They had a detailed list and they knew exactly how many bodies there were."

"Judge: What was the grinding machine?"

"Welichker Wells: It was a large concrete machine. They were like large cement mixers with big steel balls inside. They would put the bones inside the machine and the steel balls would pulverize them. This was the process: First we would burn the bodies. They would become ash. We would put the ash through a large sieve and it would catch the gold and the bones. We would grind the bones in the machines. About thirty-one months later we came to the same grave we had searched in vain for hours looking for a single body that was supposed to be there. It was supposed to be my body . . ."

This testimony left me restless, my soul distraught. I was alone with my thoughts, out of school and away from my friends due to the teachers' strike. Not only that, up until then all of the conversations I'd had with my family about their murdered relatives were not in the context of the Holocaust.

My parents had emigrated to Israel in the 1930s as Zionist pioneers and their ties with their relatives in Europe were severed on the dawn of World War II in 1939. I learned to recognize the faces of our European relatives from the faded photographs at our home. The personal loss my parents suffered was not a subject that we talked about routinely at home. As far as I can remember, they didn't follow the trial either. Did they simply suppress their pain and grief? It was impossible for me to tell.

Two days after this testimony, I was still shaken up by it. That night at dinner, I heard my father tell my mother that he'd heard that someone from his shtetl was a witness in the trial. This came as a surprise to me. Typically, the Holocaust and my parents' personal loss was not a topic of conversation in our home and as far as I knew, they weren't following the trial.

Hausner was from Lvov, where both of my parents lived during their youth. My father called Hausner and learned that the witness from the shtetl was staying at the Reich boarding house in Beit Hakerem, not far from our home. "I called him," Father said. "He'll come tomorrow for Shabbat dinner. I also invited my sister Sabina (whom my father rescued from that shtetl in 1939)."

When the doorbell rang on Friday evening, I opened the door and the witness was standing there, smiling from ear to ear with a bouquet of flowers in his hand. The shtetl that he came from was my father's small town—Stoyanov. At the dinner table, the guest, my father, and his sister mainly just reminisced about Stoyanov. It was all nostalgia, and not a word was spoken about the guest's testimony in the Eichmann trial or what became of Stoyanov during the Holocaust. They shared memories about people, the shtetl, and its landscape. Eventually, I had to leave to go to a meeting my youth movement was holding at its clubhouse. The guest asked which youth movement and I told him it was the HaTnua HaMeuchedet movement and bragged about my plans to live on a kibbutz. After our guest was informed what a kibbutz is, a fierce argument about socialism developed, pitting the young Israeli patriot (me) against an

American professor who had become acculturated in a capitalist society that had absorbed him.

About two years later, during hikes after parachuting in the Negev, as part of my army service, the profound memory of the guest's inexhaustible vitality still resonated. This was a Jew who had emerged from the inferno to build a life full of meaning. That Friday evening, I realized, had changed my life.

About forty years ago, I visited an exhibit of the work of Jewish photographer Roman Vishniac at the rabbinical school of Reform Judaism in Los Angeles. Vishniac used his camera to document the life of the Jewish shtetl on the eve of the Holocaust. One of the pictures showed a Jewish boy with dark, kind eyes, opened wide. His side locks were tucked behind his ears and his face was optimistic, good-natured, a world away from the evil which would be unleashed against the Jews of Europe and which would cut his future short. Many Israeli offices have a copy of a famous picture of Israeli F-15s flying over Auschwitz during a visit to Poland in 2003. In my offices, though, I have always kept the photo of that long-lost boy, whose name I have never known. This picture, and not one of Jewish fighter pilots in the sky over Poland, fortifies my Israeliness.

As I see it, the attempt to bypass many generations of our history was doomed to fail from the get-go. In the decades to come, a new Israeli culture flourished, nurtured mainly by the revival of the Hebrew language. This revival was led by members of the *Haskalah* (Jewish Enlightenment) movement who sought to renew Hebrew as a secular tool (as opposed to a language of prayer and liturgy) for developing a Jewish nationalism detached from religion. The Zionist movement inherited an abundance of Hebrew prose and poetry, Hebrew translations of world classics, and, of course, Hebrew magazines and newspapers. As successful as this new culture was, though, it never created a strong enough foundation for a new and autonomous Jewish identity that could provide the secular basis for democratic life in Israel. The fact that no solid foundation was created for a new secular Jewish identity is inextricably linked to the Zionist deficit. This gives rise to another assumption I will need to address: the failure to create a solid foundation for a new secular Jewish identity meant that no solid alternative was created to oppose the religious counterrevolution that emerged from the womb of the secular Zionist revolution.

The revival of the Hebrew language went hand in hand with the decline of Yiddish. This was a tangible expression of the way our parents in the founding generation of the State of Israel cut us off from our past. It goes without saying that Yiddish was an integral part of the Jewish world and its culture for nearly a millennium. Yiddish works of literature became treasures of our cultural heritage, like *Tzenah Urenah*, which was compiled from texts written in the sixteenth and seventeenth centuries. In the eighteenth century, Yiddish became the language of the Hasidic movement and the *Haskalah* movement. And in the nineteenth century, this Jewish language brought to life the literature of Mendele Mocher Sforim, Sholem Aleichem, Sholem Asch, Y. L. Peretz, and others. As a symbol of its glorious contribution, Isaac Bashevis Singer was awarded the Nobel Prize in Literature in 1978. Across all of Europe, the Yiddish theater was a Jewish institution and theaters stayed packed night after night. Yiddish was the language of Jewish journalists who were the primary source of news for their communities over the course of centuries.

Yiddish paid the price of the revival of the Hebrew language, the biggest cultural achievement of Zionism. It was not phased out gradually—it was purged by a Zionist movement who saw it as inferior, representing a weak and groveling culture of the exile. Yiddish was the native tongue of most of the Jews of the Diaspora, so rejecting Yiddish was one and the same as rejecting the Diaspora.

Not all Zionists shared this view. Two Zionist authors wrote about what I and many others who grew up in Israel feel: something is lacking, we are missing part of our heritage. Micha Josef Berdyczewski wrote:

> The Jewish language, the jargon . . . is a sublime building, which one must marvel at; the Jews took nouns and verbs from the German language, from Polish and Russian and a lot from the Hebrew language and more from other languages, and mixed them together, concocted, fried, processed and made them into one language, a natural language, a language that expresses all of the emotions of the soul of Jews, and so on. The Jew poured his soul and spirit into this language, his anger, his discourse, his anxiety and his grief, as well as his joy and hope. He planted a large measure of his wisdom and intelligence in it—and his cunning; you will find his wit, his sarcasm and his jokes, his crookedness and his conspiracies in it, you will find the noses of the Jews, their traits and psyches in it. Nothing is missing. This language is spoken by most of our sons and daughters; and with its assistance, we can understand the internal lives of the Hebrew masses that are hidden from the eyes of the outsider. Because until we understand the jargon, until we know how to feel the subtle veins in the soul of the masses, until our ears learn to hear the whisper of the strings and the tones humming to us silently above the lips of the crowd, speaking to us or to each other—we will not have the true key to the locked garden, to the heart of the nation.[26]

And Yosef Haim Brenner wrote:

> Hebraists . . . love illusions in general, and thus the fact that several hundred children are speaking Hebrew in school already creates an illusion in their soul that Hebrew is the language of the young generation in the Land of Israel, and therefore, in their view, one additional effort is required, children must be

prohibited from hearing jargon on the stage—and, after all, everything here . . . for us, the few stalks of grain in Judea, the Hebrew language is precious—in fact, let's work to enhance and disseminate it . . . that is fulfilling a well-known need . . . but for this we must disturb some jargonish drama, which is also needed? For this, we won't allow the young generation to read the great things that are in the jargonish literature? . . . For this, we'll forbid our youth to become familiar with the lives of their people, and in this regard, to hear, for example, artistic jargonish monologues from an artistic reader? . . . No, gentlemen, by this, we are still doing nothing for Hebrew; by this, we are only giving ourselves an even larger badge of shame; by this, we are showing only that the main thing for us is the empty word, the empty chime, the decoration. Pardon me. . . .[27]

By negating the exile, we have become orphans. By negating the exile, we dealt a fatal blow to Yiddish, which was already decimated by the Holocaust.

After the birth of the state, the religious counterrevolution gained momentum as the earlier momentum for creating a new culture in Israel began to wane. The religious counterrevolution was also stoked by the external threats Israel faced and by the Israeli military occupation of the Palestinians of the West Bank and the Gaza Strip.

Now that I've entered my eighth decade, strolling down memory lane takes on new meaning. Looking back, it becomes apparent that over the years what was "old" has now become "new" to me. It is now obvious to me how central my Israeliness is to my Jewishness and how crucial my Jewishness is to my Israeliness.

In the early 1950s, when I was in first or second grade, my ecstatic parents were getting me ready for a trip to a festive event held by the

Harel Brigade at Kiryat Anavim. In hindsight, I understand now more than ever how important it was for those Israelis who "came from over there" (Europe) to mingle with the young pioneers of the Palmach (the commando unit of the Haganah—the formal defense force of the Jewish Agency, the official governing body at that time) and other early Israeli military forces. On the bus from Jerusalem to the conference and sitting on the haystacks outside the cemetery at Kiryat Anavim we rubbed shoulders with these warriors, laughed at their jokes, and were happy just to be with them.

My father served in the intelligence services of the Haganah and achieved the rank of captain during the War of Independence. The reverence he showed for the Palmach elevated them to the level of mythic heroes in our home. At the Harel Brigade event in Kiryat Anavim we saw the brigade commander, future prime minister Yitzhak Rabin, give a speech, followed by a band that performed old Palmach songs. My parents were pioneers who immigrated to Israel and discarded their "old Jew" identity back in Eastern Europe. Over the course of that night at Kiryat Anavim I saw their eyes swell with pride as they sat shoulder to shoulder with "the new Jews" of the Palmach.

On the other hand, for years I carried with me vague recollections of seeing Holocaust survivors wearing long-sleeved shirts in the broiling Israeli sun and struggling to hide the numbers tattooed on their forearms. A clearer memory is of the derogatory terms used for these survivors: they were referred to as "soap" and were seen as so very different from the heroic, native-born Israeli sabras.

In the heroism of the new Jew and the fallen soldiers, physical and spiritual sacrifice was celebrated. On the other hand, the spiritual heroism shown by Jews who during the Holocaust maintained their way of life even while facing certain death was not praised in Israel. For many years—far too many—the phrase "they went like sheep to the slaughter" was used to describe these Jewish brothers and sisters of ours in what can only be seen as a macabre sort of negation of the exile.

In 1951, the Knesset ruled that Holocaust Memorial Day would be termed "Holocaust and Ghetto Revolt Memorial Day." In 1953, the current name was approved and was signed into law in 1959.

I recall vague fragments from two or three "Holocaust and Heroism Remembrance Day" assemblies in elementary school. Pupils from every grade gathered in the gymnasium and I remember closing my eyes tightly during the reading of stories from the Holocaust, trying to imagine the faces of the uncles and aunts I never knew. I tried especially hard to picture Lonek, my mother's beloved brother whom she always said I closely resembled. I always felt compelled to feel sad or even shed tears, but my eyes always remained dry despite my best efforts. At home, we didn't speak much about the subject, not even during the Eichmann trial. It was as if the Holocaust was taboo, as if growing up without grandparents was just the way of the world.

My high school's ceremony to mark Memorial Day for Israel's Fallen Soldiers was different in every way from the assembly to mark the Holocaust. It was held in the school's courtyard and parents and relatives of the school's fallen alumni were seated by the memorial board where the names of the heroes were etched. Every year, a classmate read the words of the poet Haim Gouri: "Here lie our bodies, a long, long row . . ." We all felt profound empathy for the heartbroken families who left a deep impression on us just by being there. Identification with the fallen was instilled in us even earlier.

When I was young, the juxtaposition of heroism and the Holocaust in "Holocaust and Heroism Memorial Day" bothered me. For me, heroism was reserved for those who fell on the battlefield. Later, as the Holocaust and its lessons became a focus of my professional work, my attitude changed completely. The heroism of the new Jew, embodied by fallen soldiers, reflected physical, muscular sacrifice. Spiritual courage, standing for the essence of life in the face of the murderers, clinging to life in the most impossible circumstances that human beings can create, was ignored in the collective consciousness of the Israelis. For too many years, the argument that the Jews killed by the Nazis "went like sheep to the slaughter" was one of the characteristics of negating the exile and there was little interest in seeing heroism in their struggle.

At the same time, during my years as an upperclassman in high school, I discovered *Scrolls of Fire*. Reading this book was a transformative experience, the pages coming to life for me as I read it. *Scrolls of Fire* was meant to commemorate Israel's fallen soldiers. It was a collection of writings by soldiers who died in battle and gave a priceless window into the lives of these soldiers who were killed in the War of Independence. Reading it sparked my imagination, as I learned more and more about "the new Israelis."

The images of these soldiers came to life by flipping through these hundreds of fragments of their lives. The book was compiled by Reuven Avinoam Grossman, whose son Noam lost his life in the war during fighting near Jerusalem.

One of these poems was etched into my memory. I first read it fifty-six years ago as a high school junior. Recently, I have been driven to find what about the poem inspired me so much as a young man. I found the answer in the library of the Ghetto Fighters' House. It's a poem from *Scrolls of Fire*, written by Amos Finn:

Speak to me, pistol. You sit on my hip, always in my way,
When I'm walking by myself in the bushes and brambles
In the mountains and the valleys, visible and invisible
to all who would look.
You are with me always!
And when our enemies multiply on the path,
And every tree and bush says:
"Beware!" and when the darkness spreads
every shadow will look like an enemy
and a voice inside me will say
"Go back!"
You grasp my waist and say
"Continue, I am with you—I am with you."
I rest my hands upon you

And I will see that you are indeed with me

And my entire body will fill with confidence!

You, who in every one of your words has power

Over my fate, says to my enemies

"Take care!"

You give me a year's worth of rest when you lie under my pillow.

You shout thunder and lightning, you send smoke skyward
    and you

Spit metal.

"You bastard!"

You fire burning metal into human organs

You pierce holes in the heads and hearts of God's creation.

Full of life and energy, whose strength to build buildings and

Harvest orchards and make another thousand pistols just
    like you.

You become yet another inanimate object.

You take fathers away from their sons and sons from their
    mothers

And husbands from wives,

You, who cannot be used to build houses or sow an orchard

Why were you created?

"I hate you! I hate you so much!"

I am afraid to carry you, but I am required to

I will wear you under my shirt so others cannot see

But the day will come though, when no one will

Seek to take the soul of another person,

And security will surround me and I will never need to ask you

For help, you who sits on my hip.

I will carry you in my hand and I will cast

You into a volcano, where the lava will reshape you

You will become a helpless piece of metal.

And I will find a wife who is like me, and she will be on my waist
    and give

me the security of life.

These words left a powerful impression on me. They also contributed a great deal to the design of my worldview. Today, in my eighth decade, I think a great deal about my life and what was old has become new. And as I said before, my Jewishness has become a meaningful part of my Israeliness, and vice versa. And the disaster that befell European Jewry is a pillar within this identity.

❧

For decades, the way Israeli soldiers died in the defense of the homeland was the antithesis to the way Jews were murdered in the Holocaust. The Israelis died as heroes, while the Jews of the Diaspora died humiliating, helpless deaths. The *yizkor* memorial prayer could serve as a case study of the changes that occurred in Israel, by looking at its gradual transition from a new, secular emphasis, back to the religious and the "old" of the Diaspora. Here is the *yizkor* memorial prayer composed in Israel in memory of the victims of the Holocaust. Their deaths were passive, the victims helpless:

The people of Israel will remember the holy communities in the lands of exile, which were uprooted, destroyed and erased, those who were killed, victims of the kingdoms of evil, who were tortured in body and soul in the detention camps; . . . who were murdered en masse in the markets and in the streets; who were led to slaughter in death cars; who were buried alive, who were burned in holy temples on the Torah scrolls . . . and whose blood was spilled by unclean hands—in martyrdom.[28]

The *yizkor prayer* for the fallen in Israel's wars, on the other hand, portrays them as heroes slain at the height of battle:

We will remember brothers and comrades who set out with us in the battalions of fighters—we returned and they will not return again. Waves upon waves ebbed and flowed—and they remained on the beach, without returning. They set out young and strong, handsome and tall, as a plant in the field, until the lead caught them and the shrapnel of death killed them, one after another they dropped and fell in the fields, each son to his mother, each father to his children, each one who loved to those who loved him, filling the entire land.

Humiliating death versus heroic death; we are uneasy about the former, while the latter draws us in to identify with it. One death alienates and the other inspires solidarity. From the state's first years, two ceremonies developed: Holocaust and Heroism Remembrance Day and Memorial Day for Israel's Fallen Soldiers. Held close to one another on the calendar, their juxtaposition only sharpened the contrast between the two modes of death. This contrast was illustrated in the sayings that were commonplace in the early decades of Israel. On the one hand, the Jews of the Diaspora who were led "like sheep to the slaughter"; on the other, the soldiers, who "in their death, bequeathed us life."

The contrast between heroic and humiliating deaths is one of the starkest expressions of how the exile has been viewed in the collective Israeli consciousness. The exile was to be rejected and the "exilic mentality" viewed as one of passivity and death. The secular Zionist revolution saw this mentality as one of a people who are passive victims living aimless lives. This ideology saw the ancient Jewish concept of "martyrdom" as foreign and alien to the "new Jew."

In the 1980s, it became apparent that Israelis' perception of death was changing. No longer in the underdog role, Israelis began to identify their state and its battle for physical survival more as Goliath than David. The ongoing dangers of terrorism at home and abroad and the persistence of the political conflict caused Israelis to see themselves more and more as Jews who were victimized by murder and terrorism and less as the "new Jew" fighting and winning righteous wars of necessity. The contrast between unnatural death in the exile and heroic death in Israel's wars faded and the contrast between the shameful death in the exile and the heroic death in the State of Israel gradually blurred.

Meanwhile, the religious foundation of the Jewish people pushed the secular foundation of Israel aside. The original wording of the prayer for Israel's fallen soldiers was composed by Berl Katznelson in memory of those killed in the battle of Tel Hai and states that "Israel will remember." In 1976, Rabbi Goren changed the words to "God will remember." No effort was made to enforce this change until Lt. Gen. Benny Gantz's term as chief of staff (2011–15). Following fierce public debate, the chief of staff decided to stick with the secular version. This effort to reinstate a religious worldview, though unsuccessful, was just one of many. For example, in recent years only men have sung at the ceremony held at the Western Wall on the eve of Memorial Day for Israel's Fallen Soldiers, although female soldiers had sung at these ceremonies for years. This is part of a growing trend of using religious imperatives to exclude female soldiers from various activities and remove women from the public sphere elsewhere in Israel.

In the early 1950s, the newly born State of Israel was focused on the Zionist goal of the "ingathering of the exiles" in Israel, which had as its central ethos forming a melting pot in Israel that would help create a new society and the new Jew. The ingathering of the exiles was undoubtedly one of the glorious achievements and successes of Zionist action but it ultimately defeated the effort to negate the exile by bringing the exile and all of its traditions to Israel.

These traditions held strong in Israel largely due to the patronization and condescension shown to new immigrants by elitist, upper-class Jews from Eastern and Central Europe. This created feelings of discrimination and exclusion among a large underclass of new arrivals that had no connection to the Zionist elite and great difficulty assimilating or relating to its dominant secular Hebrew culture. The attempt to impose upon these proud, traditional Jews a new Israeli-ness detached from the two-thousand-year-old culture of Judaism was doomed to fail.

This is a key reason why the infrastructure of consciousness failed to take root in the Land of Israel. The secular Zionist revolution led by the revolutionary Zionist elites was short-lived. The revolutionary element that drove the wheels of Zionist leaders came up against Judaism: the central element that had preserved the national component in the collective consciousness of the Jews. The main phase of the Zionist revolution was realized with the founding of the State of Israel. In the years that followed, waves of mass immigration restored broad swaths of the Jewish tradition to the mosaic of cultures in the Land of Israel, the very same traditions which the Zionist elite had rebelled against. Over time, and paradoxically, the Zionist deficit brought the religious nuances of immigrants from Islamic lands into the belief system of religiously observant pioneers from the Mizrachi movement and strengthened the religious counterrevolution within the Zionist revolution. The religious counterrevolution is a key issue and we'll return to it later.

The new arrivals had their synagogues in what were labeled "development towns" that were spread out across the Israeli countryside. The patronizing attitude of the elites stopped at the doors of these synagogues. Inside these houses of worship, the new arrivals were their own elites. Meanwhile, the secular Zionist elites were severed from the roots of their own heritage in the exile. They tried instead to develop new secular rituals, heroes, and art, but it was artificial and unripe to form a sturdy foundation for a new national beginning. These are yet more by-products of the Zionist deficit. The changes brought by secular leaders were too drastic and they did not evolve naturally and gradually like the secularization that developed in Christian Europe.

As noted by Assaf Inbari, an Israeli historian of this current generation, "Ben-Gurion's statist-Hebrew melting pot was not a melting pot. It was the status quo. It didn't try to mediate between secular and religious via a shared platform of national identity. Instead of mediating, it offered alienated coexistence in a state whose every region is a cultural canton. The status quo served as an escape from the Zionist challenge that frightened everyone—both secular and religious. The secular feared and fear Judaism, and the religious feared and fear modernity. Both camps were afraid to open up, to get to know each other, to enrich each other and to patiently create a multi-dimensional culture."[29]

As Israeli society lacked the framework to develop a secular collective consciousness, religion remained the focus of identity for the new immigrants. The signs and characteristics of the "new Jew"—"the blue-eyed youth with golden curls," detached from the roots of his past—could not compete with "old" traditions. These traditions were preserved mainly in the culture of interpersonal relations, ways of life, and rituals of traditionalists and believers. They were preserved in the home, by family. This culture of the exile could not be negated and it posed a direct challenge to the transformation the founding fathers had envisioned.

Were religious Jewish nationalists part of Zionism from the outset or did they penetrate the movement retroactively? From the comparative perspective, we can see that the secularization processes in Christian sovereign entities evolved organically, thus preventing the development of a religious counterrevolution. In revolutionary cases, on the other hand, the act of revolutionary secularization left the religious foundations intact, even if temporarily suppressed, and imposed the following dialectic on the secularization process: in territorial nations (Turkey, Iran, Algeria), the revolution incorporated these foundations; in the diasporic case, the question of whether they penetrated later or from the outset remains unanswered so far.

If the historical conditions had existed for including Jews in the evolutionary secularization process in Christian Europe, then the idea of negating the exile may have been unnecessary. The fact is that the cultural bedrock created by the leaders of the Jewish national liberation movement was severely lacking. It was bereft of historical foundations and continuity in developing a new-secular-Jewish collective consciousness. In other words, the secular rebellion developed at the expense of the continuity that was anchored in traditional Judaism and no dialectical relations evolved between the two. Continuity is an essential condition for passing on the foundations of consciousness from generation to generation. But the negation of the exile was a complete and total attack. The scholar Michael Walzer describes and examines this process: "There actually were intellectuals in the national liberation movements who aimed at a critical engagement with the old culture rather than a total attack upon it. I like to think that had they won, the story might have turned out differently."[30]

The secular Zionist elite tried to overturn the foundations at the heart of the Jewish religion and create a secular, normative, and political focus that would offer a solution for the Jews of the Diaspora. This rejection of Jewish tradition and history motivated the Zionist revolutionaries to take history into their own hands. Metaphorically, the revolutionary founders rebelled against the core component in their own identity and acculturation: the foundations of *Yiddishkeit* from their grandparents' homes.

Considering the challenges that Israeli society faces in the twenty-first century, and in light of how the secularization of Christian countries played out, I feel that the Zionists threw the baby out with the bathwater. That is, Israel's founding fathers created a divide between their children and the sources of their heritage and culture. The past fell victim to the deliberate acceleration of normalization processes. However, in the anomalous reality of nascent sovereignty for a people with no history of political sovereignty, the exclusive pursuit of normalcy was nothing but a mirage—it only prevented Israel from contending with a reality that was inherently anomalous.

This exclusive pursuit of normalcy and the failure of the Zionist leadership to deal with the unique realities of the Jewish state meant they were unable to develop creative secular interpretations of Judaism. In the absence of a secular Jewish alternative, stewardship of the Jewish religion in Israel was left to Orthodox religious Jews.

When I think back to what I learned as a kid in the Israeli school system, it's clear to me that this constant pursuit of normalcy during Israel's early years created in the Israeli consciousness a sense of disdain toward the past. It was right there in the schoolbooks. The founders' generation put their disdain toward the Diaspora in writing, portraying their rebellion against the Jewish past as the realization of the historic fate of a dynamic people. Long after I left school, as a researcher spending years studying the Holocaust, I became convinced that secular Israelis attached the same stereotypes to religious Jews and the Diaspora as a whole. They were inclined to emphasize the passivity of Jewish martyrs slain in the Diaspora, to draw a stark contrast between the minority of European Jews who died on their feet and the helpless majority of victims who were murdered by the Nazis and their collaborators without putting up a fight. The ethos of Holocaust study was to emphasize the move from "Holocaust to rebirth," the transition from an exterminated people to a people reborn in their own sovereign nation. My generation saw this as nothing less than pure redemption—bursting forth into the light after years of darkness and slaughter.

By grouping the religious and the Diaspora together as objects of derision and sweeping stereotypes, Israel's founders avoided dealing with the centrality of *halacha* (Jewish law) in the daily life in the Jewish exile. They dismissed it outright, thus making it impossible to create a consciousness that fully linked the past, present, and future of the Jews. In addition, it meant they wrote off a historic opportunity to adapt the *halacha* to secular interpretation. In every other national culture, the political norms that guide the democracy are heavily influenced by an awareness of the connection between the past, the present, and the future.

By rebelling against the exile, the founders of Zionism also rebelled against themselves. They rebelled against their own history, their families, and their communities. Their lives were steeped in *Yiddishkeit* and their feet were always planted in the past, no matter how much they tried to bypass and reject their own history. Their identity, their culture and mannerisms, were shaped heavily by the *Yiddishkeit* of the very same world they rejected.

Zionism instilled the concept of homeland in the collective Israeli consciousness. This homeland and the revival of the Hebrew language were to be the foundation for secular Zionism even though individual Israelis were unable to find meaning and purpose in these accomplishments. This foundation was not strong enough to liberate Israelis from their problematic stance toward Judaism and did not make up for the fact that too many Israelis lacked a strong connection to their historical and cultural heritage.

It is impossible to overstate the achievements of this cultural dimension. The list of Hebrew poets and writers in the founding generation is magnificent. The revival of the Hebrew language is one of the most—if not the most—prominent manifestations of a new Israeli cultural mainstay that could oppose the Diaspora ethos. However, this cultural breakthrough largely stood alone. Without a large enough foundation of secular cultural additions to Israeli life, the door was left wide open for a religious revival in Israel.

In a letter dated December 26, 1926, German-born Israeli philosopher Gershom Scholem wrote the following to renowned German-Jewish philosopher Franz Rosenzweig:

What will be the meaning of "now" in Hebrew? Would not this abyss of a sacred language, which is submerged in our children, break out again? True, the people here do not know the meaning of their actions. They are certain that they have transformed Hebrew into a secular language and have removed from it the apocalyptic sting. But this is false. The secularization of a language is nothing more than rhetoric, empty words. It is impossible to remove these entire words until they explode without abandoning the language itself. Therefore, this Volapük, this language of ghosts that we speak here on the street, represents the same linguistic world that lacks expressions which could perhaps be secularized, but, if we were to pass on to our children the language that was given to us, we the generation of transition [to modern Hebrew and the Jewish state] will live with this ancient, rebirthed language.[31] *Do we not know that someday the religious power inside this language will not explode in the face of those who speak it?* [emphasis mine]

Will our youth take a rebellious stance toward the holy language? A language consists of names, the power of the language is bound in its name, and there is an abyss within it. Since we honored these ancient names day after day we can't just deny their force. We have awakened them, and they will appear because we have imbued them with such great power.

God will not surrender the language that praises him and allow it to come back to life. The revolution in the language—a language in which the voice of God can be heard—is something that is not being discussed in the country because the people who renewed the Hebrew language do not believe in Judgment Day. If only the frivolity with which we embarked on this apocalyptic path will not bring about our end.

Orthodox Judaism in the Diaspora, on the other hand, has a language of nationhood that is sacred and passive. It draws its cultural foundations from a fertile soil of religion and nationhood. For the people of Europe, languages were an integral part of secular life. The gradual, organic secularization process freed cultural expression—in science, education, and art—from the bonds of the church. And it appears this served to strengthen the foundations of these European languages. The connection between the language and the life of the political unit, between language and nationalism (which includes a territorial element, the homeland), also contributed to reinforcing these foundations.

The breakdown in ties with our collective Jewish history is both a product and a symptom of Israeli secularism. This break stifled the organic secularization process of Judaism, a process that itself was fragile and vulnerable.

When examining this process, we should also keep in mind the differences between the Christian and Jewish traditions. The organic processes of secularization in Christianity, especially in its Protestant branches, led to the establishment of democracies built upon a foundation of human rights. The secularization process that took place within the Zionist revolution birthed a democratic state whose normative foundations were heavy on national symbols but relatively devoid of the principles of individual rights and liberties. From the moment the secularization process of Jewish culture was derailed, secular Israelis adopted religious symbols in an artificial way. While this filled some needs, the moment the symbols (rightfully) failed to provide moral significance (which usually derives from a normative system and ethical codes), the identity crisis became more acute and distorted with many secular Israelis developing an antireligious stance and even real hatred in some cases.

Religiousness is not an alternate system of norms for secular people. Secular youths typically cannot internalize the normative meaning of religious texts, holidays, symbols, and commandments. The secular context negates the divine transcendental source of the tradition. The will of God as expressed in religious commandments and the very idea of a higher power are negated in the secular context. Secular Israelis have yet to internalize what has long been recognized by Diaspora Jews and every other Western collective that has undergone a process of secularization: that the normative frameworks of the collective were formed and galvanized during its shared history.

There is still no collective recognition in Israel that the normative frameworks of the nation were formed and galvanized during the course of seventy generations in the Diaspora, via the nation's diasporic ethos. The nation does not—and cannot—have a normative framework other than the framework that was formed and galvanized during its long history. The nature of the Jewish normative framework and its various characteristics were formed in the historical context of the Diaspora, which had social, political, and cultural dimensions. Secularism could not illuminate the past, nor could it inspire a powerful enough foundation for the democratic state founded by the Zionists.

I believe that the new Hebrew-Israeli culture did not include any alternative secular perspective or interpretation of the rich history of Jewish culture that evolved over two thousand years. If there was a tradition-oriented secular approach among the processes of liberation from the exilic past, it made no significant impact. Instead, a secular lacuna emerged that enabled the development and reinforcement of the Orthodox monopoly. Those who stepped in and seized this monopoly—the institutional rabbinate in Israel—are part of the historical continuity of religious Jewish leaders and organizations that the fathers of Zionism rebelled against.

Changes that took place in the Diaspora since the nineteenth century challenged the traditional rabbinical mold. And during the rise of increased modernity, alternative theological approaches were created in the changing Diaspora. These included the Reform and Conservative movements, which today include the majority of Diaspora Jews. The Israeli and Hebrew secular identities did help form a short-lived secular alternative to a life and country based on Jewish law. The Zionist founders were connected to Diaspora history in their own personal lives. But when their generation died out, a vacuum was created. Israeliness was "reborn" without formulating and establishing an alternative to the religious commandments of Jewishness.

Today, belief in God is missing from the life of modern secular Israelis. They are disconnected from all of the imperatives this belief entails and their Israeli-Hebrew identity has been severed from the sources of meaning and purpose. The Jewishness of Israelis remains without a definition of the substance of their secularity.

There is no sufficient secular alternative framework to Judaism in Israel that could challenge the rabbinical monopoly. Furthermore, the secular state school system cannot accommodate the spiritual mechanisms which are at the very center of the lifestyle of religious Jews. Israel lacks any constitutional guideline on freedom of religion and freedom from religion, something that in other democracies is typically taken for granted. In Israel, this has prevented the formation of a clear definition of the relationship between the individual and the collective. The cultural-political infrastructure of Israeli democracy is thin and shallow precisely at a place that should help Israelis define their identity. In a wider sense, this weakness has stifled attempts to reconcile Jewishness and democracy in the Jewish state. This has led to a failure in Israel's ability to find a balance between the universal and particularistic elements in its political culture.

Hebrew University professor of philosophy Eliezer Schweid asked:

> How will religious content have actual significance for those who are not religious? And, in particular, how will those who are not religious be able to impart this to their children? It turns out that continuity of memory, in the sense of education, is not sufficient continuity. It turns out that a relevant connection is needed between the content in the memory and the content that shapes life in the present and its image of the future. And if there is a far-reaching difference between the memory of the past and the image of the future, the question that arises is whether despite this difference, and while affirming it, will it be possible to draw content from the memory of the past that can support and shape the present? Is it possible to generate secular motivation, together with a conversion of the religious motivation of Judaism? And is it possible to discover content that is valid from the secular viewpoint within the religious content of the past and position Judaism as a secular

culture, open to its surroundings, without severing it from its religious past?

Schweid wrestles with these questions in the spirit of the philosophy of Zionist poet and cultural pioneer Ahad Ha'am. As we search for an answer to the problems of secular identity in Israel, the spirit of this philosophy and the way Schweid presents it are very important. In fact, it can completely debunk the secular Israeli assumption that secular life is the antithesis of religious life, that it is antireligiousness.

Chapter 5

The Gordian Knot

Religion and Nationhood

Since the early days of Zionism, and after more than seven decades of statehood, distinctive features of the collective identity of Jews in Israel have developed, at least in part. The Hebrew language, spoken by all Israelis, serves as a firm basis for establishing additional characteristics of a shared national identity. However, Israel's national identity still has fundamental shortcomings that stem from a disagreement over its core definition. For example, Israel's territorial identity is a subject of fierce dispute between those who seek to resolve the conflict with the Palestinian neighbors predicated on a return to the 1967 borders and those who stake a claim to all of the territory between the Jordan River and the Mediterranean Sea. Moreover, there is deep disagreement over the very definition of Jewishness. As noted, the Orthodox monopoly over religious matters in Israel leaves little space for other religious definitions, including Conservative and Reform. This disagreement lies at the heart of the crisis of identities in Israel.

The internal Israeli conflict of identities is reflected in a comprehensive survey of 2,803 Jews in Israel conducted by the IDI and the Avi Chai Foundation in 2009. When asked, "Which of the following terms defines your identity?" 51 percent responded "Jew," 41 percent "Israeli," 4 percent "my ethnic group," and 4 percent "religious" or "not religious." In response to the question: "Who is considered a Jew in your eyes?" 33 percent included in their definition of a Jew "someone who feels Jewish, and whose parents are non-Jews" and 48 percent recognized as Jewish "someone who was converted to Judaism by a non-Orthodox rabbi." In response to another question, 67.5 percent defined their Jewish identity as belonging to Israel and the Jewish people while 32.5 percent expressed Orthodox views on the essence of Jewishness. Nearly half of the respondents said that when Jewish law conflicts with democratic values, democracy should always be accorded precedence. As expected, preference for Jewish law over democracy is more salient among ultra-Orthodox, religious, and traditional Jews than among secular Jews. About 22 percent of the respondents defined themselves as religious or ultra-Orthodox, another 26 percent categorized themselves as traditional, and 46 percent defined themselves as secular (including some who defined themselves as antireligious).

These data shed only minimal light on a complex crisis of identity. For example, there are no precise data on the number of young people who choose to marry outside the auspices of the Chief Rabbinate. The estimate is that at least half of the young couples in Israel refrain from registering for marriage at the Chief Rabbinate. In any case, the connection between the Jewish religion and the Jewish nation is complicated. In light of the Orthodox monopoly over the definition of Jewishness, the rabbinical interpretation of Jewish law (*halacha*) is in constant tension with democratic values and norms. The *halacha* is a collection of rulings that accumulated over the years of exile. It formed an organic part of the life of Jews and the Jewish community. In my view, this fact raises an acute question: In a time of Jewish sovereignty in Israel, why isn't the *halacha* exclusively identified with the exile? *Wasn't it possible from the outset to separate the* halacha— *which does not address a reality of Jewish political sovereignty—from Jewish sovereign life in Israel?*

This question, which is not a topic of public discussion, encapsulates the problematic dialectic of religion and nationhood in a reality of political sovereignty. In my view, it expresses one of the central challenges of Israel's emergent sovereignty. There is an extensive and diverse literature on the role of religion in modern nationalism, which is essentially a secular phenomenon. Much has also been written on the relationship between the Jewish religion and the Jewish nation. Here, I seek to contribute another facet or nuance to this discussion. From my secular perspective, it would be less complicated today to deal with the problematic connection between the Jewish nation and the Jewish religion if the *halacha* had remained part of the exile instead of "immigrating" to Israel. If the *halacha* had become identified with the exile in the collective consciousness of Israelis—even if only vis-à-vis relations between the individual and the state—the nation-religion conundrum would have been simpler to address.

To emphasize and better understand the depth of the crisis of identity in Israel, I suggest we look at the religious components in the American identity. Two basic elements differentiate the American polity from its Israeli counterpart: the US Constitution (including all of its amendments) and religious pluralism. The United States is a religious nation, but it accords legitimacy to pluralism and primacy to the Constitution, which defines the civil religion. The overwhelming majority of Americans endorse references to God in public frameworks (for example, in the Pledge of Allegiance), as long as no specific religion is mentioned. "America is a predominantly Christian nation with a secular government," Huntington notes.[32] The civil religion in the United States enables Americans to connect secular politics to their Christian society, "to marry God and country, so as to give religious sanctity to their patriotism and nationalist legitimacy to their religious beliefs."[33] The civil religion in America encompasses four elements. First, the US government is built upon a religious foundation. The framers of the Constitution assumed that the republic would survive only among men imbued with religion and morality. Second is the belief that Americans are a chosen people, the "New Israel." Third is the use of Christian symbols in public rhetoric, rituals, and ceremonies. Fourth, national events and

ceremonies have religious overtones and incorporate religious functions. American religiosity accords legitimacy to pluralism and does
not cast any doubt on the supremacy of the Constitution.

In the Israeli context, where there is no constitution and an
Orthodox monopoly holds sway, I propose addressing the question
of Jewish nation versus Jewish religion by focusing on the particularistic element in the "Jewish" and "democratic" equation. That is,
from my secular perspective, I ask: What role does religion play in the
"Jewish" character of Israel? Is it possible to reduce the involvement
of the Jewish religion in Jewish nationalism by recognizing that the
latter was revived by secular Zionist liberators? How can the particularistic Jewish character of Israel be defined in humanistic-universal
terms and be grounded in secular humanism? And in connection to
these questions, which fundamental national characteristics contribute to the shaping of the collective identity? How can Jewish nationalism define its identity without the religious component?

In my view, there are clearly substantive differences between religion and nationalism. For example, while most of the world's religions aspire to uniformity of belief, nationalism emphasizes the
differences between it and other collectives. Israel—a nation defined
by religion—is an exception where the problems caused by the connection between religion and nationhood are intensified. Still, the
central Jewish belief in being "the chosen people" in covenant with
God is not unique. Indeed, one of the main components of national
identity is the sense of a collective mission and destiny.[34] The ancient
belief in being a people chosen by God is expressed in modern nationalism, especially among peoples with monotheistic traditions. This
can be implicit (through secularization) or explicit (preserving the
elements that sacralize this divine "chosenness").

In this sense, as Anthony Smith, a renowned historian of nationalism and ethnicity, emphasizes, nationalism is driven and inspired by
a belief in a national mission and collective fate. In the literature on
modern nationalism, various scholars note the centrality of shared
myths and memories, the connection to the historical territory, and

the emphasis on fostering and preserving the nation's unique cultural values. The idea of being chosen by God serves as a sort of glue binding a nation together. It is essentially a religious idea: people chosen by God to fulfill a mission or a specific religious objective. By fulfilling this mission, the chosen people will be recognized and blessed for their uniqueness. Their redemption—and that of the entire world—will be ensured.

In the Zionist narrative, this belief in being a chosen people—the "light unto the nations"—always clashed with the ethos of becoming a people "like any nation." The dialectic relationship between these two concepts created the potential for equality between the universal and the particularistic, between democracy and Jewishness. The second concept, "like any nation," was a clear expression of the secularity of the Zionist vision, which sought "to return the Jewish people to history." The two ideas balanced each other, and this balance mitigated the danger of ethnocentrism inherent in the idea of divine chosenness.

Smith asserts that religious myths of divine selection strengthen the national collective's sense of centrality and reinforce and give justification to the belief in the internal supremacy of the collective. As Smith stated, "The religious-Jewish perception that the Jewish people is 'the chosen people' may lead to a situation in which nationalism may become a phenomenon in whose name we, the Israelis, conduct chauvinistic politics of internal convergence."[35] In other words, the "chosen people" ethos and other such myths of divine ethnic favor have the potential to develop into ethnocentrism. This is because such myths help reinforce a separation between the chosen collective and outsiders who do not belong to the ethno-religious community and thus have no part in the holy national mission and its obligations. The contemporary Israeli ethos of "the whole world is against us" takes inspiration from the biblical "people who dwell alone and shall not be reckoned among the nations."

This reality raises the question: Could more emphasis on universal values be a solution? Also, to what extent can religious Jews resolve the dialectic between the concepts of "light unto the nations" and "like any nation"?

In the modern era, territoriality placed religion in a competitive position.[36] Secular nationality was based upon territoriality and the shared cultural elements of nations. It incorporates the collective elements of identity within the nation-state and strengthens it. The lack of territory—in practice and, no less important, in the historical memory of the Jewish people—strengthened the role of religion in nationalism. In other words, without territory or a symbiotic relationship between religion and nationhood, the connection between Judaism and Jewish nationalism was strengthened.

The Israeli author A. B. Yehoshua has emphasized a concept he terms "the weakness of the concept of homeland."[37] The Jewish nation, he notes, was not born in its homeland but in a land that was not its own: Egypt. Therefore, the primary connection between the people and their homeland does not exist in the national consciousness. God freed the children of Israel from slavery and it is God who deserves thanks for their liberty and independence. This is the very antithesis of Zionism, a movement led by secular liberators founding a secular Hebrew nation. Outside of the homeland, too, the Jewish nation preserved its identity as the people of God and its national existence—even without territory. Thus, Yehoshua asserts exile became a legitimate option within the structure of national identity and the right to a homeland is by virtue of the Jewish people's fidelity to God's commandments.

During the early stages of the Zionist movement's development, the national consciousness crystallized around negating the centrality of religion in Jewish nationalism. In practice, though, at no point during these stages was the close reciprocal link between religion and nationhood truly weakened. Thus, religious concepts such as redemption and deliverance were used to shape the national consciousness, with the clear intent of secularizing them. From the Zionist viewpoint, these concepts were designed to underline the fact that the establishment of a refuge for the Jewish people in its own national homeland was thanks to the actions of Jewish human beings: the "new Jews," not the "old Jews" who waited for redemption to come from God or the Messiah.

This viewpoint was popular with Zionist thinkers. "The national idea—that is, the view that a Jewish collective exists that has material and spiritual needs and interests, and whose existence is of value in itself—was part of the collection of outlooks absorbed by young people who were exposed to secular culture," writes Israeli historian Anita Shapira.[38] According to Shapira, "The young Ahad Ha'am argued that a person could be a good Jew without observing all of the 613 commandments. He thereby created a distinction between the Jewish religion and the Jewish people." Zionist leader Berl Katznelson, she notes, compares the religious "midnight lamentation" (*tikkun hatzot*) to the "pain of the tragedy of the secular nation."[39] "These are people whose acculturation process was only partial and whose secularization process was also incomplete. 'Children banished from their father's table,' Berl defined himself and those of his generation."

Zionist author Y. H. Brenner was particularly blunt, Shapira says. "He developed . . . an exceptionally scathing view promoting a Jewish nation detached from the Jewish religion."[40] He carried the banner of rebellion against the religious tradition, aiming to displace it from the center of the lives of the Jewish individual and the Jewish nation. His opposite was religious Zionist leader Rabbi Avraham Yitzchak Hacohen Kook, whose teachings were based on the Gordian knot between religion and nationhood and served as a foundation for the religious counterrevolution against secular Zionism. Brenner completely rejected Rabbi Kook's attempt to create a synthesis between religion and nationalism. For Brenner, this was an effort "to unite what is impossible to unite," a product of confused, contradictory thinking. "All of his confused assumptions and baseless visions end with the verse 'and the righteous man shall live by his faith.'"

Brenner notes that "beyond all of the convulsions in 'unity and duality'" and "the gyrations in 'the essence of heresy'" stand

613 commandments of Jewish law that the rabbi, "the philosopher who is concerned with the precepts of circumcision," fastidiously interprets and desperately wants the public to obey. In other words, acceptance of the authority of biblical injunctions is Rabbi Kook's source and purpose, according to Brenner.

Perhaps best illustrating their opposing views, Brenner said of a meeting held between him and Kook that "the rabbi writes about light, light, light, and I have darkness in all of the chambers of my soul."[41]

For Brenner, the concept of "national will" is central.[42] It could not have existed during the exile. In fact, as he puts it, "the history of our exile is only a history in the metaphorical sense." Brenner also agreed with the assertion that the Jewish people had no history.

It is possible that this all-out assault on the Jewish Diaspora past which the Zionists led can be seen as part of the need to jettison the central role that religion had played in the lives of Jews throughout their history. Perhaps it can also be seen as a psychological response to the failure to disconnect religion and nation in the case of the Jews.

The symbiotic relationship between the Jewish religion and the Jewish nation is central to the Zionist deficit, and to this day there is no constitutional solution in Israeli democracy. The Zionist deficit "allowed" the religious tradition to return to Israel "in a form of national-religious fundamentalism," according to scholar Tomer Persico.[43] In its modern form, religion cries out "in the name of the nation no less than in the name of God."[44] Unlike in Christian states, where religion has been separated from the state and made primarily a matter for the individual, in the Israeli-Jewish case the collectivist nature of the religion allowed it to occupy a significant role in the public space.

Chapter 6

The Transition from Sovereignty-in-the-Making to Sovereignty

I would like to take a break from the exposition of my thoughts, worldview, and biographical snippets and return to the context in which these things were written. I wrote my doctrine to describe the way I view the vulnerable and fragile phenomenon called Israeli democracy. As I wrote in the opening paragraph of this book, "This work is motivated by a feeling of partnership in a historic genesis in the creation phase of Jewish political sovereignty." This sense of living in a seminal period in Jewish history is the filter through which I examine Israeli life as we near the end of the second decade of the twenty-first century. The question "How did we get here?" was the initial motivation for writing this book and led to the conclusions I lay out in these pages. Two questions figure prominently in my analysis: Could it have been different? And will an examination of the processes and developments that brought us to where we are help us to make the reforms required for building a more secure and stable future?

The answer to the first question is basically: no. That is, the creation of a nation-state for the Jewish people in their land, the ingathering of millions of Jews and turning them into citizens, Israel's countless achievements—these incurred unavoidable costs. The Zionist deficit, the missed historical opportunity to formulate a constitution,

Ben-Gurionist statism, and the disharmonious social mosaic of Israel today are some of the repercussions of this genesis phase. Even if we are not cognizant of these repercussions, they are reflected in our lives, along with the impact of Rabin's assassination and the Orthodox monopoly in defining our particularistic identity. The repercussions of the genesis phase of Jewish political sovereignty prompted me to issue the "invitation to my Israeli compatriots to join in a common awakening," as I wrote in the opening line of this book.

The answer to the second question will be determined by whether or not we internalize the fact that we are still in the sovereignty-in-the-making stage.

German-American political philosopher Leo Strauss, in his published lecture *Jerusalem and Athens: Some Preliminary Reflections*, challenges the Zionist worldview. Strauss argues that the establishment of the State of Israel marks a significant change in the configuration of the exile but does not constitute the end of the exile because, in the religious sense, the State of Israel is a part of the exile. The state does not resolve the eternal problems in Judaism because "infinite, absolute problems cannot be solved." In the following pages, I will attempt to address the challenge expressed by Strauss.

In the Diaspora, Jews did not develop the political responsibilities that determine relations between rulers and the ruled. Zionist leaders paid little attention to the implications of this and the repercussions can be felt to this day. Against this background, I distinguish between two transitions: the transition from a state-in-the-making to a state and the transition from sovereignty-in-the-making to sovereignty. The first transition occurred as a revolutionary act on May 14, 1948, when Israel declared its independence. The second transition is an evolutionary one. I believe that it is still in process and that the state remains in an intermediate stage between sovereignty-in-the-making and full sovereignty. This reality reflects the fact that Israel is a formal democracy and not a substantive one. It has functioning institutions in all of the three branches of government. It has elections and it operates according to democratic rules. On the other hand, it lacks a constitution to regulate relations between the authorities and, in particular, the legislative and judicial branches. Also, most important, it lacks a bill of rights that would define and establish personal liberties, protect minorities, and clearly demarcate the role of religion in society.

To make matters worse, the lack of a constitution means that Israeli pupils are not being taught the basic values of democracy that are essential for participating in civil society. The reality we face today is that individual Israelis and the country's entire civil society have failed to internalize the meanings and substantive principles of democracy.

～

James Madison to Thomas Jefferson, May 15, 1787:

> Monday last was the day for the meeting of the Convention. The number as yet assembled is but small. Among the few is General Washington . . . There is a prospect of a pretty full meeting on the whole, though there is less punctuality in the outset than was to be wished.

Madison to William Short, June 6, 1787:

> The Convention has been formed about 12 days. It contains in several instances the most respectable characters in the U.S. and in general may be said to be the best contribution of talents the States could make for the occasion. What the result of the experiment may be is among the arcana of futurity . . . The personal characters of the members promise much. The spirit which they bring with them seems in general equally promising.

But the labor is great indeed; whether we consider the real or imaginary difficulties within doors or without doors.

And to Jefferson, also on June 6, Madison wrote: "The whole Community is big with expectation. And there can be no doubt but that the result will in some way or other have a powerful effect on our destiny."

The creation of the US Constitution when a nation was born is analogous to the ceremonial circumcision of a newborn Jewish male: it is a cornerstone in establishing national identity. This is what happened in the United States. Israeli democracy, however, is a ship of state that left the shipyard prematurely: not all the bolts are fastened, not all the seals are tight. The psychological gulf between the two democracies is as wide as the distance from eighteenth-century Philadelphia to twenty-first-century Jerusalem. The intellectual genius and political will of the founding revolutionaries, Anglo-Saxon gentlemen, educated humanists of the upper social classes, gave rise to a constitution which, with periodic amendments, has determined America's democratic character. This did not happen in Israel, and perhaps could not have happened.

Consider, too, the West German constitution that came into being in 1949, only four years after the defeat of the German regime that had brought such devastation to the world and upon itself. It was born of very different circumstances. But like its American counterpart, the German version was enabled by that vital convergence of intellect, sophistication, and political will—buttressed, in this case, by the victorious Allies—at the historic founding moment.

By contrast, in that very same year, David Ben-Gurion, the first prime minister of Israel, missed the constitutional moment, and since then, Israel has been Israel. High drama and volatility are the stuff of daily life. "In the evening," we joke, "the morning's news is history." The decision to formulate a constitution for Israel was cited in the state's Declaration of Independence on May 15, 1948: "We declare that, with effect from the moment of the termination of the [British]

Mandate ... [and] until the establishment of the elected, regular authorities of the State in accordance with the Constitution which shall be adopted by the Elected Constituent Assembly not later than the 1st October 1948, the People's Council shall act as a Provisional Council of State."

The first Israeli elections were held in January 1949 to elect representatives to a national assembly that was slated to produce a constitution by October of that year. The opportunity was missed because Ben-Gurion was unwilling. Why? What reason did the founding father of the State of Israel have for opposing a written constitution? My friend, the late historian Zeev Tzachor, who served as Ben-Gurion's last secretary at Kibbutz Sde Boker, offered the following explanation: Ben-Gurion wondered, for a variety of reasons, if writing a constitution was feasible or worth the effort. Given that the Jews had lacked a national territory and common language for so long—seventy generations—Israel's founding father was not certain that the nascent Jewish state would survive. (Until 1939, he never even spoke of statehood.) Ben-Gurion's great wish was to build a nation out of the multicultural, multilingual Jewish people scattered around the globe and to guarantee its independence and sovereignty. This, perhaps, explains the haste with which he set up the new nation's institutions. The tasks ahead were vast and a constitution, Ben-Gurion apparently believed, would tie his hands. Great energy was needed to build the foundations of the State of Israel—political, social, and cultural institutions, an economy, the Israel Defense Forces. The state absorbed Jewish immigrants from a hundred countries speaking scores of languages. All these efforts diverted resources that under other circumstances would have been directed to plan for the future of Israeli democracy. Given the vastness of other challenges, and despite an abundance of intellect and savvy, the all-important political will was missing, and so was a constitution.

The State of Israel missed its first historical opportunity to establish a constitution. The very first elections in the newly born State of Israel, held in January 1949, were meant to elect a Constitutional Assembly. This assembly was supposed to complete its task to frame a constitution later that year. However, only a month after the elections, under the leadership of Ben-Gurion and his Mapai (Labor) party, the Constitutional Assembly voted to change its original purpose and to function as a parliament, becoming the first Knesset of Israel. Ever since, the elected body in Israel wears two hats—as both a parliament and a constitutional assembly. As a parliament its elected members mainly focus on the next elections, while as a constitutional assembly its mission is to examine what needs to be done for future generations. The work of a parliament and the work of a constitutional assembly are like two parallel lines that will never meet.

The United States and other countries have bicameral legislatures, in which one house can (in theory) engage in political discourse with an eye to the next election, while the other, at least theoretically, acts like a national assembly, making strategic choices to strengthen the democratic well-being of future generations. The twin-headed nature of Israel's parliament, being a house of representatives and a constitutional assembly at the same time, means that tremendously important decisions are often made for petty political reasons. This system had to be reformed, but how to do it? After all, the comfortable horse traders of Knesset would never vote themselves out of existence.

The same year that Israel passed on formulating a constitution, Germans ratified a constitution of their own. They were only a few years past the trauma and devastation of World War II and had already taken a huge leap toward becoming a formidable democracy. In the United States, the principles of the Bill of Rights were instituted during the course of the nineteenth century, which included the Civil War—the bloodiest and most traumatic event in American history. Currently, Israel is still a formal democracy but far from the model of substantive democracy that prevails in stable, developed democracies.

There are several explanations for why Israel has yet to achieve full sovereignty. A primary factor, inherent in the Zionist deficit, comes from the way the founding fathers of Israel viewed the concepts of state and sovereignty. For territorial nations, sovereignty was based on agreed institutional foundations and an "old political order" which does not exist in the Jewish reality. From this old political order developed the concepts of natural law, liberty, rights, and, eventually, modern political sovereignty.

This process of establishing sovereignty included changes in the social imagination, a concept which philosopher Charles Taylor said "notes the way we collectively imagine our social life in the modern Western world."[45] Social imagination includes the ways in which people perceive social existence, how they adapt themselves to the existence of others, and their expectations from society.[46] Social imagination is the platform for shared understanding in a society. It enables shared practices and a broad and inclusive sense of legitimacy. There are significant differences between social imagination in territorial collectives with political sovereignty and a Diaspora collective that lacks any such pedigree of sovereignty. As with the acculturation process, the historical deficiencies faced by the ancient Jewish nation complicated the development of sovereignty.

Author Yaron Ezrahi writes that "the space in which democratic politics operates becomes full of many social imaginations about the desired political order," but in Israel there is no shared understanding to help the country build its social life.[47]

Unlike territorial nations, Israel simply did not go through the same transition from an old political order to a modern moral order. There was no Israeli ethos of statehood prior to 1948 or in the years after the formal establishment of the state. In Jewish history, there is no parallel to the Westphalia treaties as part of a process of secularization and the development of modern sovereignty. Therefore, the Zionist deficit is defined by shallow definitions of state, statehood, and sovereignty. The system of rules of conduct that prevailed in the Jewish communities of the Diaspora reflected the way that they and Jewish law had acclimated to the Eastern European Diaspora. This Diaspora was a world of its own, not defined by any sovereign state, and it never underwent any sort of institutional differentiation.[48]

A cursory look at the writings of the leaders of the Zionist movement reveals a curious fact that demands a closer look. The Zionist pioneers spoke extensively about the effect that exile had on Jews and the situation of the Jewish people in the new era. They also devoted some attention to the effects that modernity had on the Jewish people and their future. Nonetheless, while they gave great thought to the past, they paid little attention to what the longed-for Jewish sovereignty would look like. While the founder of political Zionism, Theodor Herzl, composed a utopia (*Altneuland*) about the future Jewish state, even the most pragmatic Zionist leaders did not come up with any sort of detailed guidelines for what the sovereign Jewish state should be like. They certainly did not bother to figure out ways to regulate the relations between the state, the society and its social mores, and the Jewish religion.

Some have surmised that this was a tactical decision by the Zionist leaders. From the outset, political Zionism refrained from declaring its "final objective" in order to avoid provoking undesirable reactions: What would the Turks say? What would the English say? And, primarily, how would the Arab neighbors react? This claim surmises that the Zionists understood how the state they sought to establish would operate. I have my doubts. The Zionist movement did not address the nature of sovereignty because it feared the internal repercussions of this discussion. It formulated and accepted political compromises that were meant to be temporary. Indeed, the character of the future state was shaped in a haphazard process in which the Jews seemed to realize that they would have only a narrow scope of influence in shaping their hard-won freedom. And thus, they refrained from establishing a constitution for the new sovereignty.

In my view, the completion of the process of achieving sovereignty depends on building the consensual infrastructure, a social contract for Israel. This would serve as the basis for defining the shared normative set of values that guide political conduct and outline the parameters of the political culture for the national collective and sovereign citizens.

What defines diasporic nations more than anything else is that they are anomalies. This unique identity is an integral part of the nation's daily life and that of the political collective living in the Jewish state. Negating the exile was a way for Zionists to normalize Jewish collective life in the Land of Israel.

An obsessive craving for normalcy was already evident in the revolutionary stage of the Zionist process. Leaders of the Zionist movement instilled this desire in the collective consciousness as an ideological instrument that also had a psychological function: to sever ties with their own Jewish heritage. The craving for normalcy among a people characterized by an abnormal existence was one of the reasons (even if not a primary one) that the intellectual and mental resources of the state were not utilized to help make the transition from sovereignty-in-the-making to full sovereignty.

Territoriality forms the bedrock for sovereignty. It enables the development of a multigenerational tradition of responsibility for political sovereignty that transcends any particular political doctrine or regime. Together, physical territory and sovereignty comprise a solid framework for continuous existence and national-cultural-ethnic survival. There is no substitute for a territorial homeland that serves as a physical basis for a collective and is not only located in its historical memory or consciousness. On their own sovereign territory, the members of every generation refashion their national institutions, government systems, and patterns of citizenship. They do so while also considering the myths, memories, values, and symbols of their past and also their social imaginations.

Although it is not easy to accept, I believe that all of these make the reality of our lives in Israel an anomaly over time. It is even harder to accept such reality when it entails facing difficult challenges and not simply a passive approach as was the Jewish tradition in the Diaspora. Israel has always had an internal clash between normalcy and anomaly, between wanting to be like all other nations and being at the same time "a light unto the nations."

Perhaps Israelis have felt that by admitting the country is an anomaly, they were somehow endangering its territorial existence. Viewing the anomaly as a threat (and not as a situation that should be accepted in order to deal with its implications) leaves a number of basic questions unresolved, such as: What are the features of the collective identity of the State of Israel? What is the Jewishness of Israel? *What question is the Jewish state designed to answer?*

This "exile versus normalcy" dialectic is lacking. I suggest we try something that is almost the complete opposite: diasporic versus the anomaly of Israeliness. In the first equation (exile versus normalcy), the exile represents the temporary element in the lives of Jews while normalcy represents the Zionist longing for the permanence and stability provided by a stable Jewish state. In the second equation (diasporic versus anomaly), the first pattern is reversed. Diasporic is presented as a permanent form of Jewish existence while the anomaly embodies the uniqueness of the Jewish nationalism that is developing in the political center of the nation today—that is, during the ongoing initial stage required for shaping a shared cultural-social-political ethos for the entire Israeli collective. This collective can be described as a kaleidoscope composed of fragments of cultures and identities in transition from sovereignty-in-the-making to full sovereignty.

A central characteristic of the anomaly that is Israel is the fact that the country lacks borders to define its territory. Borders are not only geographic or political reference points. They distinguish between cultures, languages, customs, and landscapes and help define the identity of one collective vis-à-vis another. For more than fifty years, ever since the Israeli victory in the Six-Day War in 1967, there has been no consensus on the territorial dimensions of the Jewish state.

Instead, the State of Israel is the only democracy that lacks defined borders with its neighbors. Israeli society itself is torn over the issue of where to draw the country's borders and how to determine the lines where the democratic State of Israel ends and the cultures and undemocratic states of the Arab Middle East begin. This reality hinders Israel's ability to transition to full sovereignty and also weakens Israel's democracy and rule of law. One of the main obstacles preventing the definition of our borders—the settlements in the West Bank—also pose a serious threat to Israeli democracy. This is not only because the settlements help to perpetuate a military occupation of the Palestinian people but also because of the continued attacks on the Israeli Supreme Court by supporters of the settlement enterprise.

The secular, national-ethnic view of Jewishness does not reject the Diaspora or its history. Unlike the exile versus normalcy argument, it offers to include the exile, cognitively and emotionally. It also accepts that the cultural-national life of the Diaspora was and remains essential to building a fully sovereign Jewish state.

Chapter 7

Ben-Gurionist Statism

David Ben-Gurion is considered the architect of the State of Israel, having served as its first prime minister (from 1948 to 1953 and again from 1955 to 1963). He was born in Plonsk, Poland (then part of the Russian Empire), in 1886 and received his initial Jewish education in a "reformed *heder*" established by his father, Avigdor Green, one of the founders of the Hovevei Zion movement in Poland. As a teenager, the future prime minister started the Ezra youth club to promote Zionism and the Hebrew language.

Ben-Gurion arrived in Jaffa in 1906 and became active in Poalei Zion, a socialist-Zionist party. For several years, he worked in agriculture in various settlements. In 1911, he served as a delegate to the Eleventh Zionist Congress and was elected to leadership roles in Poalei Zion. Ben-Gurion traveled to New York in 1915 with his friend Yitzhak Ben-Zvi (who later became the second president of Israel) to recruit and train Jews for a "work army" in Palestine.[49] In 1917, Ben-Gurion married Pauline Munweis (1896–1968), who had emigrated to the United States from Minsk as a teenager. A few months after the Balfour Declaration, upon America's entry into World War I, Ben-Gurion, Ben-Zvi, and others began recruiting volunteers for a Jewish Legion.[50] But by the time the volunteers arrived in Palestine, it had already been conquered by the British.

In 1919, Ben-Gurion helped to form the Achdut Ha'avoda party and was elected its leader. The Histadrut labor federation was established a year later and Ben-Gurion served as its secretary-general from 1921–35, focusing on Jewish settlement and organized labor. As a member of the Yishuv's Provisional Council (*hava'ad hazmani*) and later as a member of the Jewish National Council (*hava'ad haleumi*), Ben-Gurion helped to lay the organizational foundations for the Jewish state. He also worked to unite the labor movements: in 1930, Achdut Ha'avoda and Hapoel Hatzair merged to form the Poalei Eretz Yisrael party: Mapai. Ben-Gurion was elected chairman of the Zionist Executive and Jewish Agency in 1935 and worked in this role to foster collaboration between the labor movement and other segments of the Zionist movement. From 1920 until the birth of the state, Ben-Gurion played a role in all of the crucial decisions of the Zionist movement. In 1937, he supported—together with Chaim Weizmann and Moshe Shertok (Sharett)—the Peel Commission's partition plan, which called for establishing a Hebrew state in part of Palestine. Although the land earmarked for the Jewish state was small, Ben-Gurion saw this as an effective means of achieving the Zionist mission. In February 1939 he participated in the St. James Conference in London, which was followed by the white paper that set limits on Jewish immigration to Palestine and land acquisition by Jews. Upon returning to Palestine, Ben-Gurion declared an open struggle against Britain. The political battle against the white paper intensified after the end of World War II. On April 18, 1948, Ben-Gurion was appointed to head the People's Administration and on May 14, 1948, he declared the establishment of the State of Israel and a provisional government, in which he served as prime minister and defense minister.

In 1953, Ben-Gurion retired to Kibbutz Sde Boker in the desert in southern Israel. Ben-Gurion's decision stirred a great debate about the role of a leader, including in my home, where my parents were committed supporters of the Mapai party. Even I, just ten years old, saw Ben-Gurion's decision to resign as a mistake, though I may have been just mirroring my parents' view. My mom suggested that I write a letter to Ben-Gurion and, against all odds, the same man who was so stingy with his autographs outside the old Knesset actually wrote me back.

In his own handwriting, he clearly explained the importance of settling the Negev desert and setting a personal example for his fellow Israelis.

In 1955, Ben-Gurion returned to public life to serve as defense minister and, several months later, was again elected prime minister. He continued to live in Sde Boker while in office and the kibbutz remained his home until his death in 1973.

There is a direct link between the "statist" outlook of Ben-Gurion and Israel's missed opportunity to frame and accept a constitution in 1949. In his book *Ben-Gurion and the Constitution,* author Nir Kedar writes, "The argument over the constitution was in fact part of the broader statist polemics during the transition from the Yishuv to the state."[51] Kedar attributes the difficulty that arose in what he calls "the polemics around the question of statism" primarily to structural-institutional aspects: the transition "from the political structure of the Yishuv's federation of ideological groups to a sovereign structure of a democratic state of law."[52]

Ben-Gurion's emphasis on majority rule and the rule of law highlighted the considerable lack of attention to the essence of democracy: liberties and individual rights in general and the rights of minorities in particular. In retrospect, it appears that Ben-Gurion's statism fell victim to Israel's failure to have an intellectual or pragmatic discussion about the meaning of concepts such as state and statehood. The Zionists had no parallel to *The Federalist Papers* and, due to the

Zionist deficit, were left with Ben-Gurion's statism, which emphasized founding a state quickly.

Ben-Gurionist statism laid out the parameters of Israel's formal
democracy and hindered Israel's potential to build a substantive
democracy. He put more emphasis on the responsibilities of individuals to the state, as can be seen in comments he made to the Knesset
in 1959, in which he said, "You're talking all the time about a bill of
rights. Where is your bill of duties?"[53]

Ben-Gurion did not distinguish between state and society and was
not particularly sensitive to the repercussions of Israel being such a
diverse and complex society. He did not fully appreciate the need to
affirm substantive democratic ways of life, which in a diverse society
requires celebrating diversity and identifying the line between state
and society so that a rational discourse can take place.

Ben-Gurionist statism, an outlook that is still rooted in the Israeli
consciousness as an alternative to disagreements and rifts, seeks to
underline the aspects shared by all members of the society. This means
settling for the lowest common denominator, conceding or ignoring
disputed issues, and opting for neutrality. Statism focuses on values
of unity, consensus, and obedience, preferring them to pluralism and
critical thinking.

A nation-state that claims to be the home of Jewish self-
determination must have guidelines for defining the identity of its
collective. In the early years of Israel, there was a wide range of opinions among Zionists about what identity the Jewish state should
have. This diversity of opinions was valuable in a country with such
a multifaceted culture and collection of worldviews. In the end,
though, instead of incorporating all of these worldviews into the
forging of Israeli identity, the state adopted the neutrality of Ben-
Gurion, leaving the country with a hollow identity.

Neutrality also led to the enactment of the State Education Law of
1953, which abolished the different streams in the education system.
These streams had evolved along a number of decades in the pre-
state era. They had been affiliated, ideologically, with three branches

of Zionism: the Labor Stream, the Zionist Religious Stream, and the Liberal Stream. The most significant characteristic in each was what used to be called the educational triangle: the tight connection among school, the youth movement, and the parents' home. When the law was enacted, I was in fourth grade at the Arlozorov School for Laborites' children in Jerusalem. I remember how on May Day that year we wore our blue shirts (the color of the three youth movements affiliated with Labor) and marched from school to an assembly held in the formerly Arab neighborhood of Sheikh Bader, which later became Sacher Park. The combination of ideologically affiliated school subsystems formed a foundation for political socialization until the youth movements and certain elements of political education were removed from the school system. The State Education Law of 1953 ostensibly abolished the different political streams that had developed in the education system during the pre-state period. But in practice, it was only the Labor-Zionist education stream that was actually eliminated. The religious Zionist stream remained intact and later became known as "state-religious education." To this day, it retains the characteristics of the educational "triangle."

When I look at the way the 1953 law ended the training of pupils in the basics of participation in a democratic civil society, I can't help but think that it was an expression of the same Ben-Gurionist omission that prevented Israel from creating a constitution in 1949. It is worth mentioning that appended to the ratification of the constitution in the early days of the New German Republic, that nation laid the groundwork for "political education" (*politische Bildung*) aimed at achieving an appropriate political socialization for the future members of a democratic society.

Thus, not enough attention or sensitivity was invested in shaping a social policy for the wide variety of identities and cultures that made up Israeli society in the first year of the state's existence. This is especially true if we look at how traditional Jews from Asia and North Africa were subjected to secularization processes based on the negation of the Eastern European Diaspora. The lack of sensitivity shown to these immigrants fostered alienation among traditional Jews and perhaps lessened the chances of social integration. Author Alessandro Ferrara warned, "When religious citizens in states with secular politics are requested to 'translate' religious values into secular concepts . . . [this may generate] increasing alienation among broad groups of citizens who have religious orientations and may reduce [their] ability to integrate in cultural systems when they face a divide between institutional secular values and religious values."[54] I believe this has also latently been the means of mobilizing the traditionalists into the ranks of the religious counterrevolution.

At the dawn of Israeli statehood, Ben-Gurion sought to enforce Jewish sovereignty in a hurry, at once, immediately. His statist, unification concept of sovereignty was narrow, though, and it was insufficient to accommodate a society crying out for recognition of its diverse cultures and identities. Ben-Gurion, according to legal scholar Nir Kedar, saw "the state as an entity that should treat all of the members of society uniformly, impersonally, and equally."[55] Ben-Gurionist statism craved normalcy and it was presented as a way to achieve normalization in the lives of Jews within the borders of their political home, so that the nation would be like all nations. Focused on the here and now, the leaders of the nascent Israeli state did not focus on developing a vision for the future of a people with no tradition of political sovereignty.

Against this background, we can understand the obsession with normalcy as reflected in Ben-Gurionist statism. That said, not all of the ills of the Zionist deficit can be attributed to this political ideology. Any analysis must take into account the momentous and complex times in which Ben-Gurion orchestrated the creation of the state. Ben-Gurionist statism was born in the reality of the 1950s, when Israel was emerging from the shadow of the Holocaust and dealing with mass immigration and a series of ongoing security threats. This context must be taken into consideration. The idea of statism shook the national consciousness, disrupted cultural and political frameworks, and sometimes even overturned them. My critique of this statism should be seen as a sort of retrospective diagnosis that was impossible to make at the time.

The goal of creating a normal reality in Israel was of paramount importance to the founders of the state. At the helm of Jewish nationalism was a pragmatic leader who faced a nearly impossible reality and who lacked the ability to educate the people of his nascent state about the principles they would need to adopt. He was an illustrious statesman but not an educator and there was no political ally at his side to take this role. A contrast with the three founding fathers of the United States immediately comes to mind. In Israel there was no equivalent to James Madison, Alexander Hamilton, and John Jay. These three men authored *The Federalist Papers*, an in-depth guide for the American democracy, a sort of pedagogical manifesto that took a long-term view of the matters at hand. It is self-evident that this collection of eighty-five articles provided a blueprint for the normative foundation of American democracy. Ben-Gurion, though, was a priest without a prophet. He envisioned the creation of the state but had no long-term plan for its political content and no *Federalist Papers*. No equivalent document was written in Israel because the founders of the state and the practitioners of Ben-Gurionist statism lacked a sound foundation of political-state theory and views. This is in marked contrast to the founding fathers of American democracy, whose political beliefs were grounded in the implications and conclusions of such theories and views. There was no Alexis de Tocqueville to sum up those views and guide the actions of Israel's founding fathers. This absence is not only an attribute of the Zionist deficit but also reflects the fact that the Jewish people had no tradition of political sovereignty.

The revolutionary passion that drove the Zionist mission, together with the practical application of democratic procedures of governance, led to a series of accomplishments under Ben-Gurion's leadership at the threshold of statehood. Nonetheless, the neutral essence of statism became one of the repercussions of the Zionist deficit, joining other factors that powered the religious counterrevolution even before the state was established. Two of the accomplishments of Ben-Gurionist statism illustrate this: Israel's Declaration of Independence and the definition of Jewishness in the Law of Return. It is doubtful that these accomplishments could be achieved today considering the power of the religious counterrevolution. God is not present in the Declaration of Independence of the State of Israel and is instead replaced by the words "Rock of Israel" as an expression of the secular nature of the Zionist revolution. Moreover, the framers of the declaration deleted a biblical verse (Deuteronomy 1:8) that reads, "See, I place the land at your disposal. Go, take possession of the land that the Lord swore to your fathers, Abraham, Isaac and Jacob, to assign to them and to their heirs after them."

Israel's Law of Return, the very first bill enacted by the Knesset, has been a call for Jews to immigrate and gain citizenship. The law—which was enacted in 1950—does not define a Jew according to *halacha,* the body of Jewish law. During the 1950s, immigrants were registered as Jews under the Law of Return based on their declaration of Jewishness, including ones not considered Jewish according to *halacha,* which stipulates that a Jew is someone born to a Jewish mother. The Law of Return gave validity to the secular perception of Jewishness and sidelined the religious view. In July 1958, despite the opposition of the religious parties in the Knesset, the government reaffirmed that an adult would be registered as a Jew after declaring his or her Jewishness in good faith and as long as he or she was not a member of another religion. That same year, Ben-Gurion asked fifty Jewish religious authorities considered to be "sages of Israel" for their opinions on the criteria to adopt vis-à-vis religion and nation. The majority supported the Orthodox stance while the rest proposed defining Jewishness as a cultural-ethnic identity. The argument over the question of "Who is a Jew?" was left unresolved.

In 1970, the Knesset enacted an amendment to the Law of Return, ruling that a Jew is "someone born to a Jewish mother, or who converted and is not a member of another religion." The authors of the amendment did not define the type of conversion required and the religious parties failed in their attempt to have the law stipulate that only an Orthodox Jewish conversion would be sufficient. Moreover, the amendment to the Law of Return recognized the reality of mixed marriages and thus allowed the child and grandchild of a Jew, even if not Jewish according to *halacha*, to enjoy the rights offered under the Law of Return. This paved the way for hundreds of thousands of immigrants from the former Soviet Union in the 1990s. Some of these immigrants viewed themselves as belonging to the Jewish people, even if they were not Jewish according to *halacha*. However, there were also Christian immigrants who immigrated to Israel based on family ties.

The never-ending argument over "who is a Jew" reflects the fragility of the secular basis of Ben-Gurionist statism, which stems from the Zionist deficit. This saga began with a clearly secular definition of Jewishness to which restrictions were later imposed as the religious counterrevolution gained strength. The reality today is that about a third of the million immigrants from the former Soviet Union are defined as Jews under the Law of Return but not according to Orthodox Jewish law.

In light of these two examples—the Declaration of Independence and the Law of Return—I ask myself: In today's Israel, would a majority of Knesset members agree to sign the Declaration of Independence? Would the 1950 version of the Law of Return be enacted today? Would today's Knesset agree to remove the "according to *halacha*" clause? I doubt it. In the years after the founding of the state, Ben-Gurion statism prohibited ideological diversity in the state's institutions and schools. Subsequently, as the reins of government were gradually handed down to the next (and native-born) generation, the past was remembered in stereotypical ways and Jews' connection to their past and their sense of destiny and purpose were greatly disrupted. The harm caused to the children of Israel's founders was largely irreparable. The negation of the diasporic past also birthed a problematic attitude toward the future. In order to understand Jewishness as a dynamic ethnic and national-cultural process that is open to secular interpretation, secular Israeli Jews need self-confidence and intellectual courage, but they have been left shaken by the religious counterrevolution and their severance from their own past.

The weakness of the secular foundation of Israeli democracy can also be seen in Israeli attitudes toward the country's Arab minority. The literature discussing the question of the Arab minority's place in Israeli civil society is very rich and diverse and cannot be covered in entirety here. Nonetheless, I cannot develop my doctrine regarding the Jewish and democratic nature of Israel without addressing the country's non-Jewish minority. Their role in the country's collective consciousness and the question of how to reconcile the rights of a non-Jewish minority with Israel's identity as "Jewish and democratic" must be addressed.

To analyze the status of the Arab minority in the Jewish-majority society of Israel we must examine our readiness to include those who are not members of our people in the civil society of our state. Even a cursory glance reveals the difficulties inherent in integrating non-Jews into Israeli society. As should be expected, there are diverse views among Jews and Arabs regarding this question of integration which are expressed both at the ideological level and in behavioral practice. The founders of Zionism believed that the principle of inclusion was important to the state and the nuances of this principle were prominently expressed in Israel's Declaration of Independence:

> The State of Israel . . . will foster the development of the country for the benefit of all its inhabitants; it will be based on freedom, justice and peace as envisaged by the prophets of Israel; it will ensure complete equality of social and political rights to all its inhabitants irrespective of religion, race or sex; it will guarantee freedom of religion, conscience, language, education and culture; it will safeguard the Holy Places of all religions; and it will be faithful to the principles of the Charter of the United Nations.

Whatever one thinks of the document, my assumption is that there is currently not a majority of Israeli parliamentarians who would approve the contents of Israel's Declaration of Independence if a vote were held today. This doubt is fueled by the erosion of the principle of inclusion of non-Jewish minorities on both the ideological and practical level in Israel in recent decades. The results of the 2017 Democracy Index paint a compelling picture of how the Arab and Jewish publics in Israel perceive each other, including how national-religious and secular Israeli Jews view the Arab citizens of Israel: 78.2 percent of national-religious Jews think there is no discrimination against Arabs in Israel and said they "agree" or "largely agree" with the claim that the State of Israel is democratic for Arabs and Jews (to an equal extent). Over two-thirds (68.1 percent) of secular Israeli Jews concur. Only 14.6 percent of the religious public and over a third of the secular public disagree and apparently recognize that discrimination exists.

Only about a third (34.6 percent) of national-religious Jews agree with the statement: "The viewpoints of [both] Jews and Arabs regarding the conflict should be taught in all schools"; 59.1 percent disagree with this statement and among secular Israeli Jews, more than three quarters (77.5 percent) agree with this statement, compared to 17.9 percent who disagree.

Two-thirds (66 percent) of the national-religious community "agree" or "largely agree" that "voting rights should be denied to those who refuse to declare that Israel is the nation-state of the Jewish people." Only a quarter (24.5 percent) "don't agree" or "don't really agree" with this antidemocratic assertion. The situation among secular Israeli Jews is a bit better, though still far from satisfactory in terms of recognizing the political rights of minorities in a democracy: 54.6 percent "reject" or "largely reject" denying voting rights and 42.7 percent support the denial of this fundamental right.

In a troubling display, when presented with the statement "fateful decisions regarding the system of government, economy and society require a Jewish majority," 83.3 percent of the national-religious public and 60.5 percent of the secular public agreed, while 11.7 percent and 35.8 percent, respectively, said they reject this assertion.

The relative affinity between national-religious and secular Jews in Israel can be seen in the responses to the question of whether Jewishness denotes a religion, a nation, or both. Among the former, only 9.1 percent believe Jewishness pertains exclusively to religion, none say that it only entails nationhood, and the overwhelming majority (85.5 percent) thinks it involves both. Among the latter, 27.5 percent view Jewishness as solely a religion, 6.1 percent say it entails only nationhood, and 65.1 percent think it involves both.

In addition to these findings, I'd like to note several insights from Haifa University Professor Sammy Smooha's study, "Still Playing by the Rules: Index of Arab-Jewish Relations in Israel 2013." "The feeling of distance is a more acute feeling than discomfort," Smooha writes. "42.7 percent of the Arabs and 65.9 percent of the Jews feel distanced from each other. The Arabs feel rejected not only by the Jews, but also by the State of Israel."[56] "The alienation is also reflected in a negative attitude toward contacts with the other side, especially among Jews: 45.7 percent of Jews, compared to 29.7 percent of the Arabs, are not prepared to have a neighbor from the other side. Moreover, 38.2 percent of the Jews do not accept having an Arab boss at work . . . These findings are very severe. Refusal to accept an Arab as a supervisor at work is contrary to the basic norms of equality, human dignity, and individual rights in the ethos of democracy."[57]

These findings provide a look at a troubling reality. There is no doubt that the principles of inclusion expressed in Israel's Declaration of Independence have been eroded in Israel, as can be seen in popular attitudes toward Arabs. A partial explanation can be found in the fact that the basic principles of the Declaration of Independence were not co-opted into a constitution for Israel. Another explanation stems from a significant factor in the reality of our lives: "Citizens of my state are members of the same nation as my enemy."

The state's first fifty years were characterized by unprecedented action. In the framework shaped by Ben-Gurion, Israel built the material infrastructure of the Jewish state as well as state institutions, legal and governmental procedures, economic foundations, and a strong army. All of these achievements are impressive by any criteria and they highlight the vitality of the liberation movement of the Jewish people. The second half century began nineteen years ago. It began in the shadow of the assassination of Prime Minister Yitzhak Rabin. More than anything else, but together with other factors, the murder illustrated that Israeli society had gone astray. These problems can be closely linked to the Zionist deficit and further highlight the need for Israel to continue the work required to achieve full sovereignty.

My mom played a big part in shaping my identity. She had the charisma of a leader, but it was tempered by humility. Her Zionist values were shaped in the Gordonia youth movement and these values guided her through a series of milestones in her life: immigration to Palestine as a young pioneer, joining Kibbutz Hulda in 1934, helping to establish the Defense Ministry's Rehabilitation Department during the War of Independence and the Jerusalem Municipality's Social Work Department, working for equality for women in the Labor party, Mapai, and more. There was a range of other activities and contributions to society that I only learned about during the weeklong shiva mourning period after her death. I was fortunate to have her as my mother and I grew up a happy child, supported by her warmth and love. Mom, Etka Carmon, indeed had a profound influence in shaping my identity.

In early 1939, my father was already in a relationship with my mom when he asked the kibbutz assembly for permission to travel to Poland to bring his sister Sabina to Israel. The voices from the doomed Jewish communities of Europe apparently resonated in the Land of Israel at that time and my father felt a great sense of urgency, largely because of the stories he had heard in the letters sent by his widowed mother. Sabina was born six months after my grandfather died on the battle-fields of World War I. My father desperately wanted to bring her to Israel, but the assembly at Hulda did not approve his trip and my parents left the kibbutz and gave up their membership. Dad traveled to Poland and returned with his sister, who lived to a ripe old age in Israel. Upon returning to Palestine, my parents settled in Jerusalem. After leaving the kibbutz, my mom started to work as a nanny for Rachel Yanait and Yitzhak Ben-Zvi (the future president of Israel). Their older son, Eli, fell in battle in the War of Independence, just days before Eli was to marry. For years my mother spoke of her time taking care of Eli when he was a little boy.

In early 1956, my mom sent an invitation for my bar mitzvah to the President's Residence, addressed to Rachel Yanait Ben-Zvi. The president's wife responded: "Come visit me after your son's reading the haftorah on Shabbat."

On the day of my bar mitzvah, I read from the Torah in the assembly hall of Hebrew University High School (Leyada) in Beit Hakerem. The assembly hall became a synagogue on Shabbat and holidays, with an ark holding three Torah scrolls placed on the stage. After completing the haftorah, and dressed in our holiday finest, we rushed to the hut in the Rehavia neighborhood that served as the president's residence.[58]

The president met us at the door just as he was leaving for a Bible class. He recognized my mom and his wife welcomed us into the modest reception hall. She was sitting on the sofa with two women she introduced as friends from their days in the HaShomer, the first pre-state Jewish defense organization, both of them members of Kibbutz Kfar Giladi. One of them was Manya Shochat, a monumental figure among the early Zionist pioneers. I was still very young, but I already knew who she was and meeting such an icon of Zionism thrilled me.

Beaming with pride, my mother told the three women how her son had sung the haftarah (a section of the Torah read in synagogue on Shabbat) beautifully and the First Lady, a Zionist hero in her own right, asked if I would be willing to sing the haftorah again. Naturally, as a thirteen-year-old boy in the President's Residence, I was overcome with embarrassment, and also confused. I had yet to understand how the "values of the Labor movement," of the "new Jew," could connect with the "*Yiddishkeit*" of the "old Jew." The connection between my haftorah portion, the Hashomer organization, and the three prominent Zionist women sitting in front of me was unclear. When I finished singing, Rachel Yanait Ben-Zvi gave me a bar mitzvah present: the book *What I Chose*, an anthology of short stories. Inside she'd written a dedication, and I read it aloud right there on the spot: "To Ari on his bar mitzvah, may you walk in the path of your parents and even surpass them."

Chapter 8

The Ethos of Survival

Day after day I would wake before sunrise and race to the door to face the dawn, my heart racing as I would check that tragedy had not befallen our family. As I ran to the door, I would pray that no one in a uniform was waiting on the porch to tell me that our family had suffered a tragic loss. My heart was constantly racing and riddled with anxiety and fear for my sons, Elay and Omri, who served in the Second Lebanon War in the summer of 2006 and in Operation Cast Lead in the Gaza Strip from December 2008 to January 2009. Omri also fought in Operation Protective Edge, a two-month war in the summer of 2014 that left sixty-seven Israel Defense Forces soldiers dead and hundreds wounded. During each round of violence, whenever my sons were posted on the front lines, I found myself running, fleeing from the very possibility of darkness. The tradition in Israel is that when a soldier falls on the battlefield, a trained IDF team comes to the soldier's home to personally inform the family.

During the War of Independence, my mom was one of the founders of the Ministry of Defense Rehabilitation Department. Among other tasks, she helped found the unit that goes to the houses of fallen soldiers and gives their families the worst news anyone could imagine. This unit—which would tell families about the death of a son, husband, or brother—became part of the fears of parents whose children serve in the army, and in particular those who serve in combat units. Years later, I too became one of these parents who live in fear of these bearers of bad news and flee from any possibility that they may visit their doorstep.

My late father, Moshe Carmon of blessed memory, was born in a small town in eastern Galicia (now Ukraine) to a poor family that belonged to the Belz Hasidic sect. My father acquired his basic education in a *heder*, a religious school for Jewish children. His father, Zvi Aryeh Lokerman, for whom I am named, was forcibly conscripted into the Austrian army and fell on the battlefields of World War I. My father served as a "ghaffir" in the British Army, was a member of the Haganah's intelligence unit (Shai), and fought as a captain in the War of Independence. In the mid-1950s, my family moved to the Beit Hakerem neighborhood in Jerusalem and on the memorial days for fallen IDF soldiers, we—fifth and sixth graders—walked to the military cemetery on Mount Herzl to place flowers on the graves of the fallen. Asaf Zeitlin, of blessed memory, a classmate of mine, used to place the bouquet on the grave of his older brother, Uri, who was killed in action in the War of Independence. Every morning when I arrived at school in Jerusalem, I would see the names of former pupils etched in the memorial stones by the entrance. In the early 1960s, I fulfilled my duty and served in the Paratroopers Brigade.

During my first time performing IDF reserve duty, my battalion parachuted into the area of Tel Kisan, which is located between Acre and the Arab village of Tamra. During this jump—my twenty-third—I was injured and from then on registered as a disabled IDF veteran.

After the Six-Day War in 1967, I began visiting graves of friends of mine who had fallen in Israel's wars. The closest friend of all was Shaul Shalev, who was killed in the Yom Kippur War on the banks of the Suez Canal. I gave my son Ilay the middle name Shaul in honor of my late friend.

Since the early 1990s, some of my friends have begun visiting the graves of their own children who have died during their military service. We have joined them on these visits and our hearts have cried out along with theirs.

My two sons and two daughters have all served their country in the military. My two sons served in combat units—Elay in the Navy and Omri in the Paratroops Reconnaissance Unit—and both fought on a number of battlefields during their service. Every year on Memorial Day, Omri visits the graves of three friends who died during their active and reserves duty. My eldest granddaughter, Yarden, enlisted in the IDF in the fall of 2016 and my grandson Itai, her brother, enlisted in the Navy in September 2017.

Eran, my dear friend Shaul's son, has been like a younger brother to me. Every year or so on Memorial Day at Mount Herzl (Israel's equivalent to Arlington Cemetery), we would meet and visit some. When he was twenty-five, I saw him at the ceremony wearing the uniform of an Israel Air Force captain. After spending twenty years watching him grow from a boy to a young man and then an IAF officer, I approached him at his father's grave after the ceremony.

"This coming Saturday at 7 in the morning I will come pick you up," I told him, and on Saturday we drove in my jeep on a trail through the Makhtesh HaKatan in the Negev desert. The hours we spent together—from sunrise to sunset—were quality time for the two of us. I did most of the talking and told Eran about his father and me and the friendship between us that was cut so short.

I told him how standing outside the National Library just before a logic exam in college, Shaul and I discovered that we both happened to register for the same history and philosophy course. I told him about the unique sense of humor his father had, about his athletic prowess, and how he challenged me to a push-up contest in the locker room at the Givat Ram gymnasium. I told him about our talks, about how I could see the signs of a budding intellect, not only while we studied for exams but also in our discussions of literature. I told Eran about how his father would run, full of excitement and pride, to see his wife's exam scores and about how we drove together to

Hadassah Ein Kerem one Shabbat morning to visit Gabi just days after the birth of his first daughter, Narkiss. About our heart-to-heart talk in his parent's yard in Givatayim during his father's shiva, when we talked about our role as combat soldiers, and I told Eran about our sad meeting at Mount Herzl after the end of the Six-Day War, where we sat next to the grave of one of our professors, Shmaryahu Rivier, who had died in the battle for Jerusalem.

As we drove, I told Eran about his mom, my dear friend Gabi, and how we listened to recordings from the days of battle when Shaul was the commander of the 184th battalion of the Armored Corps. Eran asked me if I knew how his father was killed and I told him how he was hit in the neck by a single bullet while he was standing in the turret, leading the battalion next to the Suez Canal. Shaul died on the spot.

Eran asked me if it was a case of friendly fire, and I told him I had no idea.

I remained disturbed by his question long after the drive ended. Months later, Eran told me that he had investigated his father's death and learned that he was killed by enemy fire. It was very important for him to know, and it weighed on him until he was able to find the truth.

When Operation Protective Edge began in July 2014, my wife, Tzipa, and I were in New York. I was recovering from medical treatment and we were waiting to return to Israel about ten days after the fighting had started in Gaza. The entire time we were in New York I would climb the walls in fear for my sons fighting in the war. The only escape was the long walks we took those mornings in Central Park.

⟨✦⟩

Besides a few biographical details, my life story is rather typical. It is woven with the common threads that connect most Israelis, simply because they are Israelis. Our ongoing and continuous struggle for physical survival has played a central role in the collective biography of the state and in the life stories of countless Israelis. This struggle for survival, which stands at the heart of Israel's national agenda, has far-reaching repercussions on our entire way of life, most of which are unique. Here is a nation with no tradition of political sovereignty that has faced continual threats to its existence for nearly a century and has prevailed, time and again, despite having no history of defending a state and its borders. Here is a collective exercising its muscles for the first time since the battles of the Maccabees. I venture that there is no precedent in human history for building a nation and establishing sovereignty in the shadow of a continuous and protracted physical threat to existence. This ongoing struggle for physical survival may not be the primary reason for the anomaly at the center of our way of life, but it certainly underlines and reinforces it.

The massive presence of the struggle for physical survival in the very heart of our lives has far-reaching repercussions on the routine way of life in Israel. It eroded our self-confidence and engendered anxieties, prioritized military spending over socioeconomic budgeting, and, most of all, it has fueled an aggressive and sometimes violent public discourse. The unrelenting struggle gave rise to the ethos of survival from the very outset and continues to foster it nearly a century later. For decades, the ethos of survival has dominated the cultural-mental space where, in other circumstances, the ethos of sovereignty should have emerged.

The massive presence of the ethos of survival accentuated the obsessive craving for normalcy in the collective Israeli consciousness. We Israelis prefer to "grab" reality. Our obsession for normalcy has a profound behavioral impact on our political culture. It is also one of the reasons, even if not the primary one, for the squandering of intellectual and mental resources that are so essential to the transition from sovereignty-in-the-making to full sovereignty.

I believe that the way the Jewish nation has out of necessity "exercised its muscles" after two thousand years of atrophy is not what Zionist leader Max Nordau had in mind when he coined the term "muscular Judaism" (*Muskeljudentum* in German) in a speech at the Second Zionist Congress in Basel, Switzerland, on August 28, 1898.[59]

I'm not at all certain that what was then a vision, a dream, is consistent with this struggle for survival that has been so central to the national ethos for nearly a century. Nordau's dream, vision, and hope reflected the characteristics of "the new Jew," as opposed to the alienated "old Jew" of the Diaspora. In pre-state Hebrew literature, "the new Jew" was described as a "blue-eyed lad, with golden locks, silent, strong, and muscular." Images of his opposite can be found, in a sort of macabre irony, on the pages of the Nazi *Der Stürmer*.

There is no doubt that the secular foundations of the Zionist revolution were the foundation of Israel's phenomenal success in establishing the Israel Defense Forces, which have ensured Israel's existence in a hostile region, against all odds, for over seventy years. Ben-Gurion and his pragmatic political-security policy and views drew their strength from this secular, rational revolution. The greatness of Ben-Gurion's leadership lay entirely, from start to finish, in the practical, physical act of statecraft. The IDF is the clear result of Jews taking charge of their destiny and security, without divine assistance. God was not present in the minds of most of the soldiers who took part in defending the State of Israel. The secular foundation of Zionism inspired solidarity in Israel's early years and constituted a constant source of strength for the IDF.

However, the existential reality of life in Israel and the state of constant conflict with its regional neighbors place an unbearable burden on the Zionist ideological foundation of Israel, which has already been weakened by the Zionist deficit. If Israel did not face any external threats, focus could be placed on developing new interpretive approaches to Judaism and Jewish culture and heritage in the Jewish homeland. The cultural wealth of two thousand years of exile was one of the objects of destruction in the Holocaust period. These texts that were so central to our cultural heritage cry out to be submitted to creative secular interpretation. In other words, Zionist ideology should have formed the methods of interpretation necessary for creating a strong and sustainable secular-Jewish-Zionist identity. This ideology also should have defined the tools for codifying a constitution to defend the sovereignty of human beings and their freedom in the Israeli democracy. Instead, we are left with the Zionist deficit.

With our emotional and intellectual energies devoted to physical survival, we have not been able to pursue these necessary steps in achieving full sovereignty, to the extent that we are unable to demarcate our eastern border. That is, we've yet to define the parameters of the physical space in which the Jewish nation fulfills its right to self-determination.

Israel's awe-inspiring victory in the Six-Day War in 1967 introduced a new dimension to the ethos of survival: the occupied/liberated "territories" of the West Bank and (previously) the Gaza Strip and Sinai. Israel's occupation of the West Bank serves as another drain on the emotional energies vital for establishing a secular-Zionist-Israeli identity and worsens the anomaly that already exists in our lives. The presence of "the territories" at the center of our lives has turned us into a borderless democratic-sovereign collective. The fiercest argument in Israeli society centers upon where Israel's borders should be drawn. This is symbiotically connected to the act of shaping the moral fronts in that the question of the Jewish and democratic nature of the State of Israel stands at the heart of the territorial discord.

For over fifty years, the democratic State of Israel has maintained a military regime to occupy and control the territories it captured in war and the lives of its non-Israeli residents. Israel has not annexed these territories, their residents are not citizens and lack political rights, and there is an alternate set of Israeli laws practiced in the occupied territories. Thus, these territories which are not part of sovereign Israel have led to what I wish to call an artificial and anomalous "territorialization" that is the opposite of an organic territorialization. The latter defines the political borders of the collective that lives in the territory and establishes the various features of the collective's political sovereignty within these defined borders, unlike the Israeli system, where the eastern border remains undefined.

The focus on the question of borders has strengthened the territorialization of national-cultural values. It has become a dominant factor in the forging of political-economic-social policy in Israel, largely through the diversion of resources to the territories. The state has invested enormous resources to pave roads, develop infrastructure, and wage legal battles with the Arab residents of the territories, all while deploying soldiers and police within an occupied territory that lies outside the state's recognized borders. These policies have created an artificial physical separation between Jews and non-Jews. It is the height of irony that this territorialization is taking place in a diasporic nation that has no history as a territorial nation and has yet to achieve full sovereignty. Territorialization has brought a return to the ghetto ways that Zionism rebelled against. However, unlike the ghetto in the Diaspora, the ghetto in the occupied/liberated territory enjoys the physical protection of the state. This artificial territorialization has strengthened the feeling of transience and the lack of a complete sense of "being at home."

Security is always at the center of the Israeli national agenda and its prominence is directly linked to the fears of Israelis. As stated, these fears have shaped our political culture and patterns of behavior for decades. The struggle for survival imposed on Israel became the be-all and end-all. The pursuit and holding of territory became the objective instead of a means to an objective. It shifted resources to a physical goal: survival. "The security situation" is what created the constant sense of being under siege and led us to revert to our ghetto mentality and wall ourselves off. Our state has been defined by a war and a prolonged siege mentality, which can be seen in famous Israeli sayings such as "a people who will dwell alone" and "the whole world is against us." Our survival ethos has also been defined by aggressiveness as we have transformed from "the few against the many," from David to Goliath.

Physical survival has been a central concern since the 1920s, in pre-state Israel, and there is no reason to believe this will change anytime soon. Survival is the dominant ethos affecting our lives from every possible perspective: cultural, social, economic, and, of course, political. Survival relegated to the margins any process to clarify and shape the historical-cultural-ethnic foundations that define the Jewishness of our collective and how they coexist with democracy. It has fostered an aggressive mentality which in turn reinforced the growing trend of ethnocentrism. The centrality of this ethos over time has weakened Israel's ability to plan for the future of the state. Instead, we obsess about survival in the here and now.

Although Zionism succeeded in restoring the Jewish nation to history, it failed to provide physical security, a problem that had plagued the Jewish nation in the Diaspora. Feelings of alienation and hostility toward non-Jews and the fear of residing in a non-Jewish environment were transported from the Jewish experience in the Pale of Settlement to the circumstances of Israel, in particular following the Six-Day War in 1967. Gone was the sense of homeland and the hope that Jews would never again live in the shadow of pogroms. Instead, we regularly encounter the phenomenon of Jews projecting Diaspora-based stereotypes of non-Jews onto Arabs.

The problem of the territories captured in 1967 remains unresolved. Its impact on the rifts in Israeli society is only growing stronger and more significant. The main question at the heart of the internal divide on this issue relates to the national identity of Israel: How can the state remain Jewish and democratic while ruling over the Palestinians? Palestinian Arabs, including the Palestinian citizens of Israel, already comprise about 51 percent of the population living between the Mediterranean Sea and the Jordan River. The future of Israel's national identity will be determined by how this question is addressed and the relative emphasis accorded to universal values versus particularistic values.

Here are several examples that illustrate the situation, as reflected over the years in the Peace Index, a joint project of IDI and Tel Aviv University. One of the questions asked in a survey for the Peace Index in December 2011 was: "What is more important to you: a Jewish majority in Israel or Israeli control in the West Bank?" Among secular Israelis, 70.5 percent said a Jewish majority was more important while only 33 percent of religious-national Israelis chose this answer. In August 2018, 90 percent of left-wing voters supported an independent Palestinian state, compared to 68 percent of centrists and only 30.5 percent of right-wing voters. The same survey asked: "Do you currently support the signing of a peace accord based on the formula of two states for two peoples?" Among Jewish Israelis, 47 percent expressed support for an accord based on this formula and 46 percent said they did not support such an agreement. Only 25 percent of right-wing Jewish Israelis voiced support for an accord based on the "two states for two peoples" formula, compared to 70 percent of centrists and 91.5 percent of leftists. Among Arab Israelis, 73 percent of the respondents supported a peace accord based on the two-state formula.

It is important to note that a lack of trust in the Palestinians' intentions is a central variable affecting the views of Israelis. Some 66 percent of the Jews in Israel agree with the following statement: "Most of the Palestinians have not accepted the existence of the State of Israel and would destroy it if they could." This percentage has remained steady, with slight variation, since the Peace Index surveys began in June 1994. Among Jewish respondents, 84 percent of right-wingers concur with this statement, compared to 53 percent of centrists and only 20.5 percent of leftists. Among Arab respondents, 57.5 percent also agree with this statement.

Therefore, it looks like the ethos of survival is here to stay.

Chapter 9

The Centrality of Death in Israel

Shimon Koren was born in 1947 in the Wasserburg transit camp in Germany, the only son of Adolph and Rosa and the nephew of Henek Koren. (As mentioned earlier, Father was Henek's counselor in the Gordonia youth movement.) Like his older brother Henek, Adolph was rescued from the horrors of the Holocaust.

On a Sunday afternoon, March 31, 2002, during the Passover holiday, Shimon and his two children were sitting at the Matza restaurant in the Neveh Sha'anan neighborhood in Haifa. It was a favorite restaurant of the family and they ate there often. Rachel, the mother, was supposed to join them, but changed her mind at the last moment. At 2:40 p.m., Shimon and Rachel spoke on the phone. Shimon asked his wife if she wanted them to bring her something from the restaurant. She said it wasn't necessary. Moments after their conversation, a Palestinian terrorist burst into the restaurant and blew himself up. The bomb gutted the restaurant and set it ablaze, collapsing the roof on the diners. Dozens of people in the restaurant were injured in the attack and fifteen were killed, including Shimon and his two children, Ran and Gal. The look on Henek's face when he came to my parents' home to tell them the horrible story is impossible to forget.

༄

Death plays a significant role in the collective consciousness of Israelis. Young people growing up in Israel encounter death already in childhood and in a variety of ways. Boys and girls raised in secular communities—who will later serve in the army—encounter it in the memorial boards of graduates who fell in Israel's wars. Such boards are displayed prominently in most schools in the State of Israel. Children also encounter death on Memorial Day and Holocaust Remembrance Day, which occur one week apart, just after Passover. Many come from bereaved families or are closely connected to bereaved families in Israel. This is true of the boys and girls who serve in the army, including a growing minority of girls from the religious Zionist community. The reality is different for those who don't serve in the army, a group which still includes a large majority of the ultra-Orthodox and Arab citizens of the State of Israel.

The role of death in the collective consciousness of Israelis is also a paradox. On the one hand, Israeli collective imagination includes many perceptions of death spread across the entire social mosaic and reflected in a variety of behavioral expressions. These range from signs of self-confidence and a rational acceptance of this presence to various manifestations of fear. Some of these expressions are visible and some are hidden, to emerge when people are faced with the physical threats which come in and out of the lives of Israelis, often at a moment's notice. The presence of death is perhaps the single thread that connects the different segments of Israeli society in a semblance of solidarity. On Holocaust Memorial Day and the memorial day for fallen IDF soldiers, our shared mourning briefly salves the rifts that divide this society during the rest of the year. The exceptions to this are the Arab and ultra-Orthodox Jewish minorities that for the most part do not participate in the moment of silence that pervades Israel's public spaces on each memorial day.

On most days, Israel's cemeteries are cloaked in a pastoral stillness. In the military cemeteries, the silence is broken by chirping birds and the falling leaves blown by the wind among the sparse mourners who visit during the rest of the year. All of this changes on memorial days.

Even the sounds of those mourners who come in the hundreds of thousands is special. The combination of these sounds is a harmony of solidarity, making up one of the few times that we experience what we don't tend to display outside the cemeteries: a shared fate.

On Memorial Day in April 1974—the first after Shaul's death—I came to mourn the friend whose loss I would feel for the rest of my life. It was only a matter of months after his death on the banks of the Suez Canal and he was still buried in a temporary military cemetery in Kibbutz Mishmar HaNegev. Three months earlier I'd returned from the United States after finishing my doctorate, which I dedicated to the memory of Shaul. During those twelve weeks, I pushed my emotional scars deep within me. These wounds were still bleeding, and the collective soul of Israel was plagued by grief from the terrible losses of the Yom Kippur War. None of that compared to the bereaved families themselves and the heartache which had darkened their lives.

Like other military cemeteries across the country, the one at Mishmar HaNegev was packed with people on that Memorial Day. The soldiers were buried close together. It was this density among the hundreds of fresh graves and their uniform appearance that made this feeling of solidarity among the mourners ever stronger.

When I reached Shaul's temporary grave, his wife Gabi was there, along with her parents. The moment I returned to Israel from the United States I raced to be at Gabi's side, at the couple's apartment in the Talpiot neighborhood of Jerusalem. When I first saw her, right after I'd gotten off the plane, she asked me to come with her and former Israeli politician (and then general in the Armored Corps) Mordechai Tzipori to see the spot where Shaul was killed. We drove all the way from central Tel Aviv in Tzipori's Plymouth Valiant and crossed the Sinai Peninsula from east to west, ending on the east bank of the Canal.

During the ride, I learned that Tzipori was one of Shaul's commanders during the War of Attrition (1967–70) and later the Yom Kippur

War, when Tzipori was commander of the Armored Corps. His relationship with Shaul was much more than that of a commander to his soldier.

We stood on a tall dust mound and Tzipori held an aerial photograph and a map of the battlefield as he told us about what transpired during the war. His admiration of Shaul is hard to overstate. He told us of Shaul's heroism and how he saved thirty-three IDF reservists from the Jerusalem Brigade who had become trapped in the "Purkan" stronghold in the Sinai.

In "To the End of The Land," Israeli author David Grossman wrote of the battle at the stronghold:[60]

At 2 a.m. they set out. Under the full moon the stronghold looked like ruins. It was hard to believe that this box had protected them over all those days . . . They set out in two rows far apart from one another. At the front of one line marched Ilan, the commander, and at the front of the other, his deputy . . . They marched, collapsing in the dunes, soldiers falling silently, cursed only in their hearts.

We marched and marched till we reached the small wadi full of mounds and hills, and we stopped to rest . . . Over the radio we heard that there was no way to reach us, that we needed to wait a little longer . . . the bullets were constantly whistling by all around us, just like in the movies. When we reached the ridgeline we saw that it was infested with Egyptians. We thought we were done for.

They shouted at us through the radio and ordered us to start shooting flares so that they could find us. We shot flares, they spotted them. A tank appeared at the top of the ridge, an M-60 Patton coming down what was almost a straight incline. An officer poked out of the turret and called for us to get to the tank. We shouted at him, "What can we do? How?" and he kept signaling, come, there's no time. "What? All of us? Get to the tank? How? Where? Get here NOW!"

We were thirty-three men crammed in a tank that was bouncing like crazy. We smashed into a tree and tossed it aside. Bones were breaking, we could hardly breathe, everything was dust, flying rocks—all you could do was close all your holes and just live, live . . .

Shaul's heroic rescue of the reservists took place on the morning of October 9, 1973. That same afternoon, Shaul was killed.

During the memorial ceremony, I stood with Gabi and her parents next to the grave. The burial plots were placed close together and the shoulders of the mourners brushed against each other. Next to us was a family of Moroccan origin whose son was temporarily buried next to Shaul. Eventually it was time for the twenty-one-gun salute. After the first round was fired, the family next to us let out heartbreaking screams that shattered the silence. Gabi's parents, particularly nice people, were of stoic German-Jewish origin ("yekkes"). Their disapproval was soon to follow. Gabi, who was holding back her tears, whispered to me: "If I could only allow myself to act like them, to shriek with all my might."

∾

The powerful presence of death in the lives of Israelis, and of young people in particular, affects many aspects of our lives. It has affected relations between the different "tribes" that comprise Israeli society, in particular with regard to relations between ultra-Orthodox and secular Jews, Arabs and Jews, and recently also between secular and national-religious Israelis.

In recent decades, there have been signs of a disparity between secular and religious Israelis regarding death in service of the country.

This is connected to the clear differences in how the various groups contribute to the common security of the country.

The national service law states that serving in the defense of the state is required of all citizens and permanent residents of Israel. Those who are considered "veterans" are all men and women over the age of eighteen who did not receive an exemption from service. Also, not all those considered "veterans" actually served.

In the secular community, both men and women have a high rate of participation in national service, while in the national-religious sector the participation of women is still particularly low. Among ultra-Orthodox Jews, the participation of both men and women is still very low. In Israel, this disparity is referred to as "inequality in bearing the burden." The presence of death itself and the disparity in the attitude toward death affect the characteristics of the political culture and political agenda and worsen relations between the "tribes" that compose Israeli society.

The average Israeli, more than citizens in other democracies, is required to make decisions that signify his readiness to die for the state. A substantial part of the Israeli population answers the statist call to be prepared to give up their lives or the lives of their loved ones while other segments of society do far less. This raises the question: Where does this readiness to sacrifice life come from? My premise, which requires empirical examination, is that young secular Israelis and religious Zionist youths confront these life-and-death questions differently from one another. I believe this is due to their differing beliefs regarding the presence of a divine role in events.

Voluntary obedience, in contrast to blind obedience, characterizes armies in democratic states. The duty of self-sacrifice that drives this obedience is different when God is or is not connected to it. For secular citizens in a democracy, the obligation of self-sacrifice for the state awakens the tension between the rights of individuals and their obligations and responsibilities toward a particular collective. From the (secular) perspective of democracy, the Israeli reality creates several dilemmas. It seeks answers for the purpose of a particular death.

It questions the worthiness of sacrificing a life for an ideal or for land and asks whether or not it is justified only for physical survival.

Wrestling with these dilemmas is part of democratic life in Israel and the public discourse of the country. Is there a place for God in this democratic public discourse? I don't have an unequivocal answer, primarily because I respect the views of observant Jews who serve in the army. In their dialogue with those who are not religiously observant, they must take into account that democracy rests upon secular foundations. They must understand that secular people are skeptical about finding decisive and coherent answers to the dilemmas presented above. The need to cope over time with what is vague, unresolved, and indefinite is one of the challenges that characterize secular democracy. These dilemmas require human answers and do not rely on the divine or supernatural.

On the eve of the military operation in Gaza in the summer of 2014, Colonel Ofer Winter, commander of the Givati Brigade, sparked an uproar by calling on his troops to fight the enemy in the name of God. He issued this call in a letter that was unlike any previous written directive from an IDF commander. The letter—and, in particular, the fact that the uproar quickly disappeared in the public discourse—indicates an emerging problem in Israeli democracy. If we return to the voluntary element in obedience to authority, as Walzer noted, we need to reiterate that this element characterizes service in an army of a democratic sovereign entity. One of the differences between voluntary obedience and blind obedience to authority pertains to the presence or absence of God or a human leader who wields supreme power. This is why I am compelled to examine the concept of an "army of God," which is spreading among soldiers in the Israel Defense Forces.

Winter's message to the troops, as extraordinary as it was, reflects the increasing presence of theology in public spaces and in the IDF in particular. I will elaborate on this in subsequent chapters. Of course, God cannot be excluded from the army as long as religious soldiers are among its ranks. And a significant number of IDF soldiers are observant Jews. It is worth noting in this context the impressive increase in the number of religious women serving in the IDF. For decades, young women of conscription age could receive an exemption from army duty (which is compulsory for both men and women in Israel) by self-identifying as religious. In other armies, one of the roles of military chaplains is to provide emotional support to religious soldiers prior to battle and to ease their fears through prayer to divine providence. This type of religious function is performed on an individual basis, without entering the broader public space.

In October 2014, soon after the war in Gaza (Operation Protective Edge), I was at the Hoover Institution at Stanford University, where I serve as a distinguished visiting fellow during the fall semester every year. General James Mattis was also at the Hoover Institution at that time. We developed a friendship during our years together there, prior to his appointment as US secretary of defense. I shared with him an op-ed I had published in the *Haaretz* daily entitled, "Release God from the Army." The op-ed cited Winter's battle cry. Mattis showed me several prebattle directives he had issued as commander of the US Marine Corps. In one of them, before embarking on a combat mission in Iraq in February 2004, he reminded his troops that they would be fighting in an area populated by civilians: "Remember I have added 'First do no harm' to our mottoes 'No better friend, no worse enemy.' Keep your honor clean as we gain information about the enemy from the Iraqi people . . . we will move precisely against the enemy elements and crush them **without harming the innocent**" (boldface in the original).

Voluntary obedience to authority must be drawn from the normative foundations of democracy. It is based on a moral, democratic foundation that provides interpretation and meaning to behavior. In a nondemocratic collective, obedience is not voluntary—it is duty and blind obedience. Voluntary obedience to authority generates commitment and responsibility. Unlike duty, commitment springs from deep within each individual as an autonomous person. Duty, on the other hand, is mechanical and its sources are not within the individual. Commitment is always a "bottom up" phenomenon; from subordinates toward those higher up. Responsibility is a "top down" phenomenon: it entails the obligations of those in command toward their subordinates. They must impart meaning to those who obey on a voluntary basis, who are consciously prepared to sacrifice their lives. They are responsible for explaining, persuading, and inducing them to internalize the justifications for the sacrifice of life. In my view, acceptance of voluntary obedience fosters self-confidence and acceptance of the presence of death, which help people cope with fear. When God comes into the picture, it may undermine the moral elements that guide behavior in the army of a democratic state. The presence of the divine is liable to harm the commitment of the subordinates to their duty to serve and be prepared to sacrifice their lives and it relieves their commanders of responsibility.

At the time, I thought the IDF should show zero tolerance for Winter or those who write or say messages like that of his letter. I'm no longer as judgmental as I was, but it is clear to me that this letter should not be treated as an isolated case. It is symptomatic of other troubling phenomena that have surfaced in our army in recent years relating to the role of religion in the army.

It appears unlikely that the centrality of death in our collective consciousness will weaken. There doesn't appear to be a significant alternative to the ethos of survival that will develop in our political culture. Nor does it appear likely that we will achieve greater normalcy as we transform from sovereignty-in-the-making to sovereignty. The presence of all these—death, survival, and the anomaly in our ways of life—is intensifying. At the same time, our self-confidence continues to erode while the principal enemy of liberty—fear—just becomes stronger. I believe that the return of God to public spaces from which he was originally removed is connected, even if indirectly, to the growing presence of fear in Israel. Fear and the erosion of the self-confidence of the Israeli collective are among the elements that have helped perpetuate the centrality of physical survival. This has deepened social rifts, increased violence in Israeli society, and inflamed the rhetoric of demonization, hostility, and hatred. Demonization is a fact of life in the rift between different sectors of Israeli society. I believe that the increasing involvement of religion in politics inflames this chaotic reality, even if it were not solely responsible for creating it. This involvement in politics and in the political culture has eroded and will continue to erode the self-confidence of individual Israelis and of Israel as a collective.

In their book *Sacred and Secular: Religion and Politics Worldwide*, Pippa Norris and Ronald Inglehart state that "the role of personal security alongside the exposure to risks (security, economic, social, etc.) define securing the welfare of the individual and his community." They assert that the lack of personal security is a critical factor in the empowerment of religion in human societies. The core idea of security, they argue, entails freedom from various dangers. This idea is connected to ensuring the well-being of the individual and of his collective over time. They argue that the lack of personal security plays a critical role in increasing the role of religion in democracies. In Israel, the centrality of the ethos of survival keeps us from seeing the dominant place that religion holds in the conflicts taking place within Israeli society.

The enactment of "Basic Law: Israel as the Nation-State of the Jewish People" in July 2018 is a manifestation of the continuing erosion of Israeli self-confidence. This legislation defines Israel as the nation-state of the Jewish people but ignores the commitment expressed in the state's Declaration of Independence to ensure complete social and political equality for all of its citizens, irrespective of religion, race, or gender. The Nation-State Law also fails to echo the Declaration of Independence's appeal to all of the Arab inhabitants of the state to take part in building the state based on full and equal citizenship and representation in governmental institutions. Diaspora Jews may also infer from the new legislation that the Orthodox monopoly in Israel will remain, leaving no room for religious pluralism. The law is a mirror image of the Israeli demand that the Palestinians recognize the Jewishness of our state as a precondition of final status negotiations with Israel. What question does the Nation-State Law seek to address? What need does it fulfill? What drove its sponsors in the Knesset to enact a Basic Law that so blatantly undermines the fundamental principles of our state as formulated in the Declaration of Independence? Is the Nation-State Law the remedy for the conflict of identities, which is essentially a widening rift between religious-Orthodox-nationalist definitions of our Jewishness and non-Orthodox secular-liberal definitions?

The collective identity of nations is typically defined by the collectives themselves, based on culture, language, and history. These contours also determine patterns of behavior over time; they characterize nation-states in normal realities. The Israeli tendency in recent years to externalize the definition of our collective identity and ratify it by demanding that the outside world define our collective (as the nation of the Jewish people) testifies to the lack of a consensus in Israel on the components of our Jewish and democratic identity. This demand—which some call defiant and others consider pathetic—also indicates how central the anomaly is to the reality of our lives. No other democracy tries to affirm at the constitutional level the outlines of the national collective identity. These matters are assumed to be self-evident. No other state demands recognition of its identity as a condition for conducting relations, whether in the context of conflict or not. France does not seek to ratify its "Frenchness" in its constitution or demand affirmation of it when establishing relations with other states; neither does Sweden demand recognition of its "Swedishness" or Italy its "Italianness" and so on.

The State of Israel defined the basis of its collective identity as the nation-state of the Jewish people both in the Declaration of Independence and in the preamble of the two Basic Laws enacted in 1992. It is clear and obvious to all that the Jewish nation is exercising its right to self-determination in Israel. And our Jewish and democratic identity is clear and obvious because we have defined it so. But the reality of our lives is replete with characteristics of the anomaly. One of these is the ongoing struggle for physical survival. One of the derivatives of this is the fact that the State of Israel lacks clearly defined borders demarcating its territory. A border is not only a geographical coordinate, but a political one too. The border incorporates important variables that define the identity of one collective vis-à-vis another. Since 1967, the political sovereignty in Israel has lacked borders. Thus, the State of Israel is the only democracy that lacks a border with one of its neighbors. The lack of a geographic border leaves Israelis at a loss when it comes to defining their identity. This is one of the key factors contributing to the ongoing erosion of our collective self-confidence.

And thus, there is a connection between our declining self-confidence and the consciousness of the exile, which hovers like a dark cloud above our collective identity.

The Hebrew language wonderfully reinforces this thesis. It is a language constructed of three-letter roots. The root *bet-tet-het* is the basis for various words that relate to security. Security means a sense of certainty about the justness of one's conduct, which gives a person the confidence and courage to make decisions. Secondly, it means defending the state from enemies that threaten its peaceful existence. Thirdly, security also means placing trust in the democratic "rules of the game"—a condition for sustaining social cohesiveness, especially in a complex and diverse society.

In Hebrew, "security" (*bitahon*) can mean not only confidence but also psychological security and physical security (which is the responsibility of state authorities). The resilience and confidence of individuals in a reality of ongoing threats to their physical security is an expression of their ability to cope with ambiguous situations that generate fear. The ability to cope with ambiguous, vague, fear-inducing situations stems from the centrality of rational considerations in the individuals' behavior. In Israeli society, the cracks are widening in each of the derivatives of the root *bet-tet-het*. Under Israel's Declaration of Independence, the non-Jewish minority among us is granted civil equality. One of the victims of our diminished self-confidence, and of the Jewish Nation-State Law, is the non-Jew living among us.

From my perspective, there is a direct connection between rational considerations and the secular foundation in democracy. This secular foundation determines that authority comes from the individuals who comprise the democratic society.

The narrative surrounding death can shed insight upon the diversity of Israeli society. Secular Israeli society includes the former elite of the country's public life. For them, authority comes from human beings. During the transition from a state-in-the-making to a state, during the decades prior to 1948 and a bit afterward, the death narrative was associated with a sense of mission. The secular majority was then part of a society that had a direction and a path, whose basic orientation was toward the future. In their eyes, their mission was immortal and death was endowed with transcendental meaning. Later, as the society's direction and path became less clear, the components that imbued death with meaning have diminished—if not totally disappeared—and coping with death has become more difficult.

Religious Zionists draw their authority from God. They were also part of the same mission as secular Zionists, but there was a duality to their attitude toward the democratic source of authority. As the sense of a shared collective mission has waned in recent decades, religion has gained more and more prominence in how authority is viewed. At the same time, fewer religious Zionists now hold a dual view of the source of authority. In particular, the narrative of death became linked to the transcendental source of authority. Thus, I conclude that the narrative of death reflects a struggle with the experience of death waged by a society that has lost its way. Literature discussing the narrative of death connects it to the phenomena of aggression, violence, and intolerance. In the divided Israeli society, we've witnessed various manifestations of these phenomena for a long time, though mostly just verbally. These manifestations reinforce what I argued above: that Israeli public discourse doesn't seek out consensus as a behavioral principle. Instead, it focuses on defining the "others."

It's worth repeating that religious groups and communities in Israel are not monolithic in any way. They have incorporated liberal elements in order to cope with moral dilemmas that arise between religious and secular principles. These liberal elements are the source of self-confidence and future partnership between secular and religious Israelis in facing the challenge of rebuilding social cohesion. However, those whose religious identity does not include these liberal foundations (such as Yitzhak Rabin's assassin Yigal Amir or religious extremist settlers in the West Bank) believe that a "supreme power" will make sure that "everything will be okay," thus neutralizing the need to struggle with unclear situations or build consensus with people different from them. At the same time, these beliefs stifle the autonomy of these individuals, who turn to a religious authority above them to deal with their fears and stress.

In this context, I recall some of the important things that the late Israeli professor Karl Frankenstein wrote a few years after the Yom Kippur War (October 1973), consistent with several basic assumptions underlying my doctrine:

> It turned out . . . that the Israeli's conspicuous and arrogantly exaggerated confidence itself is rooted not only in his positive-objective traits, but also in an unrealistic and irrational view of the other, whether the "other" is the exilic Jew with his negative character, in the eyes of the sabra, or whether the "other" is an Arab.

> The structure of their illusions [of many Israelis] is built upon stereotypes, self-idealization, denial of the existence of certain traits as intrinsic to the Israeli character, projection on the Arab or the exilic Jew of what is denied—this entire structure collapsed the moment that reality forced us to recognize the existence of those traits, in actuality or in potential, in all human beings.

In his article, Frankenstein points to the changing reality in Israel between the 1967 Six-Day War and the 1973 Yom Kippur War.[61] During this time, Israelis' point of view began to change. The settlements assumed a central role (and continue to do so today). That said, this reality portrays in a painful way what already existed, latently, long before 1967:

> Inside the city of Hebron, the settlers grabbed for themselves several buildings in the center of the Muslim city, and the only thing they can say to themselves, and rightly so, is that they are surrounded. They arranged a ghetto for themselves, which is first of all a mental matter. The sense of being pushed into a corner and its opposite—the urge for absolute control—are expressed in the myth of Masada . . . Masada is a great work of architecture amidst a spectacular landscape . . . [Its story] is the story of being pushed into the corner. . . . We must compulsively remain the victims of 1929 and Kishinev. . . . And thus, events such as the Beita incident we paint in black, even if the facts prove otherwise. We continue to be the victims, even when others are the victims and the occupied, when we're the occupiers.[62]

Israelis don't realize that their reality is still new. This is the source of the cognitive gap between the reality, in which the foundations of the Israeli democratic political culture have yet to be fully constructed, and Israeli individuals' perception of their country. Israelis do not accept this reality and have not learned to live with the repercussions of the state's incomplete foundations. This means that they will apparently not see in their lifetime integration and social cohesion, normalization, or the onset of peace. Israelis do not confront this reality; they only learn to accept the repercussions that flow from it. They also do not actively contend with the challenges posed by their young democracy or try to make a personal impact on the collective effort to search for meaning and purpose for Jewish life in the State of Israel.

Part Two

The Religious Counterrevolution

Chapter 10

The Interaction between Governance and Religion

In Sophocles's *Antigone*, we read:

CREON: Now you, tell me, not at length but concisely, did you know that these were forbidden by proclamation?

ANTIGONE: Yes. Why would I not? It was public.

CREON: And you dared anyway to transgress these laws?

ANTIGONE: Yes, Zeus was not the one who issued these proclamations for me, nor did Justice, who dwells with the gods below, define such laws among mankind. I did not think your proclamations so strong that you, a mortal, could overstep gods' unwritten and unshakable traditions. Not today or yesterday but always they live, and no one knows when they appeared. I was not about to pay the penalty before gods for neglecting them out of fear for a man's thought. I knew very well that I would die (why not?) even if you had not issued your proclamations. But if I shall die before my time, I declare it a profit; for whoever lives beset, as I do, by many things evil, how does he not gain profit by dying?[63]

A proclamation by the gods versus a proclamation by the king: which takes precedence? The halacha *versus democratic values: which takes precedence?*

Antigone's decision is clear: a proclamation by the gods takes precedence over a proclamation by the king because the gods are eternal, while the king's proclamation is significant, perhaps, only in this world. Antigone also notes that death ultimately awaits every person and declares that even if she dies before her time, she would view this as an advantage because she would be leaving the kingdom of evil. Sophocles's play, which is over 2,400 years old, raises a question that has resonated throughout the centuries: the need to decide between obeying the divine or the earthly, with all its implications. The argument between Antigone and Creon moves onto the personal level when Antigone claims that she represents the entire nation, which is afraid of the king and therefore does not express its opinion.

The dilemma over the primacy of the source of authority in the Jewish state is clearly central in the Zionist religious counterrevolution and its implications. This question, described above as the "dilemma of obedience," turns out to be both universal and ancient. In the historical reality of Athens in the fifth century BCE, Socrates raised this question. He was tried by a court formed in accordance with the rules of Athenian democracy and sentenced to death. Socrates did not accede to his pupils' pleas for him to flee from jail and thus save his life. He accepted the sentence because he believed that since he lived in Athens, was aware of its laws, and hadn't rebelled against them, he was bound by these laws. Antigone represents the position that contradicts the Socratic principle. Sophocles's Antigone does not challenge the existing government, but she confronts the king with the will of the gods.

In the modern era, the "dilemma of obedience" only exists in political sovereignties in which democracy is a way of life. In democratic regimes, it is seen when a contradiction arises between the individual's conscience and enforcement of the law. In the universal dimension, this entails a possible conflict between the conscience of individuals and the norms underlying societal behavior. In our particular context, the discussion of the implications of the religious counterrevolution, this entails a possible clash between the values of democracy and *halacha*.

In his article "Obedience and Democracy," Israeli professor of political science Shlomo Avineri suggests formulating a rule to define the right to refuse to obey laws in a democratic society. According to this proposed rule, the right to refuse is legitimate only if it meets the test of universal moral values—that is, when it does not cause an internal contradiction or undermine the political system itself. According to Avineri's view, the refusal to obey a law in a democratic country for reasons of conscience cannot be universalized and such refusal expresses the arbitrariness and condescension of a particular position of conscience. Giving precedence to the dictates of the *halacha* over the values of democracy when the two clash appears to be an "Antigone choice" in light of the dilemma of obedience that often arises in religious Zionism.

Democracy, as such, cannot support an alternative to "Socrates' choice." Therefore, my discussion of the religious counterrevolution led me to a rude awakening. I grew up believing in the historical alliance between the labor movement and religious Zionism. This belief stayed with me throughout my years at the Israel Democracy Institute. The realization that at the profoundest level this sort of alliance was never possible has been difficult.

∾

We do not live in Israel by virtue of a divine promise. On the contrary—we are here because we rebelled against the belief that the Messiah would come and redeem us from exile and bring us to the Land of Israel.

This is my Zionist motto. After more than two decades of establishing and leading the Israel Democracy Institute, I can say that the State of Israel's politics, culture, and society are affected by the repercussions of the religious counterrevolution that emerged from the secular Zionist revolution, which aspired to free the Jewish people from its diasporic ways. I set out to study the possibilities of a shared future for the entire Israeli society in light of the repercussions of this counterrevolution. The following pages are devoted to my attempt to describe and analyze the characteristics and ramifications of the religious counterrevolution and the story of its development within the Zionist process. This is part of an ambitious effort to develop a multicultural and multi-identity approach to the definition of "Jewish" in the "Jewish and democratic" Israeli collective. It involves searching for openings in the Jewish religion for accepting and living in peace with democratic ways of life.

This process includes an attempt to clarify the existing dissonance, in the absence of a constitution, between the prevailing views of secular and religious Israelis concerning the presence of religion in the state's public spaces, especially in the political agenda. It is also important to examine the role of *halacha* and its rabbinical interpreters, in particular how they interact with Israeli politics. To what extent can the democracy, with its inherently secular foundations, institutions, and norms of operation, reconcile *halacha* and politics?

Underlying the study of this subject is the assumption that the religious Zionist community of Israel is not monolithic. Based on this assumption, I'll try to develop parameters for ranking the diverse attitudes toward democracy among the national religious groups, ranging from liberal national-religious Jews on the top end of this continuum down to people like Yigal Amir, Prime Minister Yitzhak Rabin's assassin, and extremist settlers, such as those who commit the hate crimes called "price tag" attacks in Israel, on the bottom.[64] We'll refer to this as the *descending continuum of believers*. Two questions serve as guidelines:

- Democracy is inherently inclusive. Religion is by definition exclusive. Civil society in any democracy includes all of the groups, sectors, and segments that compose the common sovereign collective. To what extent does the religious counterrevolution impede the containment of the exclusive within the inclusive?

- Is it possible that the religious counterrevolution has complicated the procedural transition from sovereignty-in-the-making to sovereignty? That we are not advancing toward internalizing the implications of accountability for political sovereignty? That the transition from today's formal democracy to a substantive democracy "like all (democratic) nations" has been slowed down?

From the outset, religious Zionists saw independence as the beginning of the realization of the messianic vision.[65] My friend and colleague Professor Avi Ravitzky wrote, "What is the nature of this historical return and how do we identify its place in the context of tradition? . . . Can redemption be possible, or even the beginning of redemption, without being founded upon Torah and repentance, and without entailing a revealed messianic appearance?"[66] He concludes that the Zionist movement was a harbinger of partial and concrete salvation and implemented its message in a secular way. This raised two challenges in Ravitzky's view: national Jewish secularization and historical activism. He quotes Gershom Scholem: "Can Jewish history manage to reenter concrete reality without being destroyed by the messianic claim?" This unfortunately remains unanswered in the framework of the counterrevolution.

Clearly, the champions of the counterrevolution viewed the Zionist awakening as a human, secular, and defiant initiative. Some of them regarded its leaders as heretics.

∿

Though they were separated by three months, in my memory the two events happened side by side. The first was a national holiday, the second a national tragedy. The first was the United Nations vote in November 1947 to partition the British Mandate into a Jewish state and an Arab state. The second was the explosion on Ben-Yehuda Street in Jerusalem on February 22, 1948.

On the day of the UN vote we were living in Mea Shearim in Jerusalem in an apartment with two rooms, plus a kitchen we shared with another family. My father was glued to the radio's shortwave broadcast of the UN vote at Lake Success, New York. When the voting was over, a *Machal* soldier from England let out a shout from the roof of our building.[67] This sparked a stampede of Jerusalemites toward the British compound (Bevingrad), which was cordoned off by barbed wire. They climbed onto the British armored vehicles and celebrated, and this image instantly became part of my Zionist book of memories.

Today, in hindsight, I lament that I didn't try to find out what is now impossible to know: What were my parents feeling on that very Sabbath, as they prepared for the UN vote? They were in their thirties and young by any measure. Only a dozen years had passed since they left their families behind in Europe and it had been years since they'd heard from them. Did it make them hopeful about the fate of their loved ones? Did they ponder what would be the consequences of the vote in Lake Success?

By the time the vote took place, a chilly November night had fallen over Jerusalem and it was very late for a four-year-old boy who crowded around the radio with his parents and the neighbor Avraham and his wife. All these years later, I can still recall the sound of the shortwave radio frequencies and my father pushing his ear up against the radio and trying to hear the votes being announced, one by one. My memories of that night have been shaped by listening later on to repeat broadcasts of the vote and the monotone narrator counting off the yes and no votes and the "abstains." Between the sounds of the radio and the voting there was silence which enveloped the entire apartment and the surrounding streets of Jerusalem, which was under curfew at the time. This silence was interrupted time and again by a British armored truck that would drive down the deserted street outside the balcony of our apartment.

And then it happened—a shout so intense it shattered the tense silence: "A Hebrew state! Free immigration! Down with the white paper! Long live the blue and white flag!" These were the cries that pierced the silence of the tense evening of November 29, 1947.

When the final vote count was announced, we could hear the foreign IDF volunteer from England who was standing on our rooftop shouting. How this soldier was connected to our building I have no idea. Still, his cry signaled an onslaught of Jerusalemites who broke the curfew to swarm the streets of their city between the barbed wire and the armored trucks.

There were some 100,000 Jews living in Jerusalem at the time, more or less about a sixth of all Jews then in the Land of Israel. And although maybe not all of them ran out to the streets to celebrate that night, to a four-year-old bouncing around on his father's shoulders, the celebrations sounded like nothing less than an earthquake.

Israeli author Amos Oz was a young boy in Kerem Avraham at the time. He writes of that night:

After another two or three seconds of astonishment, of standing with our lips spread apart and our eyes wide open, our street on the outskirts of Kerem Avraham in north Jerusalem erupted with an awesome cry that tore through the darkness and the buildings and the trees. It was not a cry of happiness. It sounded nothing like the shouting in sports, it did not resemble a celebration of a worked-up mass of people, maybe it was more a shriek of horror—a deranged shout of catastrophe that could freeze blood. It was as if all of the dead and all those who would die in the future suddenly were able to cry out. In an instant the horror was replaced by joy and shouting and Israel was born. Someone tried to start singing the anthem and the crowd—both men and women—began to move together as if they had been put in a giant blender and there was no such thing as forbidden or not forbidden.

One morning almost three months later, a shocking, monstrous sound shook the city of Jerusalem. It was about 6 a.m. and the explosion was to the south. I recall my father and I racing to the balcony of our home to see the shock wave shattering windows all down our street. I still remember being puzzled by the delay between the sound of the explosion and the shock wave that followed.

By the time the bombing on Ben-Yehuda Street took place, Israel was already fighting the War of Independence, which broke out when the UN declaration in November was followed by the gunshots of seven invading Arab armies. The terror attack on Ben-Yehuda Street was planned by Abed al-Kader al-Husseini and carried out by terrorists who had deserted the British Army. Three buildings on Ben-Yehuda Street were levelled, including two hotels and a residential building. The shock waves shattered windows across the city following the explosion, which killed fifty-eight people. The celebration of independence—a national holiday of the Jewish people—was enmeshed with this tragedy, just as today celebration and tragedy are constantly intertwined in Israel.

Twenty years later, on November 22, 1968, at 9:30 in the morning, I again experienced the delay between the sound of an explosion and the shattering of glass by the shock wave. On that Friday morning, I was finishing a course, just a young man of twenty-five, teaching history at a high school in Jerusalem. The school was next to Jaffa Road and the Davidka Square, just on the perimeter of the Mahane Yehuda market. During the class, a car bomb exploded in the market. For several long seconds, I wondered whether or not to evacuate the students from the class (but to where?), after which the windows in the classroom shattered. I was writing on the blackboard with my back to the students when a piece of glass shot deep into my lower back.

I was lightly wounded and became part of the statistics of the bombing. After I got patched up, I learned that one of the twelve people killed in the blast was the father of one of my history students, and the father of another student was badly wounded. My students mainly came from the lower socioeconomic classes, and the fathers of both boys worked at booths in the market.

How ready were the spiritual, political, and social leaders of national-religious Jewry to accept the fact of a secular state? This question underlies the discussion of the religious counterrevolution in the heart of secular Zionism. For example, this leadership sought to establish customs and symbols that impart religious content and significance to Independence Day, a holiday that is quintessentially secular. They did so to attribute religious legitimacy to the holiday and incorporate it in the religious world and to give religious interpretation to the Zionist narrative.[68]

Juxtaposed against my secular view of independence is the religious Zionist view that (in Ravitzky's words) "the Jewish religion is a *halachic*, social, and national religion . . . It deals with communal values and seeks to shape the public realm . . . When the three come together, they provide a firm political character to the Jewish religious tradition."[69] Yedidia Stern writes, "The prevailing Torah-based view asserts that all of reality is perceived in *halachic* categories."[70] Avi Sagi writes, "*Halacha* is regarded as all-encompassing: a system that pervades all areas of human life. It shapes [the] entire experience of the observant Jew."[71] This view raises a number of questions: Must a person committed to Torah and Jewish law live sequestered within the confines of his community? What is his attitude toward other normative frameworks? At the top end of what I called the descending continuum of believers are those who assert that Jewish law not only enables membership in additional communities— it mandates it. Under this view, religious Jews can be a member of both a *halachic* community and an additional normative value-based community.

But is membership in a liberal democracy consistent with member-ship in the *halachic* community? Comments made by my religiously observant colleagues—those at the liberal end of the continuum, who insist that Jewish law tolerates membership in additional communities—indicate that in the event of conflict between the democratic-sovereign and a *halachic* directive, the *halachic* impera-tive always takes precedence.

When I began examining the vulnerability of Israel's secular democracy, I was operating under a particular assumption. I thought that the worldview that gives priority to *halacha* could be traced to the lack of political sovereignty for Jews in the Diaspora. I thought that this Torah-first approach could only have developed in the Jew-ish Diaspora, which was defined by political passivity, waiting for the Messiah, and complete dependence on the laws of the countries Jews lived in. While this presumption makes sense, it does not explain the rabbis' aspiration to establish the *halacha*'s public standing in the sovereign Jewish state. Central questions in my examination of Israeli democracy included: Can a Torah-centric view that originated in a reality bereft of sovereignty be applied to one in which Jews have their own democratic state? Can the intellectual mix of historical reality (its revolutionary secularism) and metaphysical messianic tradition coexist? How compatible is Zionist ideology with the tradi-tion of exile and redemption?

The historian Ella Belfer claims that "Judaism as a civilization, as a history, as a system of belief cannot be contained within the politi-cal category and does not require this sort of inclusion." She suggests neutralizing charged concepts like "Judaism" and "democracy." For Belfer, the test is whether it is possible to mix the revolutionary and religious ideas that define the two different Zionisms. Should their relationship be loosened or tightened? When I (and others like me) address these questions, we encounter the following obstacle, stated by Yosef Ahituv:

Anyone who reviews the efforts of religious Zionist adjudicators of *halacha* to place the reality of the State of Israel in a *halachic* perspective since the founding of the state cannot avoid the impression that they have yet to internalize the phenomenon of secularism and of the reality of secular Jews as an ongoing phenomenon in the foreseeable historical time frame— neither in the philosophical system nor in the *halachic* system. This phenomenon is still perceived as a transitory phenomenon, starting from the days of Rabbi Herzog in his memorandum at the time of the Peel Commission, and to this very day. Therefore, the vision of a Torah state was not harmed by the reality of a secular majority in the Jewish people and there was no pressure to consider this reality when weaving the image of the Torah state.[72]

These words are difficult for Israelis to hear. For a Zionist looking for a way to create a shared basis for a stable civil society in the Jewish nation-state, these words are almost unbearable. The statement was made by the religious Zionist intellectual Yosef Ahituv, a man of great integrity who sought to build bridges with secular Israelis like me. Like many others, Ahituv focused on the threads that wove together the heart of religious Zionism's worldview. These threads are the foundation for my description and analysis of the religious counterrevolution.

For the sake of fairness, it's worth considering how much the rejection of secular life by observant Jews is a mirror image of secular Jews who reject religious Jewish life. Understanding the sources of our mutual fears of one another would be a starting point for coexistence within the frameworks of democracy.

The literature on this question grapples with many questions, such as: Is religious involvement in politics a response to a sense of injustice on the part of the authorities when normative worlds clash?[73] On this question, author José Casanova asks why religious people feel threatened by a secular state.[74] Do they fear that a clash between normative secular and religious cultures might distance the next generations from religion? Similarly, is the motivation to involve religion in politics defensive? Is it meant to lessen the repercussions of the state's intervention in what is considered religious observance?

Belfer is among those seeking a shared path. She speaks about a dialectic relationship between two conflicting Zionist heritages. This dialectic system is also reflected in the reciprocal connection between the concepts "a light unto the nations" and "a nation like all nations." The question of whether there can be an ideological mix of these two heritages is another way of expressing the basic question underlying my doctrine: To what extent is it possible for the separate spheres of Judaism and democracy to be inclusive of each other? This is a reoccurring question for me as I write this essay because the vision that guides me views such inclusiveness as vital. This inclusiveness is made more distant by a number of impediments raised by the religious counterrevolution which must be removed if we seek a shared life.

And so the question remains: How can religion and politics live in harmony? Is there a place for *halacha* in the constitutional foundation of the Israeli democracy? How can the inclusive incorporate the exclusive?

Ahituv asserted that while there used to be a shared discourse between the secular and religious in Israel, in some circles a closed religious discourse has developed instead. He argues, "The attempt to incorporate [inclusive] secular Zionism and not to be incorporated within it, is the mother of all sin."[75]

༄

On December 12, 1995, five weeks after the assassination of Yitzhak Rabin, my late colleague, journalist, and author Israel Segal and I convened a group of rabbis and observant Jews with nonobservant, secular Jews for some soul-searching in the framework of the IDI's George Shultz Roundtable Forum. Scathing, painful statements were made during the meeting. The opening remarks of Professor Uriel Simon—from Bar-Ilan University, one of the senior figures in religious Zionism—echoed throughout the meeting:

> Worst of all in my eyes is the religious rulings of *din rodef* and *din moser* against the prime minister of Israel.[76] I don't know whether it will be possible to legally prove that a particular rabbi indeed taught the murderer this ruling or responded to his students' questions, but those who are immersed in the community, like my religious friends and me, know there was an atmosphere among our public in which this dreadful ruling was given very serious consideration and had quite a few supporters. Religious people should not hide what they did; they should repent. It is a moral imperative to recognize sin, to admit it and to take it upon ourselves to completely avoid it in the future. Why didn't at least one courageous and honest rabbi stand up and declare before God and man that he had sinned in not unequivocally disavowing this ruling attributed to him? That he is sorry, wholeheartedly, for not considering the possibility that an abstract ruling could be interpreted by fanatics as a practical *halacha*, and that he seeks forgiveness if he unintentionally facilitated the spilling of blood? This type of repentance of one rabbi would cleanse the Jewish religion of the heavy guilt of facilitating the national tragedy that befell us, and we would have no need for the campaign of self-justification that we are witnessing . . . We have a clash between the law and the *halacha*. They come and demand that for the sake of statism we declare that we recognize the supremacy of the law over the *halacha*, and the supremacy of the values of democracy over the values of the Torah. This is an impossible demand, because

for a believing Jew the law is transitory and the Torah is eternal; the law is human and the Torah is divine. A sound democratic state refrains from pushing its citizens toward this type of clash by establishing the freedom of religion and worship as basic civil rights that are beyond any legislation. The Knesset must not enact antireligious laws (and indeed, it has refrained from doing so), and it must be very careful when it enacts religious laws. At the same time, adjudicators of *halacha* must also restrain themselves and refrain from issuing rulings on matters of political controversy.[77]

Chapter 11

Diverse Characteristics of the Counterrevolution in Religious Zionism

The reciprocal connection between religion and politics was, is, and will continue to be a common thread in the evolution of human history. It seems that so far in the twenty-first century we are seeing this connection strengthening anew. The broad, global context of our focus on the interaction of religion and politics in Israel may shed light on what affects and strengthens this connection. When discussing the emergence and development of the religious counterrevolution, the comparative context centers on two issues: the *interaction between governance and religion* in general and the *presence of the religion in public spaces*. The comparative context looks at what Christianity, Islam, and Judaism have in common in terms of the relations between the institutionalized religion and the governmental institutions and how they differ. In other words, what drives institutionalized religion to become involved in politics? In the case of Christianity, this largely revolves around the Westphalia treaties. Starting in the seventeenth century, religious involvement in areas of government gradually diminished. One generalization we can make about modern Western democracies is the various constitutions that establish the principles of freedom of religion and freedom from religion. Also, in secular democracies the state oversees the church.

In the Islamic world there typically is no separation between religion and state. Muhammad was a political leader and the last prophet and emissary of God. He united his followers from a series of tribes and formed a single political entity. His successors—the caliphs—were leaders who had both religious and political authority. They were his successors but not his heirs, in the sense that Muhammad was the final prophet according to Islam. But it would have been impossible to rule the Muslim world without religious authority, due to the fact that the community expressed its very political existence largely through religion.

In other words, Islam creates cultural and communal frameworks that are broader than any specific political arrangement. It is impossible to decide to be non-Muslim and create an entirely secular form of politics. On the other hand, creating an Islamic form of politics does not completely sacralize it either. Politicians do not need to get religious approval at crucial moments, due to the fact that Islam is part of the very fabric of politics from the beginning. It would be impossible to lead the Muslim community without any sort of religious authority, due to the fact that the community by its very existence defines faith and politics as two aspects of a complex identity.

The Jewish case is unique because throughout the history of the Diaspora there were no Jewish governmental institutions and because there was no separation between religion and the public domain in the Jewish experience. Both of these factors had an effect on the evolution of the religious counterrevolution.

One of the questions to address is: What motivates religious involvement in politics in democratic entities? Is it possible to distinguish between religious motivation within and outside the framework of a democracy? In other words, to what extent does the interpretation of *halacha* or *shari'a* directly influence political decisions and the stability of democratic structures? (The Christian case is different because of the absence of religious law, written or oral.)

When it comes to the presence of religion in public spaces, in Christian democratic nation-states public spaces have become secular, while in general, religion is regarded as a private matter. In the Muslim case, the political role of religion dictates its place in the public sphere. Muslim countries do not recognize the Western distinction between "religious" and "secular," private and public, or the absolute versus here and now. Islam is capable of accommodating all of these concepts simultaneously.

The Jewish case is built entirely upon the internal logic of premodern tradition. It does not recognize the need for separate places for the secular and the religious in the public space. Sagi writes, "Contrary to the Protestant religion, which places the individual in the center of religious life, the Jewish religion is intended for the nation and the entirety of its life."[78] Today, from the religious perspective, the renaissance of the Jewish nation in a sovereign framework means redefining the public arena. In this sense, the Jewish state assumes responsibility for the spiritual values and national goals of the Jewish people.[79] According to this view, there can be no separation between the religious and national dimensions. This viewpoint has expected repercussions on religion's connection to politics and again raises the question of whether or not it is possible to restrain the presence of religion in the battle over the public domain.

Our focus here is on the specific connection between *halacha* and politics in Israel. This requires contending with existential questions for Israeli democracy, including: Does the Jewish religion tolerate independent political life? Can religious Zionism keep religion out of politics? *Will the State of Israel survive the Jewish religion?* This question, and the way it is worded, is not intended to be provocative or defiant by any means. It does not ignore the fact that, as Belfer wrote, "The entire religious-Zionist ethos [is based upon] the obligation to practically apply the Torah in concrete political life, [and this is] a religious obligation that is not an 'innovation' of religious Zionism. Rather, it is the fulfillment of an ancient religious duty that Moses already expressed in the Torah."[80]

Professor Dov Schwartz, a religious Jew, points to what he calls the deep gap between the theological and ideological dimensions of religious Zionism.[81] He asserts that while religious Zionists are full partners in everyday democratic life, they are connected to the theological dimension, which means a comprehensive worldview. In this perspective, "the secular Zionist idea is a shell that covers authentic religious content . . . Zionism is the fulfillment of a divine plan, and the absolute majority of religious Zionism—if not all of it—closely identified this plan with the realization of redemption."

To what extent can religion accept the secular foundation of democracy? There's no one all-inclusive answer to this question. Still, we cannot ignore the fact that the rejection of the secular foundations of democracy and the failure to accept the fact that the state is secular create what the scholar Avi Sagi calls the "crisis potential."[82] Whether or not the secular nature of the democratic state is accepted tests a number of basic values—such as equality—which are at the intersection of the universal (democracy) and the particularistic (Judaism). The "crisis potential" is part of our daily lives. It is difficult to assess the likelihood that this crisis will occur or how far-reaching it could be. I believe the very existence of this potential poses a threat that must be addressed. The Israeli public has grown accustomed in recent decades to hearing "Torah sages" and "the settlers' rabbis" issue rulings on political topics. They assume there is internal *halachic* legitimacy to rule on these matters.[83]

Professor Stern states that "the application of *halacha* in a path of public leadership, in parallel to the Torah path, is a common process in the history of *halacha*," and notes that "we see a fascinating cultural phenomenon of consistent and ongoing multigenerational dialogue between a religious system and a government system, expressed in the normative language of *halacha*."[84] Stern seeks a way to establish "a modern, yet authentic, *halachic* approach to the systems of public leadership that determine the prevailing normative code in the State of Israel. From an understanding of the dynamic of the *halacha*'s development and in coordination with it, it is possible to establish a system of *halachic* meaning, relevant for today, for the output of the legislative and judicial branches in Israel."[85] This approach is certainly problematic. This very attempt to reveal the prerequisites for a *halachic* opinion on political questions presumably grants legitimacy a priori to a *halachic* opinion.

Unlike Stern, I believe we must completely refrain from searching for what he calls "a direct practical connection between the scope of the legal reality in the religious system of law and the secular system of law"—if only to avoid suggesting that there is symmetry between these systems of law.[86] In the past, I believed that in searching for this practical connection he was trying to establish religious restraint of *halacha*. However, the following attempt is unacceptable to a secular Jew: "We should consider the possibility of divine choice in narrowing the authority of the *halacha* vis-à-vis certain parts of human reality" and in creating "*halachic* spaces in which decision-making is left to the person, public or other normative system."

Naturally, I am comfortable with the approach of legendary Israeli intellectual Yeshayahu Leibowitz which he adopted later in life and remains exceptional in the arena of religious Zionism:

The lack of a real statist function for the Jewish nation was the condition and basic premise for shaping the *halacha* in the form in which it reached us. The entire Torah constitution dealing with society and state, with organizing and arranging them and in meeting their needs, were never designed to fulfill a historical reality. Rather, it was an ideal picture of messianic days.

The crisis of religious Judaism in our days is that it only has *halacha* that is based on an assumption of the exile. The narrowing of the *halacha*'s boundary is not only the result of historical circumstances of life in exile. The nonfulfillment of the political reality in *halachic* parameters is "immanent" and was never intended to be realized in the historical reality.

Unfortunately, the crisis potential stems from a reality that is far removed from Leibowitz's arguments. Sagi writes, "In cases of conflict between a directive of the democratic sovereign and a directive of *halacha*—a directive of *halacha* takes precedence."[87] These words resonate strongly in the political socialization processes in the state-religious education system. The significance of this statement is reflected in the findings of surveys conducted by my friend and colleague Tamar Hermann at IDI's Guttman Center that illustrate the problem.[88] She writes: "Most respondents attribute great importance or considerable importance (58 percent) to rabbinical rulings on political issues . . . [in their view] the religious leadership has an important role not only in ordering the lives of the individual, family and community, but also on political-public issues. About a third do not share this view."[89] Some 57 percent of secular respondents were opposed to government funding for Reform and Conservative communities and rabbis and only about a third (36 percent) supported it. In my view, this reflects the weakness of the secular foundation in our civil society, together with the strength of the prevailing mood in Israeli society, a product of the repercussions of the religious counterrevolution.[90]

Only 13 percent of national-religious respondents said that the Knesset is the supreme authority for signing a peace accord that would require giving over land to the Palestinians. Half stated that the authority belongs to the Jewish citizens of Israel only while 16 percent stated that the authority lies with all Israeli citizens—Jews and non-Jews alike—and 14 percent assigned this authority to the rabbis who issue *halachic* rulings.[91]

About 64 percent of the graduates of pre-army academies believed that they should refuse to carry out an order to evacuate settlements. These graduates today comprise a significant part of the more than 40 percent of the IDF's junior officer corps who are religiously observant. (The question of refusal will be one of the main questions addressed in the discussion on the role of the *halacha* in the army.) How does religious Zionism reconcile the contradiction between religious directives (*halachic* rulings) and the secular foundations of democracy? My observations indicate that religious Zionism, in general, simply does not reconcile this contradiction. The liberal part of this community, the minority, learns to live with the contradiction while the majority reconciles it by according primacy to *halachic* rulings.

Another scholar, Gideon Aran, argues that religious Zionism reconciles the contradiction by expanding the concept of religion in an unlimited way, until it becomes possible to reject and affirm secular Zionism at the same time.[92] He also asserts that a system that is both messianic and mystical can accommodate this paradox. At the center of this system, messianic redemption is identified with political Zionism and its enterprise in the Land of Israel: "Redemption is happening in front of our eyes and with our participation." This soon leads to leveraging what is opposed to the secular foundations of the state—an emphasis on the supremacy of Israel's sanctity.[93]

From the perspective of a religious Zionist with a simple view of reality, modern secularism has taken over many important areas of life that had always been the domain of religion. Religious Zionists felt threatened by modern secularism, particularly because of Zionism's aspiration to restore a complete Jewish framework encompassing all aspects of the Jew's existence. The secular revolution built secular entities from scratch but was not able to build a strong enough foundation for Israeli democracy. These weaknesses have allowed the system to become permeated by religious models. For example, in the absence of a constitutional establishment of freedom of and from religion, the country is forced to make concessions to religious parties for the sake of governance. The secular foundations have further eroded and weakened due to the lack of a constitution while the religious counterrevolution strengthened, driven by the assumption that only by applying religion to diverse areas of life—secular and otherwise—would Jewish life be restored to its original fullness.

Aran wrote on this subject: "Zionism saved Judaism. It was [Zionism] and not the religion that fulfilled the vision of reviving

Judaism . . . and it did so not in terms of the sacred and in traditional models, but through their exact opposite, via the content of modern secularism. Believers faced frustrating dissonance, which constitutes a primary challenge to religious thought and emotion."

Against this background, I wonder: *Would it be correct to assume that from the outset the Zionist revolution had no chance of achieving its objectives?* Was the Zionist deficit, which enabled, indirectly and unintentionally, the formation and growth of the religious counterrevolution, inevitable? To what extent is the tie between nation and religion a dominant variable in the Jewish case?

The Zionist deficit not only did not block the religious counterrevolution—it enabled it. For over a century, secular Zionism built a flourishing culture and Israeli identity that were founded on the revived Hebrew language. In parallel, the religious counterrevolution emerged and has since become more powerful. This is no contradiction.

Other than the establishment of Jewish self-determination, I do not believe that the way of life and fundamental values of today's Israel are consistent with the vision and worldview charted by the country's founders. The secular revolution of the Jews did not last long enough to build a secular foundation that could offer alternative sources of interpretation and meaning for Judaism. No cultural transformation took place and the "new Jew" sketched out by the secular Zionist founders was short-lived. On the other hand, the "old Jew" regained its dominance, albeit in a new Israeli incarnation. The immigrants of the 1950s swelled the numbers of the "old Jew" and those who identified with this image. Today, only 43 percent of Israelis define themselves as secular. Some 33 percent of Jews identify as "traditional," a sort of blending of religious tradition and secular life, and 15 percent and 7 percent define themselves as religious and ultra-Orthodox, respectively. As Walzer says, "We need to turn our backs on the old ways and overcome them—entirely. However, the old ways are held precious and close to the hearts of many of those who led the [revolutionary] change. This is the paradox of the liberation."[94]

According to Belfer, Zionist statism saw the religious-*halachic* stagnation as a meaningless, anachronistic remnant and viewed secular nationalism as a temporary deviation for the Jewish nation and its eternal presence in history. Belfer added that the dilemma was between the revolutionary and the historical and that the struggle to determine Israel's political definition (secular or "holy land") was primarily a battle against ambiguity.[95]

On the one hand, the secular foundation in Zionism eroded the historical consciousness of Jewish continuity, while its religious foundation, on the other hand, countered the revolutionary change that fueled secular Zionism. To state this in starker terms, it was a clash of fundamentalist actualization and Western secular interpretation. The dilemma is twofold—how do we unravel *the State of Israel's cultural entanglement* that contains both revolutionary secular foundations and *an ethnocentric particularistic orientation*? Any drastic or unilateral decision would inevitably lead to a culture war and is thus out of the question.

∽

The triangle formed by King George Street, Ben-Yehuda Street, and Jaffa Street in Jerusalem was a secular area in every definition of the word. Observant Jews who lived there and on the streets surrounding the triangle were swallowed up inside their secular surroundings. One of these observant families was the Jacksons. The parents and their four children lived in one of the ground-floor apartments of our building. Every time I came or went, I passed by their front door. I was in first grade and studying at the Arlozorov (secular) school just after we moved to the Hillel Street building from Mea Shearim. I befriended the Jacksons' son, Yossi, who was my age. He later became a famous journalist and travel writer who went by the name "Jacksy." The family was always happy to have me over at their apartment and this made it a little easier to be a latchkey kid with hours to kill after school. It was in their house that I was first exposed to the rituals and way of life of an observant Jewish family.

Their two children played all the same childhood games and their daily routines were defined by the same aimless pursuits of childhood, just with the added commandments of a religious home: keeping kosher, separating meat and dairy dishes and utensils, walking to synagogue on Friday and Saturday, and building the sukkah (a temporary outdoor shack built during the Jewish holiday of Sukkot) where they were hosting me. And, of course, all of their conversations dealt with these subjects and were part of my socialization process to their way of life.

Around this same time, my father got our family's first car, a 1939 Ford, with the license plate number "Jerusalem 1828." The Jackson family lived on the first floor of our building and we in a small apartment on the fifth floor. They were the only religious family in our building. When my parents planned to travel on the Sabbath to visit family in Jerusalem or elsewhere, Father would go ahead of time to park the car on another street "so as not to offend the feelings of those who observe the religious commandments." That's the way my parents raised me.

The religious counterrevolution, from its nascent stages through its maturation, roughly overlaps with the Zionist process from the secular revolution through the founding of the state and to the current day. Throughout this period, the religious counterrevolution has strived to infuse the *halacha* into the democratic ways of life, with an emphasis on the variables that pertain to politics and the role of *halacha* in shaping public spaces.

When the State of Israel was founded, religious Jews faced a twofold challenge. They had to define *halachic* positions on questions of governance and adopt a stance vis-à-vis the "Jewish public domain" which had developed along secular lines. These issues made collaboration and ideological partnership between religious Zionism and secular Zionism problematic from the outset. The religious Jews who helped to build the Zionist identity were supposed to accord legitimacy, indirectly if not directly, to the desire to secularize the cultural-identity foundations of the Jewish nation. But this could not be reconciled with religious belief. Nonacceptance of secularism is inherent in the patterns of behavior and ideological ways of religious Zionism. Religious Zionism, Sagi writes, not only "rejects the normative status of secularism in the Jewish nation, but it claims that on the factual level the Jewish people by nature cannot be transformed into a secular people."[96] **"Religious Zionism has always believed that the Jewish state must be a state of *halacha* [emphasis mine]."[97]**

These are facts that cannot be disputed or ignored. The ratification of a constitution that defined relations between religion and the state might have resolved this matter. With this matter left unresolved, the religious counterrevolution—and its impact on relations between the state and religion—became fact. Within religious Zionism there are many opinions on these issues; understanding that the national-religious public is not monolithic may provide an opening for creating a basis for shared life. I'm searching for allies in the national-religious public. After all, this is the purpose of my doctrine—development of a multicultural, multi-identity definition of being a Jew.

Ravitzky argues that the modern conflict between religion and the state stems from the clash of two perceptions of authority and sovereignty. He also distinguishes between metaphysical authority and political authority.[98] From the metaphysical perspective, the ideal state may be envisioned as the manifestation of divine law ("a state of *halacha*"). It would be a platform for the presence of God ("the foundation for God's throne in the world") or even as the embodiment of this presence ("a divine state"). This is an absolutist approach to politics. However, it is also possible for the believer to see the state as an efficient organizational tool and assign it to defend against violence. That is, it is possible for a supporter of a "state of *halacha*" to accept internal and external conditions, national and international norms, as well as secularization and the rights of individuals, non-Jews, and women.[99] These are two of the approaches underlying the diversity of views in religious Zionism. Ravitzky also distinguishes among three approaches to messianism and Zionism: (1), the approach that unconditionally adheres to the messianic conception and regards Zionism as an anti-redemptive process (most commonly held by ultra-Orthodox Jews); (2), the activist messianic view that sees Zionism as a step in the course of redemption; and (3), a view that tries to separate Zionism from the hope of redemption with the coming of the Messiah.[100]

Stern described the early view of religious Zionism (the Mizrachi movement, Rabbi Yehuda Leib Fishman) as holding, "In matters pertaining to what is prohibited and what is permitted, we will ask the rabbis, but in matters of life in the marketplace, they should ask us."[101] In the context of our discussion here, Stern says that the Orthodox public must decide between two approaches: adherence to messianic redemption or acceptance of secular sovereignty. The latter requires surrendering the former. The bulk of the spiritual leadership of the Israeli ultra-Orthodox public continues the experience of exile, whose primary characteristic is a lack of accountability for political sovereignty. The national-religious public seeks to square the circle. Stern suggests that we should "consider the feasibility of divine selection in reducing the authority of the *halacha* vis-à-vis certain parts of human reality" by creating "*halachic* spaces where decision-making is left in the hands of a person, public or other normative system."[102] In this way, I think he exemplifies the attempt to square the circle. The effort to restrict the involvement of *halacha* in issues of society and state in a sovereign reality is essentially an effort to accommodate the *halacha* in these matters. A secular democrat would find this unacceptable.

In the months before Israel withdrew its settlements and military installations from the Gaza Strip in the summer of 2005, my colleagues and I at the IDI held numerous meetings with leaders of the settlement movement. Our motivation was clear: regardless of our political perspective on the issue of the settlements and the Gaza withdrawal in particular, we saw ourselves as obligated to do whatever we could in order to prevent violence—even bloodshed—during the withdrawal. I can't say how many meetings we held, but there were very many. Some were very uncomfortable and we found ourselves facing a dilemma. On the one hand, our settler friends claimed that the Israeli government headed by Prime Minister Ariel Sharon acted in an undemocratic fashion in the way it approved the withdrawal. On the other hand, there was no reasonable basis to make this argument. When Sharon dismissed two cabinet members who opposed the withdrawal, my colleagues at the IDI, Avi Ravitzky and Motta Kremnitzer, rebuked the prime minister publicly.

Their emotional opposition to the democratic decision made by the Israeli government prevented them from accepting it. As the date of the beginning of the evacuation of the settlements approached, the potential for violence was in the air. I arranged an "intimate discussion" to be held at the IDI between heads of the settlement movement and the leaders of the institute. There were moments in which it felt like at any second we'd manage to break the ice and reach a breakthrough, if just barely. About ten minutes before midnight, Rabbi Meidan indicated that some members of the meeting still needed to do the evening *arvit* prayer service, so we—secular Jews to the core—helped them complete the *minyan:* a group of ten Jewish men necessary to hold a Jewish prayer service. In the days to come, my colleagues and I held meetings with law enforcement officials in order to get a sense of how they would mitigate potential conflict and contain the actions of extremists.

My unease continued. My colleagues and I decided to hold another meeting one night at the West Bank settlement of Kedumim. It came after the friendly, amiable meeting held earlier at the IDI and it was starkly different. We rode out to the settlement in an armored bus, many of us crossing the Green Line into the West Bank for the first time. The meeting began around 11 p.m. and didn't end until about 3 a.m. We had expressed our good intentions and desire to find common ground with our hosts, but the only moment when there was a semblance of agreement was at the end, when we came together to sing *Hatikva*, the Israeli national anthem.

Eventually, the fateful summer of the Gaza withdrawal arrived. I don't remember quite how, but Yedidia Stern and I found ourselves in two separate meetings in the office of the pilot Ran Packer, who was then the business partner of Major General Yom Tov Samia, the former head of the Southern Command. We discussed the ongoing dilemma of how Israeli authorities would prevent bloodshed during the withdrawal and how they were planning to ease tension across the country. The meetings were held around the time of the March to Come Together, which was when thousands of religious Zionists marched on the Gush Katif settlements in the Gaza Strip and were surrounded by police and soldiers, as well as settler leaders who heroically stepped in to defuse the situation. Our meetings with Packer were held at the same time that the IDI was under criticism for allegedly not doing enough to stop the "undemocratic" breakup of the march.

And when we stepped out of one of those meetings, Stern told me with undisguised enthusiasm that some rabbis were trying to formulate rulings that would provide a *halachic* basis for obeying the state's directives. I wondered: How can you accept *halachic* interference, whatever it might be, in the affairs of state? It was the first time that a random comment spurred me to think about the implications of *halachic* involvement in the affairs of state. As someone whose roots are in the Labor Zionist movement, my attitude toward religion-state relations at that time was a product of the myth of "the historical alliance" between the state's founders. I was a captive of the myth of the great alliance formed between the leaders of the Labor Zionist movement and religious Zionism. From my vantage point today, as I attempt to formulate my doctrine in the context of a reality formed by such perspectives and with the premise that a culture war is not an option, I'm trying to latch onto the moderate streams in national-religious Zionism and to see them as possible allies.

I would like to present two quotes from Stern's writings. Rabbi David Halevy (the chief rabbi of Tel Aviv from 1973 to 1998) stated that the *halacha* applies in principle to political issues. However, the *halacha* narrows the authority it accords only in order to establish "principles and foundations."[103] It does not define what is prohibited and what is permitted in political matters. This it leaves to the free choice of the people in each generation. According to medieval Jewish scholar Maimonides, *halachic* norms that depend on the king's commandments are not intended to be implemented in the historical reality of our day. Maimonides's preference, from today's perspective, is to prevent the practical application of *halacha* to political issues.[104]

And against the background of these assertions by Maimonides, I wish to present my questions. Stern argues, among other things, that the *halacha* is not "exempt from formulating a normative stance vis-à-vis the secular way of life."[105] And I wonder, what role could there be for a *halachic* stance in regard to a reality in which the Jewish public domain is fashioned "in accordance with the accepted norms of the secular majority?" And also: "Democratic values sometimes stand in contradiction to the world of values reflected in *halachic* norms." And I again wonder whether the question "How does the *halacha* deal with these contradictions?" is only pertinent to internal religious discourse and is totally unrelated to the ways of the civil society that incorporates the religious groups. In other words, what is the meaning and what are the implications of this call for the *halacha* to take a stance on wholly secular matters in a democracy?

Yosef Ahituv proposes four reference models within religious Zionism vis-à-vis democracy and its values. The first is the *model of acceptance*: "Today, there is no alternative to adopting democratic values . . . this is a model of after the fact and of no alternative. As noted, it differentiates between the *halachic* moral view and the democratic moral view, while seeking ways to approve partial recognition of the democratic system." The second is the *reconstruction model* in which "the universal values have always been found in our sources." In this framework, a real interpretative effort is made to show that there is no contradiction between the universal and the particularistic (democracy and religion). The third is the *model of development* which suggests a new reading of the sources. This model accepts the changes in the views of morality, "acknowledging the superiority of the moral views of today." Finally, there is the *technical model*, which "prefers mixing a 'lean' *halachic* language with a 'technical' view of democracy." This model entails relinquishing the idea of a state of *halacha*.[106]

Hebrew University Professor Avinoam Rosenak categorizes the different views of religious Jews in Israel in accordance with an article by German-Jewish educator and philosopher Ernst Simon.[107] In this article, written in 1952, Simon distinguishes between a "Catholic approach" and a "Protestant approach." Rosenak suggests that we view religious Zionism as a revolutionary movement that contains dialectical tension between modernism, which recognizes the essentiality of secularism (Protestantism), and traditionalism, as embodied in (Catholic) ultra-Orthodox thought. Unlike the ultra-Orthodox, the religious Zionists did not reject modernity. But the "Catholic" trends within religious Zionism led it to consume secularism and modernity by translating them into traditional internal religious tools. However, by doing this, religious Zionism rejected the independent value of secularism. The "Protestant" thinkers understood that secular independence is one of the foundations of the modern revolution with which moderate religious Zionists sought a partnership. Many of the prominent members of the "Catholic" group of religious Zionists studied at the storied Merkaz HaRav yeshiva in Jerusalem and were disciples of the legendary Rabbi Kook, who founded the yeshiva and is seen as one of the most central figures in religious

Zionism. This "Catholicism" was expressed in a vision of creating a state of *halacha*. The "Protestant" position sees this as a false vision that fails to contend with the actual reality of modern Israel.

The work of Tamar Hermann, who heads the Guttman Center at the Israel Democracy Institute, uses quantitative measures to break down the different groups in religious Zionism. Hermann and her team assert that the identity of the national-religious camp is based on three components: religiousness, nationalism (Zionism), and a certain degree of openness toward modernity.[108] The religiousness component represents a continuum that includes ultra-Orthodox and conservative views, mainstream Orthodox views, and liberal Orthodox views. Nationalism in the national-religious sector, according to the study, rests on the parallel existence of "open messianism" and a "moderate messianism" that blurs the connection between Zionism and messianic redemption. With openness to modernity, we can see an affirmation of science and general culture as well as diverse identities. On the other hand, we also see a denial of the legitimacy of secularism. There is no uniform model for the response to modernity. This is clearly expressed in what we refer to as compartmentalization of the believer's world into the sacred and secular, with the secular component disconnected from the world of Jewish observance and belief. Among religious Zionists, there is a wide range of approaches to modernity, from a minimal, controlled openness to the modern world to a nearly complete acceptance of all of the trappings of the modern secular world.

The following data can shed some light on the diversity of national-religious thought when it comes to democracy and secularism.

The data found that 31 percent of those affiliated with religious Zionism self-identified as national-religious, 11 percent as ultra-Orthodox, 6 percent as nationalist ultra-Orthodox (*hardal*), 12 percent as liberal religious, 24 percent traditional religious, and 9 percent nonreligious traditional. Surprisingly, 3 percent identified as secular even though they are affiliated with the national-religious camp.[109]

In regard to the democratic principles, the survey noted three approaches among self-affiliated national-religious Jews. The adjustment approach blurs the tension between the *halacha* and democracy. Proponents argue that the principles of democracy can be found in the *halacha* and in the practice of the Jewish religion. The second approach states that there is no alternative to democracy so it must be supported and efforts should be made to ease the tension between it and *halacha*. The third approach seeks to adapt the democracy to the demands of *halacha*.[110]

From my perspective, it is important to note that studying in religious pre-military programs (*yeshivot hesder*, considered an elite school option for religious Zionist youth) does not foster liberal viewpoints concerning freedom of expression. About half of those who studied in such programs believe that there is excessive protection of freedom of expression in the State of Israel. (I'll return to this later when discussing the role of religion in the army.[111])

Two beliefs supported by a wide spectrum of national-religious Jews are especially relevant to our discussion.[112] They are:

- Identity and religiousness. There is nearly complete consensus in the core national-religious group regarding the importance of maintaining religious political parties in the Knesset in order to protect the Jewish character of the State of Israel.
- Religion and state. A majority in the core national-religious group views rabbinical rulings on political issues as being important to society (58 percent). Some 48 percent say that Knesset members should be subordinate to the rabbis while 46 percent disagreed with this assertion. A majority opposes granting citizenship to non-Jews (they would not have approved the Law of Return) and an overwhelming majority considers Independence Day a religious holiday.

In the introduction to *Judaism: A Dialogue Between Cultures*, the book's editors write: "The experiential dissonance between practice [daily life] outside of religion and religious belief led many to adopt a defensive strategy of severing 'inside' from 'outside,' with each of the two its own independent compartment in the experience of the modern believers. From the outset, the religion is the only significant context for the believers. On the other hand, and in retrospect, they recognize the functional importance of the other contexts of reality. In this way, the believers find themselves in a schizophrenic life of duality, shaped by different contexts of meanings, and they are not interested in mediating between them or confronting one against the other."[113] This dissonance felt by observant Jews often surfaces in regard to issues of democracy and Jewish law. It is essential that observant Jews acknowledge this dissonance as part of efforts to develop tools for shared life and mutual recognition in our civil society.

The pursuit of these essential conditions is integral to my doctrine and will be the central focus of the fourth part of my work. I'll already say here that recognition of this experiential dissonance by believers and observant Jews, along with the ability "to live with it," places them at the upper end of the descending continuum.

The variety of views and approaches in religious Zionism is quite clear and distinct. I've presented a sampling of the work by Hermann's team as well as the diagnoses of religious Zionist thinkers. I examine these diagnoses according to two criteria: their attitude toward the reciprocal link between the *halacha* and politics and their reference to the place of religion in public spaces. Based on these criteria, I believe that nearly all of the approaches, from the most moderate to the most conservative, from the "Catholic" pole to the "Protestant" pole, are located along the descending continuum of believers. All of these approaches accept, in principle, that there is room for the presence of *halacha* in the public domain—including, directly or indirectly, in politics.

As noted, outside of this continuum lies the approach of Yeshayahu Leibowitz and a minority like him who assert that the *halacha* can have no say on political issues and that there is no place for God in public life. As noted, the top end of this continuum consists of those who are able to side with democratic values when they clash with Jewish law and can live within their schizophrenic duality. At this pole, and near it, are those who adhere to liberal principles to some degree. At the other end, as noted—at the bottom of the continuum—are extremists like those who commit "price tag" hate crimes and people like the assassin Yigal Amir. For everyone situated on the descending continuum, the very existence of this dilemma confirms that democracy is secular. This is true regardless of whether the dilemma is resolved and is even more resoundingly clear if *halacha* is accorded precedence over democracy.

Bar-Ilan University Professor Dudi Schwartz writes, "The religious Zionist is always anticipating the moment when the peels will be removed and the covers taken off, and the secular Zionist will collectively return to observe the *halacha*. The longed-for theocracy is imminent and will materialize the moment the secular Zionist sees the true path, with complete worship of God. *The religious Zionist is waiting for the moment when secularism will collapse and disappear forever* [emphasis mine]."[114] I would like to suggest that one of the key indicators of where an observant Jew stands on the descending continuum of believers is the seriousness he or she ascribes to this statement. A descending continuum can also be drawn between those who view the disappearance of secularism as a utopia signaling the coming of the Messiah and those who regard such a possibility as a positive commandment. In this sense, as I've contended ever since Rabin's assassination in November 1995, the assassin was no solitary rotten apple. There were numerous rabbis who used their authority to inspire Amir, who reacted in kind.

I realize I may be going out on a limb by placing liberal religious Zionists on the same continuum as extremists like Amir and the thugs who carry out the "price tag" hate crimes. In my view, all of the components of religious Zionism should be considered to some extent partners in the religious counterrevolution that emerged from the secular Zionist revolution. This is not an indictment and it is not meant to be a critique or to provoke. I am merely trying to send a very clear warning: mixing *halacha* and democracy can lead us down a very dangerous path. I'm calling on my liberal religious Zionist colleagues to take action to prevent the country from heading down this path.

Here's an analogy: For me, and for all those who seek out freedom and justice, the Holocaust should be a warning signal. We must see ourselves as living at the far end of the same continuum as the SS officers in the death camps and assume responsibility for our values and actions so we can stay on the right side. I seek to use the descending continuum as a means to foster coexistence and to send a warning that where we stand on the continuum is not static. It can change at any time. This demands a moral stance: What must I, a believer and observant Jew, do in a democratic environment in order to avoid slipping down the slope?

Chapter 12

The Counterrevolution
in the Chronological Mirror

The rich, diverse story of religious Zionism has already been written from various points of view. My interest here is to outline the stages of the religious counterrevolution and the implications of its growth, past and future.

The starting point for this outline is clear and it serves as an initial milestone on a path that took a very divergent course. It all starts with Rabbi Isaac Jacob Reines, the founder of the Mizrachi movement, who viewed the national revival as separate from religious redemption. He disconnected the Jewish hope for messianic redemption from the secular national initiative.

For Reines, the Zionist idea did not pertain to messianic redemption. In his view, a religious Jew could be involved in the historical political effort and be part of the separation between Zionist activity and messianic redemption: Zionism does not carry any sign or mark of the idea of redemption, and does not touch upon anything referring to it, and it is only an endeavor to improve the material situation of the nation and enhance its fate in dignity. The Zionism of Rabbi Reines was not intended to advance divine redemption. That task is of God and His alone.

It was Rabbi Avraham Yitzchak Hacohen Kook who led religious Zionism away from the path blazed by Rabbi Reines. Contrary to

Reines, Rabbi Kook ascribed religious-messianic meaning to the
Zionist movement and erased the distinction between nationalism
and religious redemption. Ella Belfer wrote about Rabbi Kook's
doctrine, which she saw as "*a 'counterrevolution' vis-à-vis secular
Zionism* [emphasis mine]" and part of the struggle for the soul of the
country.[115]

Rabbi Kook was regarded at the time as a man of compromise on
religious matters and was tolerant toward secular Zionists.[116] In retrospect, this was a false impression. His ostensible alliance with secular Zionists was limited from the outset. Partly due to the Zionist
deficit, the secular elite of Rabbi Kook's time lacked the tools to
understand the rabbi's doctrine. Thus, they accorded a type of author-
itative legitimacy to Rabbi Kook that enabled them, the nonobservant, to see themselves as "chosen."

According to Aran, the rabbi's doctrine sought to remove secularism from the Zionist enterprise itself.[117] He argues that in response to
the danger that the leaders of the Zionist revolution might "national-
ize" the religion, Rabbi Kook aimed to "religicize" the nationalism.[118]
Kook believed that Judaism and Jewish nationalism are intrinsically
linked and complement one another to form the original, complete
Jewishness. Kook asserted that Jewish nationalism was distinguished
and enhanced by its underlying religious quality.[119] In any case, the
assertion that "Zionism has nothing to do with religion" is false. The
national liberation movement is a movement of reviving the sacred.
Zionism is "a divine yearning," a movement of repentance. These
statements and the shock waves they produced in the evolving counterrevolution emerged from the vacuum created by the Zionist deficit,
which stymied ideological debate on the ties between religion and
state in the Jewish case.

Ravitzky expressed "great doubt" about Aran's thesis, even though
he admitted that Kook's doctrine gives viable status to Jewish statehood.[120] Ravitzky asks: How will his (Kook's) heritage endure when
encountering an Israeli reality in which secularism refuses to disappear and earthly politics dictate the ways of life? Ravitzky asserted

that Kook's doctrine will lead religious Zionists to believe that they should not remain bystanders in the Zionist story and should take the reins of the state in their own hands: "This [Kookist] conception, from the moment it spreads in the public, will lead the religious Zionist to abandon the traditional place assigned to him by his fathers, members of Mizrachi, as a passenger or escort in the Zionist convoy: It will demand that he take the reins in his hands."

In other words, Ravitzky asserts that Kook's view establishes the fact that "the national-religious movement reinforced the averseness to a hastening of the end [apocalyptic fervor] by humans. The fathers of the movement spoke of the constant presence of God, but not so much about the anticipated messianic breakthrough, singular and transcendental, toward the future."

Sagi portrays Kook's teachings as the embodiment of a "Catholic doctrine" that offers a total solution.[121] It's a solution that holds a "transcendental view of reality" and strives for harmony: "The religious Zionist [is able] to live the real history, while interpreting it in advance in the framework of general metaphysical plans—messianic utopias."[122] Kook provides a solution by ascribing religious value to the entire Zionist enterprise, even though it is at its core a secular endeavor.

In my view, Ravitzky summarizes the essence of the threat that religion poses to democracy. He points out how Kook sees the Jewish state as deeply interwoven with religious moral standards. "Our state, the State of Israel, the foundation for God's throne in the world," is a "divine state," the rabbi famously stated.[123] In addition, Kook developed an entire ideology out of the redemptive conception of the Zionist revival.[124] On the one hand, this ideology presents the idea of a new national revival that will protect Zionism from the ultra-Orthodox, while on the other hand, it utterly rejects the trends of national secularism. The ideology holds that the Jewish people have an organic, inseparable connection to the divine.[125] In my view, these statements and others like them are part of the foundation of the growing demands since the founding of Israel for *halacha* to play a greater role in politics. As Avi Ravitzky argues in his article, Kook's doctrine does not leave room for an ongoing secular reality.[126]

Ahituv is among those who believe that the conundrum can be traced to Kook's doctrine.[127] Ahituv laments the metaphysical discourse which stems from Kook's teachings and its complete dominance of the religious Zionist discourse. This burgeoning discourse shifted toward a messianic path and purported to not only interpret reality, but to actually steer public and political reality as well. Ahituv also points to the mystification of Israeli nationalism and the depiction of the Israeli nation as the embodiment of divinity itself.[128]

The argument with Kookist views reflects the fact that diverse variables—both within and outside religious Zionism—affected the character and path of the religious counterrevolution's development from the outset. That is, the development of the counterrevolution was not one-dimensional. This stirs hope for the possibility of dialogue that could pave the way toward a shared life and coexistence between religion and politics in the Israeli democracy. Here are two examples that illustrate this hope-inspiring diversity. First, it is noteworthy that religious Zionist leaders not only refrained from opposing the content of the Declaration of Independence but were also among its signatories. As stated earlier, in light of the widening rift and crisis of identity in contemporary Israel, only a very few political and religious figures in religious Zionism would be inclined to sign the Declaration of Independence today.

The second example involves the views of political leaders and rabbis in religious Zionism vis-à-vis a written constitution for the State of Israel. Already in the 1930s and 1940s, as Rabbi Kook was formulating his doctrine, there were explicit references to the issue of a constitution. Most prominently involved was Zerach Warhaftig, a member of Mizrachi, an attorney, and a politician. In 1947, Warhaftig led a constitutional effort, believing that it was impossible to establish a state without a constitution. After the proclamation of independence in May 1948, a Constitution Committee chaired by Warhaftig was appointed to draft a complete constitution.

David Ben-Gurion bears primary responsibility for the failure of this constitutional effort. And as already noted, his opposition is one of the clearest signs of the Zionist deficit. The failure of the constitutional effort testifies to the sources of the vulnerability of the secular foundation of Israeli democracy and the loss of a historic opportunity for the leaders of religious Zionism to be partners in this effort. Religious Zionists did not reject the existence of a legislative secular authority but expected it to be founded upon Jewish tradition— including the *halacha*. In particular, they expected that the secular authority would not clash with the *halachic* tradition.[129] For the purpose of our discussion, between Kook and Warhaftig, there is no doubt that Kook's legacy was the dominant milestone in the development of the religious counterrevolution.

In the early 1950s, as a young teenager in Jerusalem, I would go with my friend Menachem Baram on Saturday mornings to soccer games at the YMCA field. We would walk down Hillel Street toward the Schmidt School (the home of the Jerusalem Conservatory and also the meeting place of the Mesuah Scouts troop for observant Jewish youth), continue toward the open fields that are now a green park, past the giant pool on the eastern side that filled with rainwater every winter, cross over to Mamilla Street, and walk past the American Consulate to the YMCA. All along the way, we were joined by religious youngsters coming out of synagogues. Most of them were Mizrahi and Sephardi Jews (Jews whose families came from North Africa and the wider Middle East). Some were still wearing prayer shawls (tallitot) and they would stuff them into embroidered bags as they walked. Sixty years later these walks are memorable to me largely because of the tolerance demonstrated by these young teenagers. They learned this tolerance in their homes, which were full of culture and acceptance and an environment of embracing others. On those walks we'd smoke cigarettes on the way to the game (as long as a "Shabbat goy" lit them) and experience real camaraderie between secular and religious youth. We'd walk on streets that were not closed to cars on the Sabbath, and at the time, all of this seemed self-evident to us.

This stood in stark contrast to the violent protests of the anti-Zionist Neturei Karta group of ultra-Orthodox Jews in the nearby Mea Shearim neighborhood. I remember walking one Saturday with my parents on the outskirts of Mea Shearim, where we had lived a few years earlier. Many hundreds of ultra-Orthodox Jews wearing *shtreimels* (fur hats) and black clothes—obviously Ashkenazi Jews—were throwing stones at a solitary command car that drove through Shabbat Square, their cries of "Shabbes" rising up to the sky. Also, sitting in the stands at the YMCA, Menachem and I rooted for different teams than most of our religious Mizrahi friends. They were fans of Beitar or Maccabi Jerusalem, while we were forever loyal to their arch rivals, Hapoel.

On the one hand, there was the tolerance, acceptance, and shared experience of the religious Mizrahi Jews in Jerusalem (who dressed just like us). On the other, there was the fanaticism, hostility, and alienation we felt from the Ashkenazi ultra-Orthodox Jews, whose style of dress could not possibly have been more different from our own.

In the period between the founding of Israel and the Six-Day War, a baseless myth prevailed in Israel about the "historic alliance" between Mapai/the Labor movement, and the Zionist religious movements Mizrachi and Poalei Hamizrachi (which later merged to become the National Religious Party). This tenuous myth persisted until it finally lost credibility when the National Religious Party (NRP) underwent a transformation following the Six-Day War. The NRP's political foundations were built upon the earliest underpinnings of religious Zionism. The NRP, while acknowledging the fact that Israel is not a Torah state, opposed its definition as secular. The creation of the state was perceived as a "*halachic* category" and as a commandment from the Torah. In exchange for concessions to its principal demands in areas such as Shabbat, kosher food in public places, and, in particular, establishing the role of Orthodox *halacha* in matters of personal status, the NRP usually would agree to join government coalitions. Mapai's concessions to religious Zionism gave the ruling party broad freedom of action on other issues.

The NRP provided a significant vehicle for carrying the religious counterrevolution forward. No less significant role, though, was played by the mass immigration of the 1950s, which had an important impact on the growth of the counterrevolution. This wave of immigration played an important role in exposing the weaknesses and vulnerability of the secular foundation of the Zionist revolution. Within eighteen months of the establishment of Israel, the number of Jewish residents doubled from about 650,000 to 1.3 million. It rose by 310 percent by the end of the state's first decade. The Zionist vision was to gather the Jewish people from the four corners of the earth and forge a single nation in the Land of Israel. This long-term goal was guided by the "melting pot" ethos. However, without the infrastructure for acculturation, the leadership of Israel in the 1950s adopted an approach of "paternalistic monopoly" of information. In this situation, the citizens did not have access to the information required for making informed decisions.

The mass immigration of the 1950s tested the strength and sustainability of the concept of the "new Jew." The leaders of the national liberation movement developed secular rituals, heroes, memorial ceremonies, poetry, literature, and the foundations of culture. For a certain period, there was indeed a sense of a new beginning. But the newness appeared artificial, not fully formed—and vulnerable.

The attempt to assimilate this wide range of cultures into the secular Zionist model failed. The country's leaders sought to rapidly assimilate the immigrants within the existing culture in Israel and treated their unique cultural traditions as secondary and even irrelevant. As noted, the vision of the ingathering of the exiles and its central ethos—the melting pot—were the focus of Zionist activity in the State of Israel's early decades. This ethos aimed to mold the ingathered exiles in the image of the state's founding fathers. But the elites that headed the nascent state were ill equipped to shape the identity of the new immigrants. Most of the immigrants from Islamic countries and some of those from Europe (primarily Holocaust survivors) were religious. The new immigrants were not driven by Zionist ideology. About half of them arrived in rescue operations from Islamic countries that were at war with Israel; the other half were Holocaust survivors who had already begun arriving on Israel's shores in clandestine immigration missions prior to the establishment of the state. Against this background, two elements should be emphasized. First, the principle of "negation of the exile" had no chance of taking root in the consciousness of those whose identity was steeped in the Jewish tradition. In fact, the most dramatic effect of this immigration was that it brought "home" the tradition, despite the effort to negate the exile. Second, in the process of absorbing the mass immigration— fulfilling the vision of the ingathering of the exiles—a geographic periphery was created that became, almost from the first day, a cultural periphery. The geographic-cultural periphery was perceived in the collective consciousness and in its own consciousness as secondary, if not to say inferior.

Combating illiteracy was one of the significant challenges in absorbing the wave of immigration. A census conducted in 1961 found that about 250,000 Jews in Israel above the age of fourteen did not know how to read or write in any language. Zalman Aran, the education minister in 1963, said in an interview with the *Haaretz* daily: "It is shame and disgrace that the 'People of the Book' includes illiterate people, and we must erase this stain. It will not only help to connect the different communities of Jews in Israel; it will also connect the generation of parents with the generation of children."

∽

Beginning in fourth grade and throughout my youth, my youth group was a big part of my identity. I was a proud member of the HaTnua HaMeuchedet youth movement, which in many ways was a continuation of my parents' youth movement, Gordonia.

Our youth group met in a little green shack on Narkiss Street, which by the standards of the time was considered big. There were about half a dozen rooms where we held activities, which were scattered around a fairly large assembly hall. The hall had a stage and hosted all types of gatherings including lectures, Sabbath dinners, and dances. It was big enough for all the members of the youth group, and for us it was like a second home.

During a rainy Jerusalem winter in the mid-1950s, my classmates and I were gathered at the green shack for a meeting with Yaakov Maimon, a pioneer of Hebrew stenography. Ben-Gurion had tasked Maimon with recording the meetings of the Mapai party and other early state institutions. In the 1930s, Maimon was invited to take part in multiple Zionist Congresses in Europe and in 1951 he was appointed the first official stenographer of the Israeli parliament, the Knesset.

In the 1950s, Maimon founded the Hebrew language education project in the *maabarot* (transit camps for new immigrants). Maimon was obsessed with trying to eradicate illiteracy for every man, woman, and child in Israel.

When the bespectacled Maimon walked into our assembly room at the green shack, he gave off an air of modesty and restraint. He wore a khaki shirt and pants and a weathered jacket that had seen better days. His attire gave off a sort of message of solidarity with the modest ideals of the Israeli public at the time.

He told us—a gathering of students preparing for their bar and bat mitzvahs—of his work battling illiteracy and that he needed volunteers to work with him in the *maabarot*. And volunteer we did. Once a week, on Mondays, if I'm not mistaken, trucks driven by volunteers would pull up outside of tent encampments in the Jerusalem area and the volunteers taught reading and writing.

I spent months riding with my friends from the youth group every Monday to the Mevaseret Yerushalayim rec center. In the winter its leaky roof would let the rain in and during the summers the blazing sun would turn it into a furnace. We would sit and try to teach fathers and mothers, grandparents, and children. There was a thick air of embarrassment in the room when we—only teenagers ourselves— would sit and try to teach people much older than us, who were often traditional and observant. We had to find a way to fight this embarrassment.

I remember seeing a woman in her forties, who was holding a baby in her left arm while in her right hand she held a ballpoint pen for the first time in her life. She began writing first in print and then in cursive. We were young boys and trying to break the ice however we could. By Hanukkah in 1956 or 1957, we even managed to become comfortable teasing our students a bit, the jokes becoming part of the atmosphere and joy of the holiday.

Thinking of those days always fills me with nostalgia and longing for the feeling of solidarity and togetherness that could be felt from Maimon and his language lessons. Maimon won the Israel Prize (Israel's highest civilian honor) in 1976 for his "special contribution to the state and society."

This paternalistic, arrogant policy—which portrayed the immigrants as backward and primitive Middle Easterners—was doomed to fail. At the same time, there were complaints that the state was engaging in antireligious coercion, including clipping the sidelocks of Ortho- dox Jewish immigrant children.

Without a constitution and bill of rights, the Israeli democracy— certainly in its early days, but later too—did not guarantee a minimal degree of equal respect as part of individual rights and the rule of law. Furthermore, the reality of a territorial-cultural center trying to impose its values on the periphery via the melting pot made it impossible to accord an equal degree of respect. The deficit of respect developed in the geographic and cultural periphery and created feelings of discrimination that persist today in various levels of intensity. The unanswered demand for recognition of ethnic identity in the periphery led the immigrants to enlist in the religious counterrevolution. Today, decades later, the politics of identity is strengthening, reinforced by the deficit of respect, and looms as a persistent conflict. As Fukuyama notes: "Current understandings of identity . . . threaten free speech, and more broadly, the kind of rational discourse needed to sustain a democracy. Liberal democracies are committed to protecting the right to say anything you want in the market place of ideas, particularly in the political sphere. But the preoccupation with identity has clashed with the need for deliberative discourse. The focus on lived experience by identity groups valorizes inner selves experienced emotionally rather than examined rationally."[130]

In the early 1950s, my mother was one of the founders of the social services department of the Jerusalem municipality. This was during the early days, when the country's welfare system was still just beginning to take shape. During the 1950s, my mother spent countless days walking the paths of the Talpiot transit camp as part of her work with the social services branch of the municipality. It was only when we sat shiva for my mother that I learned about some of the kind things she did during those difficult days. The Talpiot transit camp was one of around two hundred that were built across Israel. During Israel's first decade, more than 900,000 immigrants arrived and the country's population grew by over 150 percent. This is a statistic that is unmatched by any other "immigrant country" in the world. A massive population growth like this over such a short period of time caused a shift in the population balance between new immigrants and ones who had been in the country for far longer. It required the immediate formulation of creative solutions.

This is why, in the first half of the 1950s, the country built ninety-eight transit camps inside older communities, in addition to thirty-one that were built far from any settled area.

These were the solutions that the young state came up with. The temporary housing conditions were threadbare at best. In 1954, there was an average of 3.4 people per household in the transit camps, 14.9 per indoor bathroom, and 15.9 per shower. In the majority of the transit camps, the trash was only picked up three times a week and in the Talpiot transit camp there was only one shower for one hundred people. Twenty-five families had to share a single faucet and 155 used a single dumpster.

The journalist and commentator Ze'ev Schiff described what he saw during a visit to a transit camp:

"The three sanitation workers with their one run-down vehicle were incapable of clearing out the piles and piles of garbage. There was no discipline of hygiene . . . the bathrooms were beneath all contempt. On average around one hundred people would have to share every bathroom. As I passed one of these buildings, which had about ten toilets, I was overcome with nausea. The tin walls were open and children would make their way in and play inside this filth. Any person looking to wash themselves or take some drinking water would have to head over to the main faucet or the general "shower," which was really not much nicer than the bathroom."

The winter of 1952–53 was particularly rainy and cold in Jerusalem. My mother, who wore rubber boots every morning to walk to the Talpiot transit camp, told us one evening that she wanted to let a young girl from the transit camp stay with us, so she could at least give one child a warm and dry home. I cleared my small room and moved into my parents' room when she arrived. She was about twelve years old and she huddled inside our house, quiet, refusing to speak a word or change her clothes into the ones my mother prepared for her. She also hardly ate the entire two days she stayed with us. It was immediately apparent how different her world—that of a new immigrant living in a transit camp—was from that of "veteran" Israelis like us. In the end, my mother took her back to the transit camp after forty-eight hours and expressed her hope that "perhaps, nonetheless, she'll get used to it."

My memories from those two days are those of a ten-year-old boy. Nonetheless, those two days left me with a clear insight about the differences between my world and that of this young immigrant girl from the transit camp. Our modest little 650-square-foot apartment was like a warm, safe palace that isolated and distanced me from a new Israeli experience taking place nearby, which was already leaving deep scars in the new country. Sometimes I wonder which of us—the veteran Israelis or the new immigrants—deserved to be seen as the outlier in society. I also think often of my mother, who was among the very few people who tried to build bridges between these two worlds.

∽

I would like to note that I'm looking here at the mass immigration of the 1950s through the narrow prism of the role it played in bringing the religious counterrevolution to fruition. In every other aspect, especially from the perspective of Zionist objectives, the ingathering of the exiles was an unprecedented historic achievement. In regard to the religious counterrevolution, mass immigration brought home to Israel the culture that was supposed to have been negated in the Diaspora. What the Zionists failed to finish during their revolution, the Zionist state would later complete.

In a roundabout way, mass migration restored the foundation against which the Zionist liberators of the Jewish people had rebelled. The fact that they lacked the tools to build a new consciousness (and without a constitution) provided a boost for the messianic-redemptive element in religious Zionism. The leaders of secular Zionism remained blind to the processes that later strengthened traditionalism and religiousness and which took place right under their noses. The religious counterrevolution picked up momentum after the Six-Day War and was buoyed by the rank-and-file Israelis who identified with it. Many of them had emigrated to Israel in the 1950s and came from traditional families which had more in common with the religious Zionists than the secular elites who carried the banner of modernism.

An element of messianic redemption had assumed a central role in secular Zionist consciousness since almost the beginning. Secular Zionism transformed redemption into a sustainable process whose inherent messianism is actualized through working the land. Still, Israel's overwhelming, lightning victory in 1967 sparked a sense of messianic imminence in the religious imagination. Among the militants in religious Zionism, the military victory in the Six-Day War reinforced the idea that the existing nation-state was only an instrument for advancing divine politics.

While secular Zionism saw territory as an instrument for establishing sovereignty, the redemption faction in religious Zionism regarded sovereignty as an instrument for redeeming the Land of Israel. As historian Uriel Tal writes, the messianic approaches that surfaced after 1967 applied categories of holiness to the political reality and turned metaphysics into an actual plan. Tal states that this model characterized not only the messianic religious movement but also secular movements in Israel. He notes that Carl Schmitt's political theology is especially apt for describing the secular politics in which religion only remains in the sphere of collective and state identity in a secularized reality. This political theology, which combines a rejection of liberalism with ethnocentric elements, became the link connecting religious and secular proponents of the Greater Land of Israel. The messianic language and the security-political-diplomatic language have always gone hand in hand, not only among settlers but also among members of the Labor movement. Redemption can be expressed in sovereign terms and sovereignty can include aspects of redemption.

Former religious Zionist politician Hanan Porat described the settlement enterprise as being derived from the recognition that the state "is the foundation for God's throne in the world."

Tal identifies two streams in religious Zionism: the stream of political messianism and the stream of political restraint. The former sees the Six-Day War as a sacred act that has breathed new life into the divine presence. This stream views the victory as a divine miracle, our period as "the era of eschatological redemption," in Rosenak's words, and the return of parts of the Land of Israel to the Arabs as "handing over the divine presence to the forces of evil."[131] The second stream is primarily important because of the content it introduced to the internal religious discourse in religious Zionism. The Oz Veshalom movement and later the Meimad party were the political-ideological expression of this second stream.

Oz Veshalom: The Ideological Circle for Religious Zionism was registered as a nongovernmental organization in 1981. Its founders were primarily intellectuals and academics. This movement took root in the mid-1970s, led by members of the moderate branch of religious Zionism, as a response to the Gush Emunim movement.[132] Its more moderate leaders included Moshe Unna, who wrote to then foreign minister Yigal Allon: "In light of the troubling signs of political chaos in the public and the unrestrained imagination guiding parts of it, as blatantly expressed in phenomena such as Gush Emunim's declaration of building one hundred settlements in Judea and Samaria, it is very important to learn that there are people in the top government echelon who do not succumb to such things."[133] Netivot Shalom was later founded by Aviezer Ravitzky and registered as an NGO in 1983, later merging with the Oz Veshalom movement. The union of the two movements served as the foundation for the Meimad party. The goal of this "stream of political restraint" was to pursue peace with the Palestinians, even at the price of territorial withdrawal. Members of this movement tried to show that their political orientation did not contradict Jewish sources at all. Their concrete goals included presenting an alternative expression of religious Zionism, promoting the ideas of tolerance and justice as central to the Jewish tradition, opposing fundamentalism and extremism in religious Zionism, promoting coexistence and supporting equality for Arabs in Israel, and expressing support for the peace process, including the establishment of a Palestinian state.

~

I can still recall a conversation at the Israel Democracy Institute in the 1990s in which Avi Ravitzky boasted proudly that "at least half of the worshippers at my synagogue are members of Meimad." Someone responded: "And half of the worshippers at your synagogue comprises the entire Meimad movement."

The roots of political messianism in religious Zionism were planted at various times during the history of the Zionist movement. After the Six-Day War, Gush Emunim became the leader of this stream. We can identify three salient and interconnected aspects of Gush Emunim's impact, all inspired by Kookism: its contribution to the narrative that portrays the state as a holy entity; its emphasis on the territorial dimension, placing it above the imperatives of political sovereignty; and the political rhetoric of its spokespersons that incited extremists like Yigal Amir.

The dramatic shift from religious Zionism to a Zionist religion is the essence of Kookism and it encompasses all of the threats to democracy.[134] Indeed, it undermines the political sovereignty that Zionism aspired to establish. Ehud Sprinzak, who conducted groundbreaking research on Gush Emunim, devoted an entire book to examining the sources of criminality in the political culture of Israeli democracy. The sanctification of the state, stemming from the religionization of Zionism, reaffirmed this skirting of the law. In their actions, Sprinzak asserts, Gush Emunim members acknowledged that they were going against the legal government of the State of Israel. For them, the government and its laws are not the be-all and end-all. Government action that blocks settlements may be legal, but it is not legitimate. Thus, the illegal actions of Gush Emunim were based on the view of the state as a state-in-the-making, as a pre-state.[135]

Gush Emunim's rejection of the government's legitimacy opened the way to *halachic* interpretation of political events and rabbinical involvement in politics. This has served to return the Israeli consciousness to the ghetto existence of the Diaspora, precisely what the Zionist movement had rebelled against. The Land of Israel became as important as the nation and even as important as the Torah itself. Religious Zionism was defined by three pillars: the nation of Israel, the Land of Israel, and the Torah of Israel. Gush Emunim shifted the primacy from the nation of Israel to the Land of Israel. By doing so, it paved the downward path of the descending continuum of believers to "price tag" attackers and the assassin Amir. In the early twenty-first century, the primacy shifted again, with nationalist ultra-Orthodox (*hardal*) ideology placing the Torah of Israel above the nation of Israel and Land of Israel.

Israeli society, including religious Zionism, has undergone many changes in recent decades. The watershed event in this period was the assassination of Rabin in November 1995. From the perspective of our discussion, it was the era from the end of the Yom Kippur War in 1973 up until Rabin's assassination that bred the extremists on the lowest layers on the descending continuum of believers. The foundations that nurtured these lowest levels were laid by the religious counterrevolution decades earlier and paved the way for *halachic* involvement in politics. Israeli settlements in the West Bank and the Gaza Strip were a major accelerator of this. The Oslo Accords and the political fallout that resulted from their signing served as a major catalyst for this increased role of *halacha*. The forces that challenged the decisions of a democratically elected government had been mounting for a long time and finally erupted after the agreements were signed.

Prior to Oslo, other events in the winding, twisting history of Zionism played a role in shaping the reality of Israeli sovereignty. The pragmatic and earthly characteristics of Zionism clashed with the growing religiosity in Israeli public life, in particular during two events earlier in the twentieth century: the peace treaty with Egypt and the religionization of politics. Both are related to the upheaval that brought Menachem Begin and the Likud party to power in May 1977. In fact, I regard the clash between the earthly and the divine as the signature feature of Begin's premiership and as underlining the growing threats to the Zionist vision.

The peace treaty with Egypt dealt an initial blow to the "people who will dwell alone" messianic worldview. This view that "the whole world is against us" was fueled by the fact that Israel was surrounded by enemy states who sought its destruction. This narrative reinforced the ethnocentric inclination that exists on the margins of many national movements and which seeks out an enemy, persecutor, or representative of evil. In 1977, the peace accord with Egypt proved that peacemaking is possible, even with the most powerful Arab state, which had for years been one of Israel's most bitter enemies. Not only this, but peace is possible through a secular international agreement and does not require divine intervention. Those who believed "the whole world is against us" were forced to face the fact that the peace agreement required Israel to relinquish a large amount of territory. For many Israelis, in particular those on the right wing of the political spectrum, this was a traumatic price to pay. In retrospect, we can see how the evacuation of occupied territories in general, and the violent evacuation of Yamit, the Israeli settlement in the Sinai Peninsula, in particular, foreshadowed subsequent events.

The election of Begin and the religionization of Israeli politics was of no less significance than the peace accord with Egypt. In fact, it can be seen as the negative image of the first event in that it leveraged and strengthened the transcendental in the secular lifestyle of a nation that was learning to bear responsibility for political sovereignty. When Begin decided to run the state "in a Jewish style," it was not the Jewishness of Ze'ev Jabotinsky, the founding father of Begin's political movement. Fragments of Orthodox religious rhetoric accompanied Begin's decisions to grant a sweeping exemption from military service to yeshiva students and to prohibit El Al from flying on Shabbat. (It is true that David Ben-Gurion was the first to exempt yeshiva students when he allowed four hundred yeshiva students to remain in the "tent of Torah" in 1948.) Over the years, the number of exemptions grew to several thousand. But Begin was the one who opened the floodgates by lifting the restrictions on the yeshiva student exemptions. In 1977, the same year that Begin was elected, the number of exemptions jumped tenfold. An examination of Begin's considerations requires a separate discussion. But whether his decision derived from an affinity for *Yiddishkeit*, appreciation for religion, a desire to strengthen his paternalistic role among traditional-minded Israelis, or simply cold coalition calculations, the repercussions of his "Jewish style" catalyzed the religionization of politics. The creation of the ultra-Orthodox Sephardi party Shas in 1982 was connected to Begin's conduct and to the presence of "Torah opinion" in politics.[136]

The religionization of politics in Israel in the late 1970s and throughout the 1980s converged with the radicalization taking place in religious Zionism. This radicalization intensified in light of Rabin's peace policy in the first half of the 1990s and underlines the strengthening of marginal groups within religious Zionism. However, the overall picture of the national-religious sector, or religious Zionism, is much more complex. It includes the development of other fascinating trends which I place at the top levels of the continuum. For example, the rise of organizations of observant women, such as Kolech (Your Voice), whose vision and objectives courageously challenge traditional mores.

༄

In early 2012, following a series of incidents in which women were excluded from public spaces—including an IDF officers' training base and a private bus line in Jerusalem—we convened a roundtable at the IDI on the exclusion of women. I left that evening with a clearer understanding of this subject following two anecdotal remarks by participants.

I told the roundtable participants that in the late 1950s, "I would go to dance in the streets of Jerusalem on the eve of Independence Day, together with boys and girls from the various youth movements. Often, we held hands in a circle with girls from the (national-religious) Bnei Akiva movement." At the IDI in 2012, the former IDF chief rabbi, Avichai Ronzki, responded: "[Carmon] spoke about radicalization [within the religious Zionist movement]. This is totally untrue. I have been engaged with the teachings of *halacha* for many years and this is what happened since you danced together with [religious] girls . . . [then] the teaching of *halacha* were to a much lesser extent or even not at all. A religious Jew is [obliged] not to touch hands with females, and it is prohibited . . . to listen to a woman's voice singing. This is the *halacha*. So how can you say about zealously *halacha*-observant Jews that they have been radicalized?"

I was stunned and couldn't believe that he could say this. I couldn't believe it. This is an Israeli rabbi saying this? The former IDF chief rabbi? As far as I remember, I was the only one who seemed taken back by Ronzki's claim that the rabbis of the 1950s didn't follow Jewish law sufficiently. Nonetheless, a fitting answer was given by a religious woman who in my eyes is a great role model. Ayelet Vider Cohen, the head of Kolech, spoke up and said the words that to this day still sound like a warning:

In my view, the discussion about modesty shapes the representation of men and women in the collective consciousness . . . making the woman out to be a sex object, one who is judged . . . The woman is submissive and she must be protected . . . the *halachic* and religious messages are in fact symptoms of this same phenomenon, of relating to women, girls, and young women as sex objects and of men as creatures who cannot control themselves. I think this degrades both sides equally. I think this discourse is one of hypocrisy and not modesty.

In an article I wrote a few months later for Makor Rishon—a conservative paper identified with religious Zionism—I stated that Vider Cohen's courageous words were testimony to the fact that religious Zionism is not monolithic, it includes natural allies who can help the Zionist movement solve the tremendous problems it faces. I also emphasized that Zionism's legacy—a source of great pride—includes a series of great female role models, including the poet Rachel,[137] Hannah Senesh, countless courageous female fighters in Israel's military, groundbreaking politicians, Nobel Prize winner Ada Yonath, a significant number of female scientists, and my late mother.

The women of Kolech are potential allies in the effort to repair the Israeli identity crisis. On the Kolech website, one of the organization's founders, Hanna Kahat, states, "We are fighting back against religious extremism, exclusion of women, the fanatic craze of modesty which serves as a form of discrimination against women. More and more synagogues, even if they don't practice complete equality, are more aware of the issue of equality and are thinking about it more than ever. There is also a process of consideration of gender and sexual orientation. . . . I do feel that something is happening."

Organizations like Kolech and their supporters, who are clearly at the upper end of the continuum of believers, can be allies in building a Jewish and democratic country defined by coexistence and cooperation between the different sectors of society.

As I write these words, I am hopeful that in the future we'll see more cooperation between Kolech and other religious and secular groups, in particular as we work toward strengthening the humanistic and egalitarian values of Judaism. On Army Radio, I recently heard the following from host Yael Dan on her talk radio program:

About a year ago the suicide of Esti Weinstein made major
waves. She had suffered greatly as the wife of a member of the
Gur Hasidic sect before "going out to the question,"[138] becoming secular. Her decision to divorce herself from the ultra-
Orthodox way of life cost her everything. She lost all contact
with her seven daughters and eventually decided to take her
own life. Her story inspired the publishing of a book that fea-
tured the stories of other "bereaved mothers" from the Hasidic
world. These women suffered in their married lives and decided
to leave the fold and were cut off from their children against
their will.

YAEL DAN: Shalom, Aviva.

"AVIVA," GUEST: Hello and God bless.

DAN: What are you doing for the holiday?

AVIVA: This is the fourth Rosh Hashanah that my children won't be
with their mother. There is a four-year hole within them filled
with longing. I am also spending my fourth Rosh Hashanah
without my children.

DAN: Do you speak with them? Do you hear the longing they feel,
how much they are in need?

AVIVA: I have six children and am in touch with only the two eldest.
It's only a small connection, and not enough at all. This is what
they are allowed, and what is denied of the younger children.
But the little that I did see them here and there, in the houses
of rabbis or in other places, I saw that they very much miss me
and are in need and people who see them tell me, "It's hard for
them, they need their mother."

DAN: How did it happen, that the connection was severed with
your children?

AVIVA: This happened as part of my process of becoming secular.
Long before I looked like a secular woman. When I said to my
ex that I want to leave . . . they tried to convince me to recon-
sider. He opened a case at the rabbinical court and they told

me, "You will be cut off from your children," and they upheld
this.

DAN: They told you in court that if you leave your husband you are
deciding to cut yourself off from your children? That's what the
rabbinical court said?

AVIVA: The court said that because I'm not religious, they will need
to give custody of the children to the father.

DAN: He has custody, but why take the children from you?

AVIVA: They said that the decision is that the father needs to bring
the children to the mother twice a week.

DAN: And?

AVIVA: They made this decision but it isn't enforced. It doesn't
make any difference to make a ruling that appears fair and
then afterward there is no way to dispute it or sue the court
because it's a rabbinical court . . . if we judge it by the results,
you [the court] don't ensure that the children will see me . . . or
that they can grow up like they should.

DAN: Did you turn to a civil court?

AVIVA: That's not allowed. There is a mixture of authorities in
charge. I tried a few times, I even issued a higher court appeal
and they told me there are no procedures available in this
court. . . . What happens in practice is that despite the fact that
the rabbinical court ruled that I have the right to see my children, they aren't allowing me to do so. I think that a child
needs both parents and if shared custody is possible I'd be
very happy. They tell us that there are dozens of women in my
position who did whatever it took in order to keep from killing
themselves like Esti Weinstein . . . They leave their families, the
bad family life they had.

DAN: Sometimes these women are pushed out, not all leave on
their own.

AVIVA: But at the cost of losing their children?!

DAN: There's no such thing as "the cost of losing their children."
It's not a price—it's an injustice. Some of them lose contact

with their children, and with others their children are turned against them.

AVIVA: On this Rosh Hashana, a year after Esti Weinstein's suicide, more and more mothers will be without their children.

DAN: Think of how sad that is. These mothers are grown women but children are sensitive and think about them, about hundreds even thousands of children like this. It's sad. It's sad.

AVIVA: Thank you.

DAN: I hear this and I think to myself, is this Jewish? Can we—women in particular—stomach this phenomenon? Where is the protest from religious women in the religious Zionist movement? The violence which is intertwined in the lives of Gur Hasidim is, it appears, a desperate response to the breakdown of the walls surrounding the Haredi "ghetto" and the influx of modernity in their communities. How does the religious Zionist world relate to this phenomenon? I have no doubt that there is a wide range of sentiments among those on the upper rungs of the continuum of believers, including rejection and denunciation and even those who close their eyes to it.

In lieu of a lengthy presentation and analysis, I'll quote from a single document that reflects what I described above and does not require much interpretation. In February 1995, nine months prior to Rabin's assassination, Rabbi Eliezer Melamed of the West Bank settlement Har Bracha sent letters to about forty rabbis and heads of yeshivas in Israel and abroad. The letters were also signed by two other spiritual leaders of the settlement movement: Rabbi Dov Lior and Rabbi Daniel Shilo. All of the bold emphasis is in the source.

The more this evil government gives in to the Arabs, the more the terror attacks throughout Israel intensify. . . . Upon implementation of the Oslo agreement and granting rule to the

Palestinian Authority over the territory and the roads, the danger has greatly increased. . . . This evil government aims to continue to implement the agreement throughout Judea and Samaria. . . .

And so, men and women, among the settlers in Judea and Samaria and other parts of the country, have asked us, beseechingly, what the law is concerning this evil government and the one who heads it. . . .

A. . . . and therefore the question of whether the members of the government are considered accomplices in the acts of murder that were perpetrated and whether according to the *halacha* they should be indicted, and what their punishment is if they are considered accomplices to murder. And, of course, we know that there are very many sides to the problem; that on the one hand, the government is authorized to act for the good of the people as it deems fit. However, on the other hand, perhaps the law changes in regard to the government that has no Jewish majority and relies on the votes of Arabs.

B. . . . but the more difficult question is: According to the *halacha*, what is the law concerning the government if it continues to implement the aforementioned agreement in Judea and Samaria? . . . There is a need to define: What is the law pertaining to elected officials who carry out such activity in the framework of their duties? And also, what is the *law on informing* [emphasis mine] that is done unintentionally, while covering the eyes and ignoring the facts and the opinion of the Jewish majority? . . .

D. If indeed it is possible to punish them in court, is every person in Israel obliged to act to bring them to trial, in rabbinical court, or if there is no other option in a secular court?

E. Are public leaders, the rabbis and officials, obliged to warn the prime minister and his ministers at this difficult hour that if, after the bitter experience of the Gaza and Jericho agreement they continue to implement it throughout Judea and Samaria, they will be obligated by Torah law to apply the law of Jewish *halacha* to them, as the law of the informer, who delivers the souls and money of Jews to gentiles? . . . and we know the fear that even raising such a question is liable to stir, heaven forbid, a fierce dispute among the people. In light of the reality on the ground, we fear and dread that the situation will become so severe, heaven forbid, that such questions will become prevalent and feelings of revenge will arise in the hearts of many of the victims, and each person will act as he sees fit. Therefore it is best to be proactive and to first discuss [these questions] in the beit midrash . . .[139]

Rabbi Dov Lior	Rabbi Daniel Shilo	Rabbi Eliezer Melamed
Rabbi and	Rabbi of Kedumim	Rabbi of Har Bracha
Court President	settlement	settlement and yeshiva
Hebron and		
Kiryat Arba		

When I read these lines, which are full of incitement to murder democracy itself, I feel frustration and shame that Israeli society has yet to fully investigate the role that leading religious Zionist rabbis played in preparing the ground for Rabin's assassination and their passive complicity in the murder itself. I have no doubt that the failure to investigate this is connected to the Zionist deficit, including the vulnerability of Israeli democracy, which lacks the infrastructure necessary to protect itself against such dangers. In any case, today I wish to assert that these rabbis and others like them reinforced the very worst of their community, the bottom of the continuum of religious Zionism which includes the assassin Amir. In a conversation with Carmi Gillon, the head of the Israel Security Agency (known by the Hebrew acronym Shin Bet) at the time of Rabin's murder, he noted that Rabbi Dov Lior, one of the three who signed the letter cited above, also influenced the members of the "Jewish Underground." These terrorists carried out a series of attacks against Arabs in the 1980s, when Gillon was in charge of the Shin Bet unit investigating them.

The religious nationalist concept—the nation of Israel, the Land of Israel, the Torah of Israel—stood at the ideological center of religious Zionism. Until 1967, the nation of Israel was accorded primacy in this triangle. Since 1967, the "young NRP" and Gush Emunim moved the Land of Israel to the top of the pyramid. The primacy extremists accorded to the Land of Israel could be seen repeatedly in the 1980s and during the time of the Oslo Accords. Perhaps this triangle can be used as a diagnostic tool. It could be used to locate various groups in religious Zionism on the descending continuum of believers, with those who assign primacy to the nation of Israel on the higher end of the continuum and those who prioritize the Torah of Israel located toward the bottom. My intention is not to be confrontational, but rather to develop a diagnostic tool to help identify possible allies who share my concerns for life in the Israeli democracy.

One of the important developments for understanding the growth of the religious counterrevolution in recent decades is the establishment of the *hesder* yeshivas and pre-military preparatory programs. As my colleague Tamar Hermann observes: "The blossoming of the Zionist world of yeshivas, including the *hesder* yeshivas, brought a new type of leadership to the forefront—the national-religious rabbinical elite, whose views have an increasing impact on the party's stance."[140] Yuval Cherlow writes, "In classical Zionism, the rabbis' authority was limited to matters of *halacha* and they were only consulted on political questions in special cases. Now, rabbis enjoy greater prestige as intellectuals whose opinions are also sought on political and other matters. This is expressed in the efforts to subordinate the party's decisions to the 'Torah opinion.'"[141]

Over twenty years have passed since Rabin's assassination and Israeli society has yet to fully grasp the significance of this tragedy. The assassin was punished, but justice was never meted out to his numerous accomplices and enablers—first and foremost, the rabbis and adjudicators of *halacha*. During these twenty-plus years, religious Zionism, like all of Israeli society, has undergone many changes and there are various scenarios for how the religious counterrevolution could affect Israeli democracy in the future. This is primarily due to the fact that these changes are dynamic, reshaping and redefining the various tones and nuances within religious Zionism. "Torah opinion" has undoubtedly strengthened and continues to strengthen in the political consciousness of national-religious Israelis. That is, the status of *halachic* rulings on political questions has risen, and this has not been met with any political, cultural, or other response in Israeli civic society.

The catalyst for the strengthening of the status of "Torah opinion" is, of course, the future of the Palestinian territories. To what extent will a democratically elected government let its hands be bound by a *halachic* decision? This is not a theoretical question. IDI researcher Kalman Neuman notes that there is a disagreement among rabbis on whether they have the authority to rule on the question of conceding territory.[142] How many rabbis are on each side of this dispute is an open question, but the fact that this dispute exists is troubling in itself. The very fact that some rabbis argue that a decision to withdraw for political reasons is an illegitimate decision from a *halachic* perspective creates an intolerable threat to democracy.

After Rabin's assassination there was an enormous effort made to obscure the role that rabbis played in the process leading to the murder. However, the evacuation of Gush Katif ten years later in 2005 turned the spotlight on some of these rabbis. In the months leading up to the evacuation, *halachic* rulings were openly disseminated by leading rabbis in religious Zionism. These rulings stated that the government decision was not legitimate. While there were no recorded cases of religious soldiers refusing orders during the evacuation, the topic of refusal became part of the public agenda and has remained there ever since. Although it would have been unthinkable a generation ago, in recent years there has been heavy debate in Israel about whether or not the state should allow soldiers to refuse to obey an order that violates a religious imperative. This dilemma is liable to prevent the state's elected institutions from acting for the public's benefit in accordance with a democratic decision. Neuman writes: "Opposition to a withdrawal that is portrayed as a *halachic* prohibition changes the nature of the internal religious discussion. If it's a categorical prohibition that can only be lifted under certain conditions, this restricts the room for political maneuvering of the government or of a political party that operates according to this sort of *halachic* view. Moreover, the expression of public will, such as a Knesset decision or referendum, cannot lift a *halachic* prohibition."[143] What makes the phenomenon of "Torah opinion" an even greater threat to democracy is what Neuman describes as "fundamental questions about the role of ideological considerations in the [*halachic*] adjudication process . . . In the field of public *halacha*, the dearth of textual material and lack of precedents make it more difficult to adjudicate with formal tools alone. In our case, it's difficult to ignore the connection between the adjudicator's religious ideological stance and the *halachic* conclusion."[144] Ultimately, "this background of the dearth of textual material and the lack of precedents" means that *halachic* rulings are merely the interpretation of certain ideologues who are ordained rabbis. I'm certain that there are ordained rabbis who espouse an opposite ideology and I ask myself: Where might we be today if the secular Zionist process had embraced the richness of Jewish history and the normative foundation and moral framework that had evolved over the generations rather than rejecting them as part of "negating the exile"?

I dedicated two decades of my professional life attempting to develop an educational approach for dealing with the lessons of the Holocaust. In the course of my work, I encountered a wealth of responses (questions posed to rabbis and their responses) which were written in the ghettos and camps, by Jews facing the most horrendous of circumstances. I remember how fascinated I was by the variety of responses, how the same question posed to different rabbis in different places could elicit such divergent responses. Interpretation, it seemed to me then and today, is an elixir of adjudication in the hands of those authorized to use it. And who authorized them to wield this authority?

An additional diagnostic tool for the descending continuum of believers could be one's attitude toward non-Jews. Like other topics, rabbinical interpretation of this subject stretches nearly from the top of the continuum to the bottom.

"On one end—which grants non-Jews maximal equality," writes Yair Sheleg, "stands Rabbi Menachem Froman."[145] Before his death in 2013, Rabbi Froman was the chief rabbi of the West Bank settlement of Tekoa and a major proponent of coexistence between Jews and Arabs on both sides of the Green Line. Froman's interpretation places him on the upper levels of the continuum: "In the world of Torah, it is actually possible to find grounds for granting a status to non-Jews that even surpasses the status accorded to them in the principles of the democratic regime." He did not view the status of non-Jews as a democratic question or a question of democracy clashing with the Torah.

Near the bottom of the descending continuum of believers are those who completely reject granting civil status to non-Jews. Rabbi Shlomo Avineri of the Beit El settlement lays the foundation for discrimination against non-Jews based on the sacred nature of the state. He views the state as a holy entity and argues that democracy "is intended, first and foremost, to serve the needs of the nation and not the needs of the individuals in it, and certainly not the needs of individuals who are not members of the nation." In other words: "Non-Jews do not need to be entitled to citizenship in a Jewish state."[146] Similarly, Rabbi Zvi Tau rejects the legitimacy of national decisions made without the support of a majority of the country's Jews. He argues of non-Jews: "Their personal rights should not be harmed in the slightest way, but at the same time they should not be accorded any national status, including citizenship, and certainly not the right to vote for the Knesset."[147] Rabbi Mordechai Eliyahu states: "Gentiles have no national status whatsoever in the Land of Israel." Based on this approach, he ruled that Jews in the West Bank can take olives grown by Palestinian farmers. Following suit, near the bottom of the continuum we find Rabbi Dov Lior, who was among those who legitimized the Rabin assassination: "Lior is one of the extremists, even in the Yesha [Judea and Samaria] camp; he's a prominent supporter of conducting a transfer of the Arabs from the territories," Sheleg writes. And in regard to the Arab citizens of Israel: "Non-Jews must not have national status in Israel, only personal status; as long as they allow the gentiles in Israel to remain a national division, we won't have peace within the state."[148]

Between the two opposite ends of the descending continuum of believers we can identify those who are prepared to accord equal rights to non-Jews. The interpretation of the rabbis (Yoel Ben-Nun, Israel Meir Lau, and Shimon Gershon Rosenberg, known by the acronym "Shagar") does not derive from an acceptance of democratic principles; it stems from their conviction that the standing of the Jewish state "would be harmed if it didn't do this."[149] Ben-Nun, who grants *halachic* legitimacy to democracy, unequivocally favors the *halacha* when democracy clashes with it. According to his interpretation, "In our days, we cannot apply the biblical law of *ger toshav* [resident gentile] to the Arabs and other non-Jews, and thus deny them full civil rights." Nonetheless, in his view, Arabs in Israel who "choose" a Palestinian identity surrender their Israeliness.[150] Lau says Israel is obligated to grant equal standing and full civil rights to all of the state's citizens.[151]

Below these three rabbis on the continuum, Yair Sheleg finds Rabbi Nahum Eliezer Rabinowitz, who states that the status of non-Jews should be like their status in Western democracies—"that is, they should enjoy complete equality in civil rights, but without any special rights on the national level or even the cultural [level]."[152]

Lower still on the descending continuum of believers, according to Sheleg's study, are rabbis Haim Druckman and Yaakov Ariel, "who slightly expand the restrictions on the Arabs' rights." Druckman, like others, assigns a religious status to the state, thus placing it in conflict with the values of democracy from the outset. Druckman states: "In principle, it would be best to have no idol worshippers in the Land of Israel. This stance allows for Muslim residents, but not Christian residents."[153] Ariel denies the ability of non-Jews to serve "in positions that symbolize the government, such as president, prime minister, IDF chief of staff."[154]

Further down the continuum are Aharon Lichtenstein and Ovadia Yosef. Rabbi Lichtenstein believes that in principle Arabs should be granted equal rights but would restrict their eligibility for governmental positions.[155] Former Shas spiritual leader Rabbi Yosef, one of the most prominent Jewish and Israeli figures since the state's founding, does not directly address the status of Arabs in Israel in his writings. "His general attitude toward non-Jews is drawn from the traditional stance of the *halacha*, which discriminates in various laws between a Jew and a gentile," Sheleg says.[156]

Further down on the descending continuum, according to Sheleg, are Yuval Cherlow and Motti Elon, who state that "non-Jews have no national standing in Israel, only individual rights."[157] In Rabbi Cherlow's view, "individual rights must constantly be balanced against the value of preserving the national identity . . . In principle, non-Jews are entitled to all of the individual rights, but have no rights at the national level."[158] According to Rabbi Elon, "Every Israeli—Jew or non-Jew—must commit not to undermine the state's authority and status as a condition for receiving citizenship."[159] Elon also requires non-Jews to accept the Seven Laws of Noah, defined as moral commandments incumbent upon all humankind.

Therefore, the broad range of interpretations only reinforces the question of a secular Jew: Who endowed these rabbis with the authority to make such decisions?

∽

I recall an incident that was very significant for me, as described in my book *Without a Constitution*:[160]

In the sweltering summer of 2008, I received a telephone call from the former head of the Yesha Council of Jewish Settlements, Pinchas Wallerstein. I was surprised. Pinchas Wallerstein was not a fan of the Israel Democracy Institute. When we invited him to one of the traditional meetings with personnel from the National Defense College on the anniversary of Rabin's assassination, he voiced harsh criticism against the institute.

"I'm calling you," he now said, "upon the suggestion of [Lieutenant General (Ret.)] Amnon Lipkin-Shahak. We're very concerned about what could happen among the settlers in Judea and Samaria. Our assumption is that during the coming years the government of Israel will make political decisions that will have far-reaching repercussions for us. I'm among those who think that about 80 percent of the settlers will comply with any decisions of the government and the Knesset. But 20 percent will not accept the decisions of the government of Israel and they're liable to start a conflagration. That's why I'm calling you."

"What can I or the IDI do to help in light of this reality?" I asked him.

"I believe," said Wallerstein, "that if we manage to show those 20 percent that the overwhelming majority of the nation stands behind the government decision, this could soften and weaken the height of the anticipated flames."

We formed a steering committee to discuss ways to implement the idea. We met: Pinchas Wallerstein, Bentzi Lieberman (the chairman of the Yesha Council during the period of the disengagement), Rabbi Yitzhak Levy (now with the IDI), Yedidia Stern, and myself. In time, the forum expanded to include about ten settlers from Judea and Samaria and about the same number of people from the other side of the Green Line.

I had extensive experience in facilitating discussions and meetings gained during nineteen years at the IDI, but this one was the most difficult of all. We met four times. The first time was on the eve of the High Holidays in October 2008. The steering committee made a point of inviting four rabbis to participate in the group, including David Stav (the rabbi of Shoham and chairman of the Tzohar rabbis), Yehoshua Shapira (head of a *hesder* yeshiva in Ramat Gan) and two who live east of the Green Line: Yaakov Meidan (from Alon Shvut) and Avi Gissar (from Ofra). Shapira is considered an authority by the most extreme elements in Judea and Samaria; his brother is Rabbi Yitzhak Shapira, author of the polemic "The King's Torah," which argued that the *halacha* permits the killing of non-Jews in some circumstances in time of war. We invited Rabbi Yehoshua Shapira with the intention of addressing the extremists and with the hope that he could cool things off if the meeting got out of control. Other participants included Pinchas Wallerstein, Bentzi Lieberman, and Sarah Eliash. Joining my IDI colleagues at the first meeting were Professor Shlomo Avineri, Amnon Lipkin-Shahak, and Dov Lautman.

At the beginning of the discussion, I asked each person to introduce himself and his views. When Rabbi Shapira's turn came, he said: "I don't know what I'm looking for here. If someone had told me a week ago that I'd be sitting at the Democracy Institute, I would've thought he was crazy. I'm not entirely at peace with the fact that I'm sitting here." Then he turned to me and asked: "I'd be interested in knowing whether you'd be willing to hold the next meeting at the winery in Binyamin. That will be my test of your credibility." I said in response that a number of people sitting at the roundtable at IDI would find it intolerable to cross the Green Line, yet I believed we would do this. And indeed, the next meeting took place several weeks later in Ofra. We arrived in an armored vehicle—an everyday matter for the settlers, but a strange experience for us.

At the start of the second conversation, my IDI colleague Professor Tamar Hermann said: "I want you to know that today is the first time in forty years that I crossed the Green Line. I vowed that I wouldn't step foot here. I did this due to a sense of the enormous importance of these meetings and in order to give them a chance."

However, despite the powerful words, the divide seemed impossible to bridge. And during the fourth and most dramatic meeting, we were relieved of any illusion that a breakthrough might occur. "We'll discuss the democratic processes that will be acceptable to us here in order to influence the general public," I began. For a moment, it seemed that addressing procedural questions would keep us away from the ideological rift, but we were unable to avoid it. The idea of a referendum was raised. The discussion was long, difficult, and revealed again and again what we were trying to hide— the gaping divide between the two camps in their respective perceptions of reality.

"I'd like to describe a possible scenario for you," I suggested. "Imagine that the State of Israel has approved a referendum. A proposal for a peace treaty is on the agenda. The government of Israel has approved the proposal, a Knesset majority has enacted a law ratifying it, and the court has rejected appeals against it. This peace treaty would include the evacuation of parts of Judea and Samaria. Now we go to a referendum and in the referendum 69 percent say 'yes.' I already hear the voices saying '20 percent of them are

Arabs'—that is, there is no Jewish majority, so the decision is not legitimate." Excitedly, Bentzi Lieberman and Pinchas Wallerstein exclaimed: "No, that can't happen. It's a democratic decision and we'll accept it, of course."

However, it came as no surprise when moments later two of the rabbis calmly stated: "You're right. It's not a legitimate decision. We won't accept it."

It's hard to describe the feeling of helplessness. And then someone said: "Friends, now we've finally come to the beginning of the discussion. Now we know the positions. Everything is out on the table. We need to think how we can move forward from here."

Today, nearly ten years later, we're still wondering how we can move forward from here.

If we look at the makeup of the group, we can gain some insight into why this dialogue failed. Politically, there were members from the left, center, and right—but that's a secondary point. Some members of the group were secular people who view human beings as the source of authority, while others were religiously observant. The religiously observant members had to reconcile two sources of authority: secular-civil-democratic and rabbinical, with the latter centered on Jewish law. To make matters more complicated, for the religiously observant the tone was set by extremist rabbis who use their *halachic* authority to rule on political issues that affect the entire public.

Throughout the many hours, we were working together to find a way to prevent bloodshed when and if the day of reckoning arrives, the boundaries of the discourse were clear. These boundaries dictated how we dealt with the political, social, and cultural issues at stake. We were able to connect and have a healthy dialogue—despite our differences—until the boundaries were breached. These boundaries were crossed when we discussed a scenario involving a majority of Israelis that also included non-Jewish citizens. A minority of the settler representatives present refused to accept this scenario, indicating that they wouldn't accept a democratic decision made by the majority and that they rejected the civil authority's exclusivity on matters affecting the general public in a democracy.

For years at the IDI, we had dealt with the dilemma of how a democratic collective could reconcile secular authority with an exclusive, religious community. Here we had a clear-cut answer.

This is difficult for me to accept. It is hard for me to recognize that there are limits to compromise: that I can only go so far in trying to accommodate someone who thinks differently than I do and whose dreams clash with mine. But there is apparently no way to get around the cold, cruel, and unequivocal realization that democracy cannot tolerate an exclusivist community's transcendental source of authority. Simply put, democracies can only be so flexible when it comes to inclusivity. Democracy cannot allow *halacha* to interfere with politics and cannot abdicate authority to those who look to divine sources for political authority.

∾

At the end of the second decade of the twenty-first century, various trends are circulating in religious Zionism. But my focus here is on characteristics of the religious counterrevolution and its growth. As Hillel Ben Sasson writes:

Today, the leadership of religious Zionism is no longer seeking a partnership with the Zionist enterprise or a central role in its vanguard. **It seeks to replace classical Zionism.** The essence of this change, and the characteristic uniting the range of educational, public, and political efforts of the religious Zionist leadership during the past decade, is the desire to reshape the heart of the Zionist ethos. From a Zionism based on the universal right of each nation to self-determination, religious Zionism is today promoting a state that understands itself as the realization of the Torah of Israel and the divine promise. . . . The fundamental objective of the leaders of religious Zionism today is to become the controlling elite in the state, to mobilize the full power of the state to further the goals of the religious-Zionist sector, and to impart the values of this elite to the Israeli public. . . . The rabbinical influence over the religious Zionist leadership during the past decade has become explicit and institutionalized. This leadership's new political program seeks to create politics that is not only driven by religious motives but subordinates the entire national experience to religious motivation. . . .

The authority of religious Zionism's rabbis is leading to a situation in which a large public of voters who do not identify with religious observance at all, are empowering a political party [the Jewish Home] that ultimately answers to the "Torah opinion" of those religious-Zionist rabbis rather than to the will of the voter [emphasis mine].[161]

According to scholar Tomer Persico, the messianic paradigm leveraged by Gush Emunim was weakened by the challenge posed by the Oslo process. Although disappointed by the hardships encountered on the road to realizing the messianic vision, religious Zionists did not become disillusioned. Instead, the disappointment engendered faith-based extremism that seeks to impose the image of redemption on a reality that opposes it. The death blow to the Kookist messianic view appears to have been Israel's withdrawal from the Gaza Strip and destruction of the Gush Katif settlement bloc in the coastal territory.[162]

Persico quotes from Haviva Pedaya's description of the extremist views in religious Zionism, views that approach the lowest levels on the descending continuum of believers: "The disengagement, for the people who underwent it, was like being torn from something real, from a point of connection. For those who were expelled, it was a breaking point that shattered the illusion that the tangible—the land—would conform to the symbolic—the state, the redemption."[163] When this connection was broken, the messianic hope shifted to an alternative symbolic focus—the Temple Mount.[164] And thus, "statism is being neglected, along with the patience required to incrementally advance toward redemption, and is being replaced by a partisan messianism and fearless efforts to hasten the end of days, to bring apocalypse now."[165]

The religious counterrevolution also generated shock waves in the secular public as it grew, intensified, and turned against the trends of Zionism. The weakness of the secular Zionist foundations could not always withstand this. Secular responses are no less troubling than the characteristics of the counterrevolution. In one of the surveys conducted by Tamar Hermann and her team, she asked for responses to the statement: "Only new immigrants who are Jews according to the *halacha* should automatically receive Israeli citizenship."[166] Some 83 percent of the respondents agreed with this statement and thus would withhold citizenship from those who do not meet the *halachic* definitions of Jewishness but are considered Jews under the Law of Return—that is, a third of the immigrants from the former Soviet Union. It's amazing that 47 percent of secular Israeli Jews agree with this and another 37 percent said they "pretty much" agree. In other words, 84 percent of secular Israeli Jews reject the Law of Return's definition of Jewishness that was applied to a third of the immigrants from the former Soviet Union.

I contend that any development whatsoever that presents a religious-institutional alternative to the state's institutions poses a challenge to the sovereign foundations of the democratic state. As such, there is a need to clarify where such developments are situated on the descending continuum of believers. Worth examining is the religious Zionist forum Takana, which Stern described as follows:

> The Takana Forum was established in 2003 by Torah sages, men and women from the fields of education, law, and therapy, with the aim of preventing sexual abuse by those in positions of

authority in the religious public. The forum's objective is to create a different way to deal with complaints of sexual harassment that are not brought to the legal authorities to handle. The forum also works to raise awareness among educators and public figures in positions of authority about sexual abuse. All this is aimed at eradicating this evil from our midst and rescuing the oppressed from his oppressor. The Takana Forum operates in coordination with law enforcement authorities in Israel.

Stern told the IDI fellows about the forum's discussions in the case of Rabbi Motti Elon, who was suspected (and later convicted) of sexually abusing his pupils. (At the time, the rabbi's name was not yet published.) Stern told us that the forum had received approval from then attorney general Meni Mazuz to continue to pursue the case behind closed doors and even to impose punishment on Rabbi Elon. I asked Stern then whether he, as a law professor, didn't think that the forum's activity created an alternative system of justice. His response underlined the dilemma: victims of sexual abuse by rabbis do not turn to the police to complain. The Takana Forum, according to its founders, created a way to address these cases behind the closed doors of the religious community and thus provide help to the victims of abuse.

The forum's code of ethics states, among other things: "There is an obligation to purify our camp from conduct that entails sexual abuse or sexual harassment. This obligation derives from [the Jewish religious edict] 'and your camp shall be holy' and from rescuing an oppressed person from his oppressor, in the sense of 'do not stand idly by as the blood of your neighbor is shed.' This obligation is consistent with the laws of the state, and it should not be interpreted in a way that contradicts the law and the judicial rulings that emanate from it. This obligation aims to apply, complete, and broaden the canvas according to Torah criteria."

To what extent does this high-minded language, laden with words like "purify," hide or whitewash the danger of establishing a quasi-judicial institution outside of the justice system of the sovereign state?

Indeed, a serious ethical dilemma. To what extent can private legal forums like Takana claim to be acting in collaboration with the authorities? Where is the thin line separating entities that engage in legitimate collaboration from those that operate independently, outside the scrutiny or control of the state? Today the rabbinical courts are operating more like the latter, conducting their work in ways that reach beyond the jurisdiction afforded them by the state. (A study is needed on the de facto privatization of the rabbinical courts. The main issues the rabbinical courts handle include marriage, divorce, alimony, custody of children and visitation rights, division of property, wills, inheritance, determination of Judaism, and conversion.)

As I worked on the final editing of this essay, the following news was published: "The large-scale sex crimes case uncovered yesterday again raises the topic of ultra-Orthodox society's attitude toward this subject. Details about the alleged offenses were recorded in the notebooks of an ultra-Orthodox politico, who ran a sort of private law enforcement system parallel to official state law enforcement. The names of the victims, estimated to number about one hundred, appeared in the notebooks next to the names of the offenders. The same politico, M., claimed in a conversation with *Haaretz*, that he chose not to report these incidents to the police because either they were insignificant or because they were already addressed within the community. The investigation revealed that suspects took the law into their own hands, and collected information [about the allegations] and conducted their own internal proceeding and determined the punishment." Thus, similar to the Takana Forum of religious Zionism, the ultra-Orthodox organization, called Committee for the Purity of the Camp, assumed the same responsibility, effectively limiting the power of Israeli law enforcement and stifling its ability to investigate or prosecute these crimes.

Today, one of the repercussions of the religious counterrevolution— in terms of the vision of implementing religious law—is reflected in the words of Rabbi Ido Rechnitz, a religious Zionist rabbi in the West Bank, during a debate with Yedidia Stern.[167] The rabbi's remarks reflect the internal religious discourse today but do not resonate in the general public. This testifies to the lack of a consensual foundation for Israeli society and the divisions within the country.

Rechnitz argues that Stern is "calling upon adjudicators of *halacha* to choose the *halachic* way in order to reduce the tension between the Torah and the state" and that this sweeping call should be rejected. "The Torah was not intended to grant legitimacy to human action, but on the contrary, to challenge it." Rechnitz goes on to assert that "the role of God is missing from Christian political science . . . which says give to God what is God's and to Caesar what is Caesar's . . . On the other hand, Jewish political science deals mainly with the question of the role of the Holy One blessed be He in public life." Rechnitz argues that the role of God in government lies in two channels: "A first channel is that Torah laws constitute the legal framework, and rabbinical sages are responsible for interpreting said laws. A second channel is that all public officials must use their authority 'for the sake of Heaven' . . . *Therefore, public officials also serve the Lord in the framework of their public work . . . The basic Jewish stance is that obedience to man cannot take precedence over obedience to the laws of the Torah* [emphasis mine]." Moreover, while Stern states that "in general, the Knesset and its laws are not seen as invalid in the religious rulings of religious Zionism," Rechnitz responds that "this assertion is erroneous. Adjudicators of *halacha* do not accept the laws of the Knesset that were designed to replace the laws of the Torah."

If there is a hint of a theocratic inclination in the words of Rechnitz, a native son of religious Zionism, his comments on the judicial branch make it as clear as can be: "The strongest point of friction between the world of *halacha* and the world of the state's authorities is the judicial branch." In his view (though he restricts his comments to civil law), the judicial branch should be in the hands of religious officials "because the law belongs to God." He goes on to say that "adjudicators of *halacha* from the various sectors have fiercely opposed the State of Israel's judicial branch when it deals with civil matters . . . because they view them as non-Jewish courts." In what could be perceived as praise for theocracy, Rechnitz states that *halachic* sovereignty "treats *halacha* as binding law whose interpreters are the members of the Sanhedrin . . . The renewal of national sovereignty is an extremely difficult process, however it succeeded and transformed the Jewish people from an ethnic group to a nation with a state and stable political culture. This type of process has yet to occur in the world of Judaism . . . *Can the world of Torah and the rabbinate today revive rabbinical statism? Perhaps the key actually lies in a combination of religion and state . . . Can God-fearing political leaders be the ones to lead a process of renewing rabbinical sovereignty?* [emphasis mine]" In response to these statements, I can say I rest my case. Professor Stern and Rabbi Rechnitz are discussing the role of religious law in the political arena. Both of them are situated— of course, at different levels—on the slippery slope of the descending continuum of believers.

These are clear signs of ethnocentrism at the extreme margins of religious Zionism, which illustrates the distinction between "otherness" and "differentness." The ethnocentric trends emphasize otherness and point to an enemy who threatens the accepted perception of reality. When otherness penetrates the relations between the groups comprising Israeli society and the conflict of identities grows stronger, one of the first victims is solidarity.

A similar phenomenon is reflected in the ascendance of exclusivist social-political movements in the United States in recent years, even if the focus is on different issues. As Huntington notes, these movements are primarily supported by white men, most of them blue-collar workers from the lower-middle class, who are protesting against what they view as a threat to white nativism: the very significant demographic changes in American society.[168] "Otherness" stirs their protest—what they perceive as a distortion of their culture's foundations, a threat to their language, and the erosion of the nation's historical identity. These movements—antiblack, anti-Hispanic, and anti-immigrant—are fueled by racism. They are the heirs to the many similar racist, exclusivist, anti-immigrant movements that shaped the

American identity in the past. As in the past, the "white nativism" movements of today are characterized by ethnocentrism. For them, "white America" is the supreme goal.

The new white nationalists—who include people of intellect and culture, graduates of prestigious colleges—are a new strain of racists, Huntington explains. They refrain from strident populism and are far different from the Ku Klux Klan members of the Deep South. These white nationalists do not preach white supremacism. For them, race is the source of culture and since there is no way to change the racial source, it is also impossible to change a person's culture. Therefore, the change in the racial balance in the United States means a change in the cultural balance. As such, it threatens the white culture that made America great. This threat comes from the nonwhite and other cultures they view as inferior.

I wish to reiterate that religious Zionism in Israel is not monolithic and thus there are various "political homes" for those who are at different stages on the descending continuum of believers. The National Religious Party was once the umbrella group for most religious Zionists. Its successor, the Jewish Home party, split in late 2018 when its two leading figures—Education Minister Naftali Bennett and Justice Minister Ayelet Shaked—broke away to form The New Right party.

Shaked, the justice minister in Israel's thirty-fourth government, attempted to explain in a lengthy article that "neither Roman law nor the tradition of the Athenian polis shaped and forged the democratic tradition of the modern era in Europe and in the U.S., but rather it was the Jewish tradition."[169] Shaked attributes Jewish roots to the doctrines of John Locke, Thomas Jefferson, and, implicitly, "countless revolutionaries, pursuers of justice and opponents of tyrannical regimes." Of course, Shaked does not address the tension between the universal values of democracy and the particularistic values of Jewishness. That same tension is, generally speaking, the source of the identity conflict and threats to democracy in Israel. In any case, she does not look for ways to resolve this tension. Her futile attempt to force democracy to fit in an environment of Jewish particularism is the product of the superficiality and vulnerability of the secular foundations of our democracy. This raises the question: How do we universalize the particular? In my view, Shaked's remarks reflect the power of the religious counterrevolution and the failure of classical secular Zionism to stifle this revolution. Is the boldness behind Shaked's presumptions drawn from the fact that her party is made up of both religious and secular parliamentarians? This mix makes the party essentially unsustainable because secular supporters empower a party that ultimately obeys the "Torah opinion" of religious Zionist rabbis instead of the will of the voter.

Israeli jurist and political theorist Haim Cohn stated that "the system of the *halacha* is anti-democratic . . . a democratic legislator will betray his mission if he adopts the *halacha* in this way . . . The state is not supposed to be Jewish unless it is democratic. The Jewishness of the state cannot be *halachic* or religious Jewishness; it must be a Jewishness that is kosher according to the values of democracy . . . when there is a conflict, democracy must have the upper hand."

Justice Haim Cohn's words emphasize the desired situation, in my view. However, the "desired" must be examined in the context of reality. In Israel today, the religious counterrevolution has reversed some of the achievements of the secular Zionist revolution, including both the structures of Israeli democracy and its normative foundations.

The secular liberation was not defeated, but it was challenged in unexpected ways and with unanticipated intensity. Since the creation of the state, more or less, two processes have developed in parallel: a gradual strengthening of the characteristics of the religious counterrevolution and a gradual deepening of the democracy's vulnerability. The significance of these two processes and their repercussions for Israeli democracy should be examined in light of the claim that Israel is a formal democracy and that Israeli society's ways of life are all in transition from sovereignty-in-the-making to sovereignty. As long as Israel does not have a constitution, the transition to full sovereignty will depend on establishing the democratic principle of inclusivity. The fact that the internal rifts in Israeli society are deepening, and that we treat those different from us as "others," indicates that we have allowed exclusivity to prevail.

The return of the old Jew of the Diaspora is one of the most noticeable signs of the backlash against the secular nature of the Zionist revolution. The return of the "negated" Jew of the exile has led to a type of religious ultranationalism that gradually became militant and has consistently transformed the political framework in our new democracy over the past decades. The return of what was negated to our ways of life is reflected, among other things, in phenomena that I allow myself to call "exilic." Examples include the fearmongering practiced by Israeli politicians and the support for the argument that "the world is against us." I wouldn't use the term "exilic" to describe the cynical political use of the Holocaust by a minority among the state's leaders, but it has definitely brought the exile to the forefront of our political lives more than it would have been otherwise. The difference between the exilic ways that Zionism rebelled against and contemporary exilic traits is that the old passivity has transformed into aggression and violence. The expression "never again," whose repeated use reflects its exilic nature and the weakening of collective self-confidence, demarcates for me the thin line that separates the victim from the victimizer.

The counterrevolution and the extremists at the bottom of the descending continuum of believers threaten Israel's ability to complete the transition to full sovereignty and a substantive democracy. However, to the best of my judgment, the religious counterrevolution has not yet defeated the project of renewal. Therefore, we can still find a way to place multicultural and multi-identity definitions of Jewishness on the cultural-political agenda and legitimize them. The basis for such definitions lies in the foundations of the Zionist revolution. These foundations were laid by those in the revolutionary movement who preferred to criticize the past while remaining connected to it, rather than mount an all-out attack against the past. Ahad Ha'am, Yosef Haim Brenner, Haim Nachman Bialik, Micha

Yosef Berdyczewski, and Berl Katznelson are some examples. Walzer writes, "I tend to think that if they had gained the upper hand, the story would have developed in a different way."[170] The liberators would have lived in peace with at least part of the nation's past, while developing innovative beliefs and practices that were still connected to familiar ways. In this way, they might have prevented the extremism in the religious revival.

It's still not too late . . .

Finale as a Prelude

Will the religious counterrevolution and its social, cultural, and political expressions ultimately undermine the foundations of democracy in Israel?

I still don't have a clear answer to this important question and I continue to wrestle with its implications. At the beginning of this essay, I noted that the Jewish nation has had no experience in bearing responsibility for political sovereignty. Israel's rudimentary stage of political sovereignty serves as a source of motivation for this "Jewish and democratic" project. The project's long-term objective is to clarify whether it is possible to propose milestones for building a shared foundation or a "consensual underpinning" for political life in Israel's very diverse society. This is of paramount importance, because the identity conflicts in Israeli life pose a challenge to the very feasibility of the Zionist endeavor.

During my twenty-four years at the Israel Democracy Institute, I conducted many wide-ranging dialogues with people from across the entire spectrum of Israel's divided society. The common theme in almost all of these dialogues was: "How do we compromise? What do I give up, and what do you give up?" But this approach did not lead us out of the conflict of identities. I believe it is not enough to formulate compromises. The conflict of identities at the heart of our collective life requires us to acknowledge and describe how we perceive each other, as painful as this might be. It means recognizing the contours of my identity and, within them, how I perceive those of people different from me. This is the profound meaning of my doctrine.

For nearly three centuries, religion was in the process of retreating from public places.[171] Huntington writes: "Modernization was seen as undermining religion, while ideologies—liberalism, socialism, democracy—supplanted religion in public arenas. These ideologies were the focus of public discussion, shaped internal and external alliances, and created models for governance. However, this trend reversed in the last quarter of the 20th century as religious political movements gained ground in countries around the world. Islamic fundamentalism and Christian evangelism are the salient examples. The 21st century began as an era of religiosity."[172]

The effort to sacralize public spaces that were previously secularized—or, as this is generally called, "bringing religion back to public life"—is a global phenomenon. In Israel, we have a special interest in this phenomenon because it entails the most polarizing and problematic aspects of secularization. One of the characteristics of secularization processes is the differentiation and independence of various spheres of life. The core essence of the secularization process, and what makes it an integral part of modernization, is the separation and independence of spheres of life from religious norms and institutions. The status of religion recedes as the political, economic, and scientific spheres become more separate and independent. Religion must then find its place as one sphere among others, recognizing their separateness and independence. As noted, in order to protect the well-being of the secular foundations of democracy and freedom, it is essential to provide security—personal, economic, and political. A crisis or a blow to security, as well as other sources of anxiety, can pave the way for the return of religion.

Secularization, therefore, entails a dramatic change in the place of religion in public and private life, and we should recognize that this change is intolerable for some religious people. Those who regard religion as a realm of absolute truth cannot tolerate the thought of according it the same status as other spheres of life, or that other spheres of life are beyond the purview of religion. This is the basic difficulty in searching for ways to coexist. Recognition of the fact that religion has the same status as other spheres is a prerequisite for inclusiveness and the acceptance of differentness, which is the foundation for tolerance. Such recognition in today's Israel means ending the Orthodox monopoly over the particularistic aspects of the shared national identity. Is this possible?

The attempt to sanctify public space and "restore" God to public life is a major threat to Israel's democracy created by the religious counterrevolution. In the Israeli case, an attempt to "re-sacralize" these places can be seen as an effort to inject transcendental authority where the source of legitimacy for political governance is the consent of the sovereign people. This attempt is not and has never been mono-lithic, unequivocal. Like the many hues of religious Zionism, the effort to "restore" God to public spaces has varying shades and inten-sities. However, from a purely democratic perspective, it seems that the combined aspects of this attempt, and its persistence over time, pose an existential threat to civil society. In general, the glue that binds members of civil society in democratic life are the unwritten propositions of a social covenant, and these propositions are devoid of transcendental characteristics. Because Israel lacks a consensual framework for these propositions, they do not exist here.

Since its early days, Zionism has been sanctified both by secular and religious Jews, and both have left their mark. While secular sanc-tification of Zionism has weakened over the years, its religious coun-terpart has strengthened. One of the most notable and extraordinary expressions of secular sanctification was in the narrative that Israelis developed around the Holocaust. A transcendental dimension was laid upon the Holocaust and it was depicted as an otherworldly, almost nonhuman event. Auschwitz was depicted as "a different planet," while the Nazis were depicted as beasts and their victims as sheep. This shows one of the drawbacks of secular sanctification. It has impaired the ability of Israelis to judge the secular, human lessons of the Holocaust, including what turns people into victimizers.

In recent decades, religion has worked its way more and more into public spaces in Israel. This is evident in all of my areas of study: education, the IDF, and lawmaking and politics. In each of these areas, we see the growing influence of Jewish religious leaders and Jewish law, which have taken a more central role in daily life, diminishing the autonomy of individuals in communities across the country. For example, a letter was recently published by "rabbis of the central stream in religious Zionism" on the issue of mixed-gender combat units in the IDF. Some of my friends were among the so-called moderates who signed the letter. These rabbis write about "the required separation" of men and women and determine that it is forbidden for women to serve in these units. "The obligation to ensure that military service will not clash with our *halachic* and moral world—is imposed on the person himself." This approach strips individuals of their responsibility and autonomous judgment. The "obligation to ensure" is not a universal obligation for all members of civil society. It is a commitment to the *halacha* and the interpretations of religious leaders, at the expense of civil society.

This message of the letter stands in clear contrast to the democratic rules that should be implemented in the army of a democratic state. In Israel, young people are expected to be prepared to sacrifice their lives for the state. The ongoing threats to the security of the state's citizens has made the experience of death central in the life of the Israeli collective in general and of the individual performing compulsory military service in particular. This reality creates numerous dilemmas: What purpose is there to a death in the line of duty? Why death? Why me? Is it worthy to sacrifice life for an ideal, or only for physical survival? And if it is worthy to sacrifice for an ideal, does this include for land or for a holy entity? Wrestling with these dilemmas is part of the public discourse in Israel. And in the democratic public discourse, there is no place for the presence of God. This is not only because democracy is based on secular foundations but also because there is no orderly and decisive set of answers to these dilemmas. The ongoing need to cope with an ambiguous and unresolved reality is one of the challenges for secular democracies. Contending with dilemmas in the democratic reality relies upon the human, the internal, and not the divine.

The cultural aspect of the sacralization of public spaces includes efforts to sanctify cultural characteristics that shape behavior. These include state symbols, myths, and rituals, as well as values and ethical-moral foundations. In this context, my work plan includes examining changes that religion has wrought in the education system: How does the religious education system address what it refers to as the "dilemma of obedience?" That is, what happens when democratic values clash with the *halacha*? And what repercussions does this have on the political socialization of a significant minority (important numerically and in terms of ethical norms) and on Israel's civic society, in which the graduates of the religious education system are supposed to integrate? The products of sacralization can clearly be seen in efforts to impose observance of the Sabbath in shared spaces where the status quo had remained largely unchallenged for decades.

The attempts to sacralize public spaces have the potential to religionize politics. This will be typified by politicians surrendering their autonomy to the authority of *halachic* commentary in decision making. The forfeiture of autonomy and critical judgment harms the aspiration to form consensus and compromises. This is one of the basic practices in a democracy's political processes. This surrender would also reflect a varying level of intolerance for other worldviews and the accentuation of "otherness" in our divided society. This sometimes reaches the level of demonizing others—whether they be leftists or Arabs. Moreover, sanctifying the state and perceiving it as endowed with religious meaning can lead to rejection of the state's supreme authority. One expression of this can be found in the attempts to weaken the Supreme Court, which serves as the interpreter of the democracy's constitutional foundations. This sanctification of politics and the role of religious leaders is part of my work plan.

In the end, the key question is whether the Jewish religion is a political religion and, if so, can it be an integral part of a democratic way of life. In other words, we must address the question: Is secularization possible, even if limited to the minimal extent necessary for modern life, without severely undermining the status of religion? An examination of this question is essential if we are to establish a shared life for all of Israel's citizens on firm and stable foundations. The answer to this question, especially in twenty-first century Israel, is apparently: No. Against this background, we can appreciate the sources of the religious counterrevolution. If modernity indeed requires a dramatic change in the accepted status of religion, this opens the door not only to the erosion of faith but also to a counterreaction aimed at regaining religion's lost hegemonic status.

However, in searching for formulas to cultivate coexistence and achieve equilibrium between the particularistic and the universal, and between religion and state, we should note that the struggle for political hegemony in the name of religion is a modern phenomenon, the result of a secularized world. Agents of the Orthodox monopoly who fight against secularization in a secularized arena are unwittingly engaged in a secular activity. Even if they win a complete victory in this struggle, this would not be a restoration of the days of old. Rather, it would establish an antiliberal secular-political hegemony that dominates a secularized space via secular means, while erasing all of the achievements of secularization—including the achievements they exploited to win their struggle. Religion cannot be restored to its earlier role through political means, not even via a modern culture war. At most, a new secularized political format can be created whose content, drawn from the religious tradition, is imposed on the citizenry in a way that is totally unlike the methods of persuasion and coercion employed in the premodern religious system.

Today, after decades of expansion and solidification of democracy worldwide, the global arena faces a series of potentially cataclysmic threats. Liberal democracy is today facing a crisis that is unprecedented since the end of World War II. Moderate signs of regression in the status of freedom and democracy were evident at the beginning of the millennium in developing democracies such as Turkey, Thailand, the Philippines, Slovenia, and others. Recently, however, an increasing number of developments in Europe and the United States have raised unprecedented doubts about the health and stability of the heart of the democratic world. The rapid growth and increased support of xenophobic, fearmongering, nonliberal parties represent the reactionary response to the universal challenges of our time. This reactionary response is a developed model of populism that exploits transparency and state-of-the-art technology. For example, reports and statements on Twitter and other social media reflect a phenomenon of distortion and the rise of "post-truth" politics based on "alternative facts." This populism appeals to fear of the other and of complex situations. It fosters a desire to surrender personal and collective autonomy to political, spiritual, or religious authoritarians.

Israeli society and our democracy today are different from what the state's founders envisioned. The developments in our democracy are part of the anomaly overtaking normality in the global arena of liberal democracies. Israel is a remarkably diverse country, but across all segments of society there is great longing for normality. For me, the characteristics and components of one aspect of Israeli society are the most critical for the existence of the State of Israel, Israeli society, and Israeli democracy. Clearly, the phenomena and tensions that stem from the religious counterrevolution in Israel are unique in many ways. Nonetheless, if we look at the threats posed to our liberal democracy and the deepening divisions in our civil society, the situation in Israel is consistent with global trends.

Do these global trends indicate an undermining of the universalistic elements of the particular? Do they hint at the return of the transcendental and the divine to the public realm? Do these global trends indicate a weakening of the infrastructure of universal humanism? What do all these have to do with rising hostility in the West toward Islam? And do the implications of these developments require a new analysis of the Zionist deficit?

Acknowledgments

I am indebted to a wide range of individuals who have accompanied me in my journey to scrutinize the elusive ways of Israeli democracy; it is wider by far than the scope of the pages of acknowledgments of this book. The preparation of the manuscript was conceived out of an extended process of discourse with friends, with colleagues, and mainly with myself. Hence, and above all, I want to emphasize that the responsibility for its content is exclusively my own.

The ideational road blocks guiding the development of *Building Democracy on Sand* were laid down throughout my years at the Israel Democracy Institute (IDI). My habitat there was created, first, through ongoing interactions with an outstanding cohort of mindful researchers, whose practical contribution to the public good and to the future of the State of Israel had always been a top priority. This company included senior fellows who brought an extraordinary, mature professionalism to the enduring internal discourse at the IDI. Similarly, I have always been enlightened by a group of young, up-and-coming researchers, whose configuration changed through-out the years but was always characterized by a zeal of commitment along with critical and fresh perspectives. My tenure at IDI has been marked, second, by constant interaction with the political, cultural, and social realities in Israel, always in a state of transition. In short, I have been fortunate to be situated at a juncture where the compo-nents for constructing a viable underpinning of ideas converged with the road maps for their implementation. I am grateful to all those who were with me in both of these arenas.

Bernie Marcus, a great American philanthropist, trusted my vision and provided me with the material means to implement it. On top of this support, I was fortunate to have Bernie's incontestable commitment to the well-being of the State of Israel translated into his coleadership of IDI.

Secretary George Shultz has served as an involved wise, experienced statesman for the work of IDI and for me personally almost from the day of the institute's inception. Working with this extraordinary man has been a unique privilege. It continued after I departed IDI and became a distinguished visiting fellow at the Hoover Institution, Stanford University, where I have spent three months every fall over the past several years. The exceptional environment in general and the intellectual milieu in particular provided an immeasurably valuable ground for writing this account. I am particularly grateful to the Marcus Foundation, whose support granted me this privilege.

A generous grant provided by Max Levit and Livingston Kosberg from Houston, Texas, enabled me to further pursue my research while residing as a senior fellow at the Interdisciplinary Center in Israel. I wish to thank both of them.

I would like to recognize Ira Moskowitz for his eloquent translation of the Hebrew version of my book into English. I further wish to acknowledge the diligent editorial team of the Hoover Institution Press, including Chris Dauer, Barbara Arellano, Darrell Birton, Marshall Blanchard, Scott Harrison, Danica Michels Hodge, Jennifer Navarrette, and John O'Rourke, as well as this volume's copy editor, Barbara Egbert.

My partner for life and best friend, Tzipa Carmon, has provided a backbone of support throughout all my initiatives and deeds, and to this product as well.

I wish to restate and emphasize: the entire responsibility for the content of this book is mine and mine alone.

Notes

Note: For quotations from works originally in Hebrew, translations are by Ira Moskowitz.

1. Muslim Arabs, Christian Arabs, and Druze comprise about 20.9 percent of Israel's population, with others accounting for 4.7 percent.

2. I wrote extensively on this subject in my book, *Without a Constitution: An Israeli Story* [in Hebrew] (Jerusalem: Am Oved and Israel Democracy Institute Press, 2012).

3. Samuel P. Huntington, *Who Are We? The Challenges to America's National Identity* (New York: Simon and Schuster, 2004), 115–16.

4. Ibid., 120.

5. Muslim Arabs comprise about 17 percent of Israel's population; Arab Christians are 2 percent of the population and Druze 1.6 percent.

6. Leo Strauss, "Jerusalem and Athens: Some Preliminary Reflections," in Issue 6 of *City College Papers*, City University of New York, collected in Volume 1 of *The Frank Cohen Public Lectures in Judaic Affairs* (New York: CUNY/City College, 1967).

7. The following is drawn from a chapter I wrote for the book *The Jewishness of Israel* [in Hebrew], ed. Aviezer Ravitzky and Yedidia Z. Stern (Jerusalem: Israel Democracy Institute, 2009), footnote 1.

8. Ibid., footnote 2.

9. Ibid., footnote 4.

10. See Mordecai Kaplan's related discussion in *Judaism as a Civilization: Toward a Reconstruction of American-Jewish Life* (Philadelphia: Jewish Publication Society, 2009).

11. Francis Fukuyama, *Identity: The Demand for Dignity and the Politics of Resentment* (New York: Farrar, Straus and Giroux, 2018), 56.

12. Ibid., 9.

13. Ibid., xvi.

14. Melissa Yates, "Rawls and Habermas on Religion in the Public Sphere," *Philosophy & Social Criticism* 33, no. 7 (2007): 880–91.

15. John Rawls, *Political Liberalism*, expanded ed. (New York: Columbia University Press, 2005), Kindle.

16. Jürgen Habermas, "Religious Tolerance: The Pacemaker for Cultural Rights," *Philosophy* 79, no. 30 (January 2004): 5–18.

17. Ibid.

18. Jürgen Habermas, "Faith and Knowledge," in *The Frankfurt School on Religion: Key Writings by the Major Thinkers*, ed. Eduardo Mendieta (New York: Routledge Press, 2004), 327–36.

19. The Jewish paramilitary group Haganah bought and outfitted this ship to carry 4,500 Jews, most of them Holocaust survivors, from France to Palestine in 1946. British forces stopped them from disembarking in Haifa and sent the passengers to Germany for detention, creating an international incident. Eventually, most of them reached Palestine.

20. See Charles Taylor, "The Dynamics of Democratic Exclusion," *Journal of Democracy* 9, no. 4 (October 1998): 143–56.

21. Ben Halpern and Jehuda Reinharz, *Zionism and the Creation of a New Society* (Oxford: Oxford University Press, 1998).

22. Yeshayahu Leibowitz, *Judaism, the Jewish People and the State of Israel* [in Hebrew] (Jerusalem and Tel Aviv: Shoken, 2005), 154–56.

23. Charles Taylor, *A Secular Age* (Cambridge, MA: Belknap Press, 2007), 299–300.

24. Acculturation is a social process in which a heritage of cultural values and norms is assimilated in a national-political collective.

25. Zvi Lamm, *Conflicting Theories of Instruction* [in Hebrew] (Tel Aviv: Sifriat Poalim, 1972), 20.

26. Micha Josef Berdyczewski, "From Language to Language" [in Hebrew], in *On Poetry and Language* (Warsaw: Tushyva, 1911).

27. Y. H. Brenner, "Grade 4" [in Hebrew], *The Land* 4 (January 1920).

28. Ibid. See footnote 31.

29. Assaf Inbari "A Melting Pot Is Needed, This Time Jewish," in *Ideas and Fragments: On the Jewishness of a Democracy* [in Hebrew], ed. Aviezer Ravitzky and Yedidia Stern (Jerusalem: Israel Democracy Institute Press, 2007), 181.

30. Michael Walzer, *The Paradox of Liberation: Secular Revolutions and Religious Counterrevolutions* (New Haven, CT: Yale University Press, 2015), 32.

31. Volapük is a language invented in 1879 by a German priest named Johann Martin Schleyer, who claimed that God had instructed him in a dream to create an international language. It was the first planned language that became a spoken language and not just an experiment. Later, it was

largely supplanted by Esperanto as an international language; today there are only a few dozen Volapük speakers.

32. Huntington, *Who Are We?*, 83.

33. Ibid., 103.

34. Anthony D. Smith, "Ethnic Election and National Destiny: Some Religious Origins of Nationalist Ideas," *Nations and Nationalisms* 5, no. 3 (July 1999): 331–55.

35. Ibid.

36. See Rogers Brubaker, *Nationalism Reframed: Nationhood and the National Question in the New Europe* (Cambridge, UK: Cambridge University Press, 1996).

37. A. B. Yehoshua, "Fusion or Welding" [in Hebrew], *Haaretz,* September 13, 2015.

38. Anita Shapira, *Brenner: A Life Story* [in Hebrew] (Tel Aviv, Am Oved, 2008), 32–33. For an English translation, see *Yosef Haim Brenner: A Life*, trans. Anthony Berris (Stanford, CA: Stanford University Press, 2014).

39. Ibid., 133.

40. Ibid., 194.

41. Ibid., 133.

42. Ibid., 278.

43. Tomer Persico, "Why Israel, India and Algeria Experienced Religious Awakening" *Haaretz Book Review*, July 1, 2015.

44. Ibid.

45. Taylor, *A Secular Age,* 146.

46. Ibid., 171.

47. Yaron Ezrahi, *Imagined Democracies: Necessary Political Fictions* (Cambridge, UK: Cambridge University Press, 2012).

48. Ehud Sprinzak, *Non-Legalism in Israeli Society* [in Hebrew] (Tel Aviv: Sifriat Poalim, 1986), 30.

49. In the Israeli parliamentary system, as in Germany and other countries, the president is a figurehead.

50. The Balfour Declaration was a document signed by the British foreign secretary, Lord Arthur James Balfour, on November 2, 1917, expressing Britain's support for establishing a national home for the Jewish people in Palestine. This was an unprecedented political achievement for the Zionist movement: a global power agreed to assist the Zionist movement in fulfilling its primary objective.

51. Nir Kedar, *Ben-Gurion and the Constitution* [in Hebrew] (Tel Aviv: Dvir, 2015), 104.

52. Ibid., 105.

53. Carmon, *Without a Constitution*, 117.

54. Alessandro Ferrara, "The Separation of Religion and Politics in a Post-Secular Society," *Philosophy & Social Criticism* 35, no. 1–2 (January/February 2009): 83.

55. Kedar, *Ben-Gurion and the Constitution*, 113.

56. Sammy Smooha, "Still Playing by the Rules: Index of Arab-Jewish Relations in Israel 2013," Israel Democracy Institute, 2013: 46.

57. Ibid., 48.

58. When Ben-Zvi was elected president, the Ben-Zvi couple refused to move to Zalman Schocken's home, which was designated for the presidents of Israel. As Ben-Zvi explained, they preferred "to continue the lifestyle to which we had become accustomed in the small hut, which was the center of the Haganah in Jerusalem, where we met members of the Third Aliyah for the first time, and where our sons Amram and Eli grew up. I learned that the government wanted us to live in the Schocken mansion, but we won't leave this spot of ours, where our hut stood. We strongly desire to continue a simple life."

59. Max Nordau was one of the founders of the Zionist movement. Born in Hungary, Nordau was a writer, physician, and orator.

60. David Grossman, *Falling Out of Time* [in Hebrew] (Tel Aviv: Hakibbutz Hameuchad Press, 2008), 563–66. For an English version, see *Falling Out of Time*, trans. Jessica Cohen (New York: Knopf, 2014).

61. Karl Frankenstein, "Israel in the Face of Crisis (Thoughts of a Psychologist and Educator)," in *In the Shade of the Yom Kippur War* [in Hebrew], ed. Adir Cohen and Efrat Carmon (Haifa, Israel: Haifa University Press, 1974).

62. Arab Muslim residents of Hebron rioted against the city's Jews in August 1929, killing sixty-seven of them. The Hebron massacre, one of a series of Arab riots that year, brought an end to four hundred years of Jewish presence in the city. Dozens of Jews were killed in pogroms in Kishinev, the provincial capital of Bessarabia, in 1903 and 1905. In April 1988, there was a clash between Jewish settlers and Palestinian residents of the village of Beita in the West Bank. A teenage Israeli girl and two Palestinians were killed. Initial reports claimed that Palestinians had stoned the girl to death. Israeli politicians continued to recite this narrative, even after learning that the girl had actually been killed by an errant bullet from an Israeli guard.

63. From Sophocles's *Antigone*, translation by David Grene, Michigan State University website.

64. "Price tag" refers to anti-Arab attacks and vandalism committed by Israeli right-wing extremists. The term "price tag" began appearing in 2008 in graffiti sprayed by the perpetrators of these hate crimes, which include throwing rocks, vandalizing mosques, torching fields, cutting down trees, and damaging other property.

65. During the pre-state period, there were voices calling for "more than sovereignty," "to complete the process of redemption through the force of arms." See Tomer Persico, "The Love-Hate Relationship Between Zionism and the Temple Mount," in *Tomer Persico–English* blog, November 14, 2014. Persico describes these proponents of messianic Zionism as more "mythic" than "religious." He explains: "They wanted to push reality to its far end, to reach the horizon and with their own hands bring into being the master plan for complete redemption. And redemption is the point at which hyper-Zionism becomes post-Zionism."

66. Aviezer Ravitzky, *The Revealed End and the Jewish State: Messianism, Zionism, and Religious Radicalism in Israel* [in Hebrew] (Tel Aviv: Am Oved, 1997).

67. *Machal* is a Hebrew acronym for "overseas volunteers."

68. Tamar Hermann, Gilad Be'eri, Ella Heller, Chanan Cohen, Yuval Label, Ronen Moses, and Kalman Neuman, *National Religious, the National Religious Camp in Israel* [in Hebrew] (Jerusalem: Israel Democracy Press, 2015), 98.

69. Ravitzky, *The Revealed End*, 12.

70. Yedidia Stern, "The Halacha's Accessibility to Statehood Issues" in *Judaism Inside and Outside: A Dialogue between Worlds* [in Hebrew], ed. Avi Sagi, Dudi Schwartz, and Yedidia Stern (Jerusalem: Magnes Press, 2000), 216.

71. Avi Sagi, "Between Closeness and Openness," in Sagi, Schwartz, and Stern, *Judaism Inside and Outside*, 168.

72. Yosef Ahituv, "On the Conditions to Internalize Democratic Values in Halacha Rulings within Religious Zionism," in Sagi, Schwartz, and Stern, *Judaism Inside and Outside*, 109–10.

73. See José Casanova, *Public Religions in the Modern World* (Chicago: University of Chicago Press, 1994); Ferrara, "The Separation of Religion and Politics," 77–91; Jürgen Habermas, "Religion in the Public Sphere," *European Journal of Philosophy* 14, no. 1 (April 2006): 1–25.

74. See Casanova, *Public Religions*, 52.

75. Ahituv, "On the Conditions to Internalize Democratic Values," 109–10.

76. *Din rodef* ("law of the pursuer") is significant as one of the few provisions in Jewish law permitting extrajudicial killings. The killing is considered a preventive measure, not a punitive one. Thus, in some situations, everyone is permitted to take action under the *din rodef* provision, even without a directive from a Jewish court of law. A person who informs on his fellow Jews is considered subject to *din moser* ("law of the informer"), which is analogous to *din rodef* in that both prescribe death for the offender, who may be killed without warning in some circumstances according to certain interpretations. The term is used to refer to a Jew who turns over a Jew or his property to a non-Jewish authority. In Rabin's case, this referred to the transfer of parts of the Land of Israel.

77. Stated in a discussion held at the George Shultz Roundtable Forum of the Israel Democracy Institute, December 1995, cited in Carmon, *Without a Constitution,* 170–71.

78. Sagi, "Between Closeness and Openness," 144.

79. Ella Belfer, "Judaism and Democracy: What Is the Discussion About?," in Ravitzky and Stern, *Ideas and Fragments,* 445–70.

80. Ibid., 464.

81. Ibid., 469.

82. Avi Sagi, "The Crisis Potential," in *Fractures: On the Unity of Opposites, Politics and Rabbi Kook's Disciples* [in Hebrew], ed. Avinoam Rosenak (Tel Aviv: Resling, 2013), 36.

83. Stern, "The Halacha's Accessibility to Statehood Issues," 216.

84. Yedidia Stern, "A Public Leadership as Halachic Authority," in Sagi, Schwartz, and Stern, *Judaism Inside and Outside,* 237.

85. Ibid., 269.

86. Ibid., 221.

87. Sagi, "Halachic Commitment and Democratic Commitment: Are They in Conflict? Thoughts of a Possible Membership in both Halachic Community and a Democratic Community," in Ravitzky and Stern, *Ideas and Fragments,* 348.

88. Tamar Hermann, *The National Religious Sector in Israel 2014* [in Hebrew] (Jerusalem: Israel Democracy Institute Press, 2015), 111.

89. Ibid.

90. Ibid., 117.

91. Ibid., 139.

92. Gideon Aran, *Kookism: The Roots of Gush Emunim, The Jewish Settlers' Subculture, Zionist Theology, and Contemporary Messianism* [in Hebrew] (Jerusalem: Carmel Publishers, 2013), 162–63.

93. Ibid.

94. Walzer, *The Paradox of Liberation,* 19.

95. Belfer, "Judaism and Democracy," 458.

96. Sagi, "Between Closeness and Openness," 148.

97. Ibid., 162.

98. Avi Ravitzky, "Is a Halachic State Possible? The Paradox of Jewish Theocracy," in Sagi, Schwartz, and Stern, *Judaism Inside and Outside,* 2, 21.

99. Ibid., 29.

100. Ravitzky, *The Revealed End,* 7–56.

101. Stern, "A Public Leadership as Halachic Authority," in Sagi, Schwartz, and Stern, *Judaism Inside and Outside,* 222–23.

102. Ibid., 224–25.

103. Ibid., 232.

104. Ibid., 236.

105. Yedidia Stern, *Halacha and Political Questions* [in Hebrew] (Jerusalem: Israel Democracy Press, 2008), 26–27.

106. Ahituv, "On the Conditions to Internalize Democratic Values," 101–03.

107. Ernst Simon, "Are We Still Jews?," cited in Avinoam Rosenak, *Halacha as Occurrence* (Jerusalem: Magnes and Van Leer Institute, 2016), 32–33.

108. Hermann, *The National Religious Sector,* 26–27.

109. Ibid., 43.

110. Ibid., 74.

111. Ibid., 97.

112. Ibid., 236–37.

113. Avi Sagi, Dudi Schwartz, and Yedidia Z. Stern, "Introduction," in *Judaism: A Dialogue between Cultures,* ed. Avi Sagi, Dudi Schwartz, and Yedidia Z. Stern [in Hebrew] (Jerusalem: Magnes Press, 1999).

114. Dudi Schwartz, "Between Time and Eternity: Thoughts on the Perception of the Temporariness of Secularization in the Religious-Zionist Idea," in Sagi, Schwartz, and Stern, *Judaism Inside and Outside,* 170.

115. Belfer, "The Jewish World between Religion and State: The Two Dimensional Principle and the Struggle over the Definition of Identity," in Sagi, Schwartz, and Stern, *Judaism Inside and Outside,* 21.

116. Aran, *Kookism.*

117. Ibid., 142.

118. Ibid., 148, 147–50.

119. Ibid., 149.

120. Ravitzky, *The Revealed End,* 168–69.

121. Ibid., 44.

122. Sagi, Schwartz, and Stern, *Judaism: A Dialogue between Cultures.*

123. Ravitzky, *The Revealed End*, 115.

124. Ibid., 120–21.

125. Ibid., 157.

126. Ibid., 164.

127. Rosenak, *Halacha as Occurrence*, 42.

128. Yosef Ahituv, "On the Use of Divine Images of Israeli Nationalism in Some Groups in Religious Zionism," in *Book of Michael* [in Hebrew], ed. Avi Sagi (Jerusalem: Kadima Reches, 2007), 383–98.

129. Sprinzak, *Non-Legalism in Israeli Society.*

130. Fukuyama, *Identity*, 116.

131. Rosenak, *Halacha as Occurrence*, 25.

132. Gush Emunim is a national-religious social movement formed after the 1973 Yom Kippur War to promote Jewish settlement in the territories captured in the 1967 Six-Day War. Religious-messianic sentiment was the primary motivation for founding the movement but Gush Emunim also attracted many secular supporters in its early years.

133. Moshe Unna, one of the moderate leaders of religious Zionism, served as deputy minister of education and culture from 1956 to 1958 and chaired the Knesset Constitution, Law, and Justice Committee in the second, fifth, and sixth Knessets.

134. Aran, *Kookism.*

135. Sprinzak, *Non-Legalism in Israeli Society*, 124.

136. The ultra-Orthodox Shas party was established in 1982 and has competed in national elections since 1984, when it won four seats in the eleventh Knesset (about 3 percent of the parliament's 120 seats). Shas, led by Rabbi Ovadia Yosef, drew its support from Mizrahi voters and reached a high of twelve Knesset seats in the 2006 elections. Its parliamentary representation dropped to seven seats in the 2015 elections.

137. Rachel Bluwstein is known by her first name or as Rachel the Poetess.

138. "Going out to the question" is an expression of the Hebrew language that refers to a process by which a religious Jew changes to a secular way of life.

139. A *beit* (or *beth*) *midrash* is a Jewish study hall located in a synagogue.

140. Hermann, "Religious? Nationalists," in Hermann, Be'eri, Heller, Cohen, Label, Moses, and Neuman, *National Religious, the National Religious Camp in Israel*, 37.

141. Yuval Cherlow, "The New National-Religious Elites," in *New Elites in Israel* [in Hebrew], ed. Moshe Lisak, Benyamin Noiberger, Hava Ezioni-Halevi, and Gabriel Shefer (Jerusalem: Bialik Institute, 2007), 334–35.

142. Kalman Neuman, *The Dispute over the State's Borders: A Question of Religion and State?* (Jerusalem: Israel Democracy Institute Press, 2013).

143. Ibid., 46.

144. Ibid., 47.

145. Yair Sheleg, *Follow the Majority? Views of Rabbis in Israel on Democracy* [in Hebrew] (Jerusalem: Israel Democracy Institute, 2006), 91.

146. Ibid., 22–23.

147. Ibid., 45–46.

148. Ibid., 59–60.

149. Ibid., 92.

150. Ibid., 38–39.

151. Ibid., 56.

152. Ibid., 70.

153. Ibid., 42.

154. Ibid., 35.

155. Ibid., 62.

156. Ibid.

157. Ibid., 92.

158. Ibid., 82.

159. Ibid.

160. Carmon, *Without a Constitution*, 196.

161. Hillel Ben Sasson, "A New Religious Zionism?" (unpublished paper, 2014).

162. Ibid.

163. Haviva Pedaya, an Israeli poet and author, is a scholar of culture and Judaism at the Jewish History Department of Ben-Gurion University.

164. The Temple Mount is a holy site located in the southeastern corner of the Old City of Jerusalem. According to Jewish tradition, it was the site of the Temple and the only place where it could be rebuilt in the future. Some religious traditions identify it as the site where the world was created. The Temple Mount is also the site of the al-Aqsa Mosque, the third holiest site for Sunni Muslims. Islamic tradition identifies it as the site of the Prophet Muhammad's night journey to heaven. The Temple Mount is under Israeli sovereignty but is officially administered by the Jerusalem Islamic Waqf.

165. Tomer Persico, "The Temple Mount and the End of Zionism," *Haaretz*, November 29, 2014.

166. Hermann, Be'eri, Heller, Cohen, Label, Moses, and Neuman, *National Religious*, 120.

167. "Debate between Ido Rechnitz and Yedidia Stern," *Makor Rishon* (weekend supplement), June 5, 2016.

168. Huntington, *Who Are We?* 310–15.

169. Ayelet Shaked, "Paths to Governance" [in Hebrew], *HaShiloach* 1 (October 2016): 37–55.

170. Walzer, *The Paradox of Liberation*, 32.

171. Huntington, *Who Are We?* 355–56.

172. Ibid.

About the Author

Arye Carmon is the founding president of the Israel Democracy Institute (IDI) in Jerusalem, and one of Israel's foremost experts on political reform. Founded in 1991 to strengthen the foundations of Israeli democracy, the IDI has become a leading think tank with a reputation for nonpartisanship, professionalism, and actionable policy recommendations. In 2009, it was awarded by the State of Israel with the prestigious Israel Prize for Lifetime Achievement.

After stepping down as president of IDI in 2014, Carmon has since devoted his time to ongoing research at Hoover Institution, Stanford University, where he serves as a distinguished visiting fellow, and at the Interdisciplinary Center in Israel. Carmon has promoted democracy and political education both in the classroom and as a board member of numerous national and government institutions. He has published and lectured extensively on Israeli democracy, education, Israel-diaspora relations, and the Holocaust.

Carmon holds a PhD in European history and educational policy studies and is the author of *Reinventing Israeli Democracy: Thoughts on Modernizing Israel's Political System* (Israel Democracy Institute Press, 2009) and, in Hebrew, *Recommendations and Obstacles to Political Reform in Israel* (Israel Democracy Institute Press, 2009) and *Without a Constitution: An Israeli Story* (Am Oved and Israel Democracy Institute Press, 2013).

Index

acculturation
  collective consciousness and, 52
  Israel and, 52, 53
  overview, 51–52, 244n24
  secular Zionist revolution and, 46
  secularization and, 45
  in territorial nations, 52–53
Ahituv, Yosef, 158–59, 160, 177–78, 188
Amir, Yigal, 144, 152, 182, 200, 201, 211
Antigone (Sophocles), 149–50
anti-Semitism, 26
Arab Christians, 243n1, 243n5
Arab Israeli men, 29
Arab Israeli minority
  Israeli Jews and, 115, 116
  Israeli society and, 114
Arab Muslims, of Hebron, 246n62
Aran, Gideon, 169–70, 186
Ariel, Yaakov, 216
Ashkenazi (Jews from Europe), xv
Auschwitz, 22, 35, 55, 57, 58, 64, 235
authority
  Israel and dilemma of obedience to, 150, 151
  metaphysical and political, 173
  obedience to, 138–39, 150–51

reactionary populism and, 239
religious Zionists on source of, 143
Avineri, Shlomo, 151, 215

Balfour Declaration, 105, 245n50
Basic Law: Israel as the Nation-State of the Jewish People, 140–41
Be'er, Haim, 6
Begin, Menachem, 202–3
Belfer, Ella, 158, 160, 165, 171
Ben Yehuda Street bombing (1948), 154, 156
Ben-Gurion, David, 54, 60, 75, 117, 126, 203
  Israeli democracy and, 108
  Israeli lack of constitution and, 96, 97, 98, 107, 109, 189
  Jewish political sovereignty and, 110
  Kibbutz Sde Boker and, 106–7
  overview, 105–7
  statism of, 107–8, 110–13
Ben-Zvi, Rachel Yanait, 118, 119, 246n58
Ben-Zvi, Yitzhak, 105, 118, 246n58
Berdyczewski, Micha Josef, 66
Bodin, Jean, 35

borders of Israel
    Israeli collective identity and, 142
    lack of defined, 102–3
    occupied territories and, 127,
       128
    territorialization of national-cul-
       tural values and, 128
Brenner, Yosef Haim, 66–67,
    91–92

Carmon, Arye
    doctrine of, 1, 13, 19–20, 23–25,
       29, 32, 35
    family history and early years,
       9–12, 33, 35, 49–51, 54–58,
       60–63, 67–70, 77–78, 109,
       117–19, 122, 154–56, 171–72,
       189–90, 193–97
    identity of, 15
    IDF experiences of family and
       friends, 121–24
    IDI and, ix, xi, 3, 4–5, 13, 22,
       152, 175–76, 200, 203–5,
       217–21, 233
    letter to Ben-Gurion, 107
    November 22, 1968 bombing
       and, 156–57
    youth group of, 193–94
    Zionist motto of, 151–52
Carmon, Etka (mother), 33, 35, 63,
    117–19, 121, 195–97
Carmon, Ilye Shaul (son), 121, 122,
    123
Carmon, Moshe (father), 9–12,
    50–51, 55, 63, 117–18, 122,
    154, 172
Carmon, Omri (son), 121, 123
Carmon, Sabina (father's sister), 63,
    117, 118
Carmon, Tzipa (wife), 9, 124

Cherlow, Yuval, 212, 216–17
Christianity, xiv–xv, 226
    in religion and politics interac-
       tion, 163
    religion in public spaces and
       Christian democracies, 164
    secularization of Christian coun-
       tries, 23, 42–43, 45, 76, 81
    secularization process of, 81
Cohn, Haim, 229
collective consciousness
    acculturation and, 52
    See also collective Israeli
       consciousness
collective Israeli consciousness
    death in, 132, 139
    erosion of self-confidence in,
       139–40, 142
    ethos of survival and normalcy
       craving in, 125
    Jewish Diaspora consciousness
       and, 45, 46
    secular Zionist revolution and,
       44–47, 79
    Zionist deficit and, 46–47
Conservative Judaism, xv
    See also traditional Judaism
Constitutional Assembly, 98
continuum of believers
    descending, 152, 157, 181, 182,
       183, 201, 214, 215, 228, 230
    upper end of, 205, 208

Dan, Yael, 205–8
death
    in collective Israeli consciousness,
       132, 139
    Israeli military service and,
       135–37, 237
    Israeli society and, 135

Israelis' changing perceptions of, 73
narrative, 143
See also fallen Israeli soldiers
Declaration of Independence (Israel), 2, 96–97, 112, 113
inclusion in, 114–15, 116
lack of constitution and, 116
Nation-State Law and, 140–41
religious Zionism and, 188
democracy
consensual underpinnings of, 16, 23–24
consent in, 25
halacha and, 180, 183, 221, 229
identity and, 195
inclusiveness of Judaism and, 160
Jewishness and, 228–29
national-religious Jews and, 180
obedience and, 150, 151
religious Zionism and values of, 177–78
Torah and, 214
US, 111
See also religion and democracy
democratic states
dilemma of obedience in, 150–51
modern threats to freedom and, 239–40
religion and politics in, 164
secularism of, 166
descending continuum of believers, 152, 157, 181, 182, 183, 201, 214, 215
religious Zionism and, 228, 230
Diaspora Jews, 8
identity of, 43
new Jews and, 59–60
as "other," 26
young, 7

diasporic nations
as anomalies, 52, 77, 101
Israel as, 26, 52, 53
differentness, otherness and, 25–26, 227
din moser, 161, 248n76
din rodef, 161, 248n76
Druckman, Haim, 216
Druze, 243n1, 243n5

education
Israeli democracy and, 109
religious, 237
State Education Law of 1953, 108–9
system, 108–9
Zionism streams and, 108–9
Egypt peace treaty, 202
Eichmann, Adolf, 60–63
Elon, Motti, 216–17, 224
ethnocentrism
of extreme religious Zionism, 227
Israeli democracy and nationalism of, 2
otherness and, 227
US and, 227–28
ethos of survival, 125, 126, 127, 128–29, 130, 139, 140
exile. *See* Jewish Diaspora; negation of exile
Exodus (Hollywood film), 60
Exodus (immigrant ship), 34, 244n19

faith, common ground for reason and, 29–32
fallen Israeli soldiers, 121, 134
cemeteries for, 132–33, 135
Holocaust victims and, 68, 72–73

fallen Israeli soldiers (*continued*)
Memorial Day for Israel's Fallen
Soldiers, 69, 73, 74, 122, 123,
132, 133, 135
new Jews and, 69
Scrolls of Fire on, 70–72
yizkor memorial prayer for,
72–73, 74
The Federalist Papers, 107, 111
Finn, Amos, 70–72
Frankenstein, Karl, 144–45
freedom
of expression and religious
pre-military programs, 180
modern threats to democracy
and, 239–40
Froman, Menachem, 214
Fukuyama, Francis, 26–27, 28, 195

Gaza, 127
Operation Protective Edge, 124,
137, 138
withdrawal of settlements in,
175–76, 210
geographic-cultural periphery
ethnic identity recognition in, 195
Israeli immigrants and, 192,
194–95
Grossman, David, 134–35
Gush Emunim movement, 199,
200–201, 222, 250n132

Ha'am, Ahad, 84
Habermas, Jürgen, 30–31
hagadot (Passover booklets), 58
Haganah, 68
halacha (Jewish law), xiii–xiv, xv, 6,
78
democracy and, 180, 183, 221,
229

din rodef and *din moser*, 161,
248n76
involvement in state affairs, 174,
176, 226–27
Israeli citizenship and, 223
Israeli democracy and, 86, 150,
151, 152, 157–58, 160, 161–62,
165, 212, 213, 215–16, 221,
229, 236, 237, 248n76
Israeli immigrants and, 223
Israeli law and, 226–27, 236
Israeli military service and, 236
Israeli politics and, xv, 152, 165,
166–68, 177, 181, 201, 212–13,
236, 237
Israeli women and, 204
Jewish Diaspora and, 86, 87,
167
Jewish people and, 91, 92
Jewish public domain and, 173,
177
Jewishness definition according
to, 112, 113, 223, 229
non-Jews and, 216, 218
Palestinian-Israeli conflict and,
168
public leadership and, 166
public sphere and, 181
religious counterrevolution and,
172, 225–26
religious Zionism and, 159, 165,
173, 181, 182
secular foundations of democracy
and, 152, 168–69, 177
secular law and, 161–62, 167
secular Zionist and, 182
settlements and, 209–10,
212–13
halachic community, religious Jews
in, 157–58

halachic rulings
  Israeli democracy and, 168–69,
    181, 212, 213, 215–16
  on Israeli politics, 201, 212–13
  religious Zionism, secular foun-
    dations of democracy and,
    168–69
Haredim (ultra-Orthodox), 49
  See also ultra-Orthodox Jews
Haupt, Georges, 21–22
Hausner, Gideon, 60–61, 63–64
Hebrew culture
  Hebrew-Israeli culture, 82
  Zionism and secular, 57–58,
    64–65
Hebrew language, 66–67
  Israeli national identity and, 18,
    85
  revival of, 2, 64–65, 79–80
  security and, 142
  Zionism and revival of, 64–65,
    79, 170
Hebrewism, xv
Hebron, 145, 246n62
Hermann, Tamar, 168, 179, 181,
  219, 223
Herzl, Theodor, 100
Hobbes, Thomas, 35
Holocaust, 22, 33–35, 57, 64, 70,
  183
  Death Brigade 1005, 61–62
  Eichmann trial, 60–63
  Israeli society and, 59
  Jewish Diaspora and, 59
  moral lesson approach to, 58,
    214
  secular sanctification of, 235–36
  survivors, 55, 68, 244n19
Holocaust and Heroism Remem-
  brance Day, 69, 73, 132

Holocaust victims
  fallen Israeli soldiers and, 68,
    72–73
  negation of exile and, 69–70, 73
  secular Israelis and, 78
  yizkor memorial prayer for, 72
homeland concept, 90
Huntington, Samuel, 18, 87, 227,
  228, 234

identity
  democracy and, 195
  See also specific topics
identity politics, 28
IDF. *See* Israel Defense Forces
IDI. *See* Israel Democracy Institute
Inbari, Asaf, 75
inclusion
  consent and, 25
  Israeli Declaration of Indepen-
    dence and, 114–15, 116
  Israeli democracy and, 2–3
  of non-Jews, 114, 115
  principle of Israeli founders, 114
Inglehart, Ronald, 140
Islam, xiv
  in religion and politics interac-
    tion, 164, 165
Israel
  as anomaly, 52, 77, 102, 239
  clash between normalcy and
    anomaly in, 102, 239
  complexity of issues facing, 16
  consensual underpinnings, 16
  demographics, 2, 243n1
  diasporic versus anomaly of
    Israeliness dialectic in, 102
  exile versus normalcy dialectic of,
    102, 103
  first fifty years, 1–2

Israel *(continued)*
    homeland concept and, 90
    immigrants and leadership of,
        191, 192
    lack of consensus on territorial
        dimensions of, 102–3
    population, 15
    president as figurehead, 245n49
    rapid changes in, 14–15, 16
    transition from state-in-making
        to state, 94
    See also specific topics
Israel, as sovereign collective
    Israeli democracy and, 23
    Israeli lack of constitution and, 5,
        16
Israel Defense Forces (IDF), 3
    Carmon family members and
        friends in, 121–24
    rabbis and, 236
    religion and, 137–39
    secular Zionist revolution and,
        126
    See also fallen Israeli soldiers;
        Israeli military
Israel Democracy Institute (IDI)
    Carmon, Arye, and, ix, xi, 3, 4–5,
        13, 22, 152, 175–76, 200,
        203–5, 217–21, 233
    Democracy Index of, 17,
        115–16
    exclusion of women in public
        spaces and, 203–5
    Gaza settlement withdrawal and,
        175–76
    George Shultz Roundtable
        Forum, 161
    goals of, 3–4
    Guttman Center, 168, 179
    Israeli lack of constitution and,
        4, 5

Peace Index, 129–30
    settlements and, 217–21
Israeli citizenship, 217
    halacha and, 223
    for immigrants, 112, 223
    non-Jews and, 140, 180, 215
Israeli collective, Jewishness of, 48
Israeli collective identity
    borders of Israel and, 142
    conflict over, 233–34
    externalization of Israeli Jewish
        identity as, 141
    Israeli democratic identity and,
        18, 24
    Israeli Jewish identity and, 18,
        24, 141
    Israeli lack of constitution and,
        x, 5
    Israeli particularistic identity and,
        18, 19, 24
    Israeli universalistic identity and,
        18, 19, 24
    neutrality and, 108
    Zionists on, 108
    See also Israeli Jewish collective
        identity
Israeli constitution
    Constitutional Committee
        (1948), 188
    religious Zionism and, 188, 189
    See also Israeli lack of
        constitution
Israeli culture
    diversity of, 25, 28
    Hebrew language revival and,
        64–65
    Hebrew-Israeli culture, 82
    Jewish Diaspora and, 53
    sacralization of public spaces
        and, 237
    See also Israeli political culture

Israeli democracy
basic laws of, 5
Ben-Gurion and, 108
challenges to, ix–xi, 13
education and, 109
ethnocentric nationalism and, 2
exclusion and, 2–3
halacha and, 86, 150, 151, 152,
157–58, 160, 161–62, 165,
212, 213, 215–16, 221, 229,
236, 237, 248n76
halachic rulings and, 168–69,
181, 212, 213, 215–16
inclusion and, 2–3
Israel as sovereign collective and,
23
Israeli lack of constitution and, 5,
23, 95
Israeli minorities and, 115
Judaism and, 31–32, 46, 152,
160, 238
lack of bill of rights and, 5, 95
as parliamentarian, 4, 245n49
political sovereignty and, 16, 35,
36
questions facing, 13, 20, 233
religion in public spaces and, 235
religious counterrevolution and,
153, 160, 212, 229, 230, 235,
238, 239
repairing, 1, 2
secular Zionist revolution and,
81, 111, 169, 229
vulnerabilities and weaknesses of,
4, 5, 16, 20, 93, 98–99, 158,
229
Zionist deficit and, 16, 46, 47, 92,
111
Zionist process and, 20
See also Israeli religion and
democracy; secular

foundations of Israeli democracy; *specific topics*
Israeli democratic identity
Israeli collective identity and, 18,
24
Israeli Jewish identity and, 2, 17,
18, 19, 24, 28, 53, 141
Israeli universalistic identity and,
17
religious Israelis and, 17
secular Israelis and, 17
Israeli founders
inclusion principle of, 114
normalcy and, 111
Israeli identity
conflict of, 26–29, 85–87, 233–34
diversity of, 32
ethnic identity recognition, 195
Israeli lack of constitution and,
x–xi
of new Israeli immigrants, 192,
195
non-Jews and, 19
Orthodox Judaism and, 2–3
religious Israelis and, 6, 17
secular Israelis and, 6, 17, 81
See also specific topics
Israeli immigrants, 2, 15, 16
assimilation of, 191–92, 194–95
citizenship for, 112, 223
deficit of respect towards, 194–95
geographic-cultural periphery of,
192, 194–95
halacha and, 223
illiteracy of, 192
Israeli leadership and, 191, 192
Israeli secularism and traditional
Jewish, 109–10
Law of Return and Jewish,
112–13
massive 1950s influx, 191–97

Israeli immigrants (*continued*)
  negation of exile and, 197
  new, 192, 195, 223
  old Jews and, 170
  paternalistic policy towards, 191,
    194
  religious counterrevolution and,
    75, 110, 191, 195, 197
  secular Zionist elites and, 74, 75
  secular Zionist revolution and,
    74–75, 191, 197
  traditional Jewish, 74–75,
    109–10
  transit camps, 193, 195–97
Israeli Jewish collective identity, 35,
    85, 86
Israeli Jewish identity
  Israeli collective identity and, 18,
    24, 141
  Israeli democratic identity and, 2,
    17, 18, 19, 24, 28, 53, 141
  Israeli particularistic identity and,
    17
  religious Israelis and, 17
  secular Israelis and, 17
Israeli Jews
  Arab Israeli minority and, 115,
    116
  Israeli political culture and, 16
  secular, 29, 114, 115–16
Israeli lack of bill of rights
  Israeli democracy and, 5, 95
  religion and, 6, 95
Israeli lack of constitution, 101, 229
  basic laws and, 5
  Ben-Gurion and, 96, 97, 98, 107,
    109, 189
  Declaration of Independence and,
    116
  IDI and, 4, 5

Israel as sovereign collective and,
    5, 16
Israeli collective identity and, x, 5
Israeli democracy and, 5, 23, 95
Israeli identity and, x–xi
Israeli society and, 5
Jewish Diaspora and, 23
religion and, 5, 6, 83
secular foundations of Israeli
    democracy and, 169
Israeli law
  halacha and, 226–27, 236
  occupied territories and alternate,
    127
  religious law enforcement out-
    side, 225–27
  Torah law and, 226
Israeli military, 3
  religious pre-military programs
    and freedom of expression, 180
  religious soldiers refusing orders,
    213
  See also Israel Defense Forces
Israeli military service
  death and, 135–37, 237
  dilemmas of, 236–37
  halacha and, 236
  religious Israelis and, 135–39
  secular Israelis and, 135–37
  yeshiva student exemptions from,
    203
Israeli minorities
  Arab, 114, 115, 116
  diversity and divisiveness among,
    6
  Israeli democracy and, 115
Israeli national consciousness, stat-
    ism and, 110
Israeli national identity
  disagreement over, 85–86

Hebrew language and, 18, 85
occupied territories and, 129
religion and, 18, 19, 85
Israeli particularistic identity
Israeli collective identity and, 18,
19, 24
Israeli Jewish identity and, 17
Israeli universalistic identity and,
17, 18, 19
religion in, 18
Israeli political culture
consent in, 25
Israeli Jews and, 16
Israeli political sovereignty, 26, 52,
101, 233
Israeli democracy and, 16, 35,
36
Israeli politics and, 16
lack of defined borders and, 103
religious counterrevolution and,
230
secular Zionist revolution and,
44
survival struggle of Israel and,
125, 127
Zionism and, 44, 99, 100, 111,
117, 201–2
Zionist deficit and, 99, 100, 111,
117
Israeli politics
political sovereignty and, 16
See also Israeli religion and
politics
Israeli religion and democracy, x, xi,
xiv, 2–6, 14, 17, 31–32, 169
majority decisions and, 220–21
Israeli religion and politics, xiv, 2–3,
20, 24
ethos of survival and, 140
fear and, 139–40

halacha and, xv, 152, 165,
166–68, 177, 181, 201,
212–13, 237
interaction of, 163
Israeli lack of bill of rights and, 6,
95
Israeli lack of constitution and, 5,
6, 83
Nation-State Law and, 140–41
religionization of Israeli politics,
202–3, 235–38
religious counterrevolution and,
163, 164
religious Israelis on, 152
secular Israelis on, 152
See also Israeli religion and
democracy; Judaism and Israeli
politics; *specific topics*
Israeli religiosity
Israeli secularism and, 160, 171
Zionism and, 202–3
Israeli religious groups, democracy
attitudes of
descending continuum of believers, 152, 157, 181, 182, 183,
201, 214, 215, 228, 230
guidelines questions about, 153
overview, 152
religious counterrevolution and,
153
Israeli right-wing extremists, "price
tag" attacks by, 152, 247n64
Israeli secular identity, 84
Israeli secularism
collective Jewish history and,
80–81
Israeli religiosity and, 160, 171
Judaism and, 83–84
national-religious Jewish leaders'
acceptance of, 157

Israeli secularism (*continued*)
    religion in public spaces and,
        234
    religious Jews and, 74
    societal, 22, 143
    traditional Jewish immigrants
        and, 109–10
    Zionist statism and, 171
Israeli society
    Arab Israeli minority and, 114
    challenges facing, 13–14
    changes in recent decades, 201,
        212
    death and, 135
    diverse identities in, 32
    diverse Jews in, 27
    diverse minorities comprising, 6
    Holocaust and, 59
    Israeli lack of constitution and, 5
    non-Jews in, 114
    otherness and, 26
    problems of, 7, 13
    questions facing, 13
    religion and, x, 5, 17, 24
    secularism of, 22, 143
    Zionism and, 19
Israeli universalistic identity
    Israeli collective identity and, 18,
        19, 24
    Israeli democratic identity and,
        17
    Israeli particularistic identity and,
        17, 18, 19
Israeli women
    bereaved Hasidic mothers, 206–8
    exclusion from public spaces,
        203–5
    halacha and, 204
    ultra-Orthodox Jewish, 206
    Zionism and, 204, 205, 208
Israeliness, 54, 82
    Jewishness and, 67, 72

Israelis
    changing death perceptions of,
        73
    conflict over settlements, 145,
        217–21
    nonacceptance of their reality, 145
    othering by, 144
    See also specific topics
Israel-Judaism connection, 86–92,
    165
Israel's creation, 190
    Jewish Diaspora and, 94
    by UN in 1947, 154–55

Jackson family, 171–72
Janowska extermination camp,
    61–62
Jefferson, Thomas, 95, 96
Jerusalem
    Ben Yehuda Street bombing
        (1948), 154, 156
    Carmon family history in, 49–51,
        54–57, 60–61, 109, 118, 122,
        154–56, 171–72, 189–90,
        193–95
    Mea Shearim neighborhood, 49,
        50, 51, 154
    reaction to UN vote to create
        Jewish state, 154–55
    secular Jews of north, 49, 50
    secular triangle in, 171
    social services department, 195
Jewish and democratic Israeli col-
    lective, 152
Jewish collective, secularization of,
    23
Jewish collective identity
    Israeli, 35
    Jewish Diaspora and, 36–37
Jewish communities
    Jewish Diaspora and, 36–38
    non-Jews and, 37

Jewish culture
    secular, 24–25
    secularization process of, 81
    Zionist revival narratives of polit-
        ical, 16–17
    See also Hebrew culture; Israeli
        culture
Jewish Diaspora, xiii, 2, 7, 8, 19,
        33–34
    halacha and, 86, 87, 167
    Holocaust and, 59
    Israeli culture and, 53
    Israeli lack of constitution and, 23
    Israel's creation and, 94
    Jewish collective identity and,
        36–37
    Jewish communities and, 36–38
    in Jewish history, 43–44
    Jewish normative framework
        and, 81–82
    Jewish political identity and, 43
    Jewish political passivity and, 14,
        43–44, 94
    Jewish political sovereignty and,
        35–38, 44, 100, 103
    Jewish voluntarism and, 37–38
    Judaism and, 39
    otherness and, 26
    secular Zionist revolution and,
        10, 47, 53, 57, 59, 65
    secularization process and, 43
    as state of mind, 36
    traditional rabbinical mold and
        changes in, 82
    Zionism and, 10, 47, 53, 57, 59,
        65, 92, 100, 102
    Zionist pioneers and, 100
Jewish Diaspora, negation of. *See*
        negation of exile
Jewish Diaspora consciousness, col-
        lective Israeli consciousness
        and, 45, 46

Jewish history
    historical Jewish people, 39
    Israeli secularism and collective,
        80–81
    Jewish Diaspora in, 43–44
    of Jewish political passivity,
        43–44
    religion and, 92
    Zionist revolution and, 7–8, 53
Jewish identity, 85–86
    collective, 35, 36–37
    of Diaspora Jews, 43
    multicultural, multi-identity, 3,
        173
    negativity towards one's, 21–22
    Orthodox Judaism and, 27
    political, 43
    secular, 65, 126, 127
    secular Zionist, 126, 127
    Zionism and, 27–28, 57
    See also Israeli Jewish identity;
        Jewishness
Jewish law. *See halacha*
Jewish nation. *See* Israel
Jewish national liberation move-
        ment. *See* Zionist movement
Jewish nationalism, 64
    Judaism and, 90, 186
    messianic redemption and, 38
    Zionism and religious, 76,
        90–91
Jewish normative framework,
        81–82
Jewish people
    as chosen people, 88, 89
    halacha and, 91, 92
    historical, 39
    Jewish political sovereignty and,
        13, 14, 26, 35, 111
    seven assumptions about, 14
Jewish political identity, Jewish
        Diaspora and, 43

Jewish political passivity
   Jewish Diaspora and, 14, 43–44,
     94
   Jewish history of, 43–44
   messianic redemption and, 38
   Zionist revolution and, 44, 46
Jewish political sovereignty
   Ben-Gurion and, 110
   creation phase of, 1, 93–94, 99
   Jewish Diaspora and, 35–38, 44,
     100, 103
   Jewish people and, 13, 14, 26, 35,
     111
   Jewish voluntarism and, 38
   transition from sovereignty-in-
     the-making to, 94, 101, 102
   Zionism and, 100
Jewish problem, human problem
   and, 24
Jewish public domain, 173, 177
Jewish religious leaders
   Israeli secularism acceptance by
     nationalist, 157
   See also rabbis
Jewish state
   UN 1947 creation of, 154–55
   See also Israel
Jewish voluntarism
   Jewish Diaspora and, 37–38
   Jewish political sovereignty and,
     38
Jewishness
   democracy and, 228–29
   halacha's definition of, 112, 113,
     223, 229
   of Israeli collective, 48
   Israeliness and, 67, 72
   Law of Return's definition of,
     112–13
   multicultural, multi-identity defi-
     nitions of, 230

   nationhood and, 116
   religion and, 116
   secular definition of, 113–14
   Yiddishkeit (Jewishness), 15, 51,
     54, 78
   See also Jewish identity
Judaism
   crisis of, 167–68
   experiential dissonance inside
     and outside, 180–81
   inclusiveness of democracy and,
     160
   Israel connection to, 86–92
   Israeli democracy and, 31–32, 46,
     152, 160, 238
   Israeli secularism and, 83–84
   Jewish Diaspora and, 39
   Jewish nationalism and, 90, 186
   particularistic and universal attri-
     butes of, 24
   as political religion, 20, 238
   in religion and politics interac-
     tion, 164
   religion in public spaces and,
     165
   religious counterrevolution,
     democracy and, 160, 238
   religious Zionism on, 157
   Zionism and, 76–77, 89, 90,
     169–70
   See also specific topics
Judaism and Israeli politics, 20, 165
   See also Israeli religion and poli-
     tics; *specific topics*

Kedar, Nir, 107, 110
Kibbutz Sde Boker, 106–7
kibbutzim, 58
Knesset (Israeli parliament), 4, 98,
   112, 113, 162, 168
Kolech (Your Voice), 203, 204, 205

Kook, Avraham Yitzhak Hacohen,
91, 92, 178
  religious counterrevolution and,
    188, 189
  religious Zionism and, 185–88
  secular Zionism and, 186–88
Kookism, 187, 188, 200
Koren, Adolph, 131
Koren, Henek, 55–57, 131
Koren, Maya, 55–57
Koren, Shimon, 131
Koren family, 55–57, 131

labor movement, religious Zionism
  and, 151, 177
labor party (Mapai), 98, 106, 107,
    117, 190, 191, 193
labor Zionist movement, 15, 106,
    176–77
Lamm, Zvi, 51
Land of Israel (pillar of religious
  Zionism), 201, 211
The Last Sea, 33–34
law. *See* Israeli law; religious law
Law of Return, 112–13
Leib, Henia (grandmother), 10–11,
    33
Leib, Hirsch, 10
Leibish, 33
Leibowitz, Yeshayahu, 39, 167–68,
    181
Lokerman, Zvi Aryeh, 122
Lonek (mother's brother), 33, 69
Lorberbaum, Menachem, xv

Madison, James, 95–96, 111
Maimon, Yaakov, 193, 194
Mapai (Labor) party, 98, 106, 107,
    117, 190, 191, 193
Marcus, Bernard, 3
Mattis, James, 138

Mea Shearim (Jerusalem neighbor-
  hood), 49, 50, 51, 154
Meimad party, 199, 200
Melamed, Eliezer, 208–10
Memorial Day for Israel's Fallen
  Soldiers, 69, 73, 74, 122, 123,
    132, 133, 135
messianic redemption
  Jewish nationalism and, 38
  Jewish political passivity and, 38
  religious Zionism and, 153, 185,
    197, 198, 222–23, 247n65
  secular sovereignty and, 174
  secular Zionism and, 185, 198
  sovereignty and, 198
messianism, approaches to Zionism
  and, 174
Mizrahi (Middle Eastern Jews), xv
Muhammad, 164
Muslim Arabs, 18, 243n1, 243n5
Muslim countries, religion in public
  spaces and, 165

nation of Israel (pillar of religious
  Zionism), 201, 211
national collective identities, 141
national consciousness
  statism and Israeli, 110
  of US, 18
National Religious Party (NRP),
    190–91, 228
nationalism, religion and, 88–89,
    91–92
national-religious Jews, 29,
    115–16
  democracy and, 180
  identity and religiousness beliefs,
    180
  Israeli secularism acceptance by
    leaders of, 157
  rabbinical elite, 211–12

national-religious Jews (*continued*)
  religion-state relations beliefs,
    180
  religious Zionism and, 76, 90–91,
    177, 179
national-religious movement, 187
national-religious public, 116, 173,
  174
nationhood, Jewishness and, 116
Nation-State Law. *See* Basic Law:
  Israel as the Nation-State of
  the Jewish People
Naveh, Eyal, 59
Nazis, 21
  See also Holocaust
negation of exile, 26, 54, 64, 67, 68,
  113, 230
  Holocaust victims and, 69–70, 73
  Israeli immigrants and, 197
  Zionism and, 10, 47, 57, 59, 65,
    73, 74, 76–78, 101, 213–14
Neuman, Kalman, 212, 213
new Israelis, 70
new Jews, xv, 73
  Diaspora Jews and, 59–60
  fallen Israeli soldiers and, 69
  old Jews and, 68, 126, 170
  traditional Judaism, 76
  Zionism and, 27, 53, 74
non-Jews
  halacha on, 216, 218
  inclusion of, 114, 115
  Israeli citizenship and, 140, 180,
    215
  Israeli identity and, 19
  in Israeli society, 114
  Jewish communities and, 37
  rabbinical interpretations on,
    214–17
  rights of, 214–17, 220–21

Nordau, Max, 125–26, 246n59
normalcy
  Ben-Gurionist statism and, 110,
    111
  clash with anomaly in Israel, 102,
    239
  collective Israeli consciousness
    and craving for, 125
  dialectic of exile versus, 102, 103
  Israeli founders and, 111
  Zionist process and craving for,
    101
Norris, Pippa, 140
NRP. *See* National Religious Party

obedience
  to authority, 138–39, 150–51
  democracy and, 150, 151
  dilemma of, 150–51
occupied territories
  alternate Israeli law in, 127
  as anomalous territorialization,
    127
  borders of Israel and, 127, 128
  ethos of survival and, 127, 128,
    130
  Gaza, 124, 127, 137, 138,
    175–76, 210
  Israeli national identity and, 129
  Peace Index and, 129–30
  Sinai, 127
  West Bank, 127
old Jews, xv
  Israeli immigrants and, 170
  new Jews and, 68, 126, 170
  secular Zionist revolution and,
    170–71, 230
Operation Protective Edge (Gaza),
  124, 137, 138
Orthodox Judaism, xv, 6

Israeli identity and, 2–3
Jewish identity and, 27
See also ultra-Orthodox Jews
Orthodox monopoly, xv–xvi, 2,
    18–19, 82, 238
Orthodox public, 174
Oslo Accords, 201
otherness
    differentness and, 25–26, 227
    ethnocentrism and, 227
    Israeli society and, 26
    Jewish Diaspora and, 26
    US and, 227–28
Oz, Amos, 155
Oz Veshalom movement, 199

Palestinian-Israeli conflict, xi, 6, 85,
    103, 115, 129, 199–200,
    246n62
    halacha and, 168
    leading religious Zionist rabbis
        and, 208–10, 215–16
    Peace Index and, 130
    terrorist bombings, 131
Pedaya, Haviva, 222, 251n163
Persico, Tomer, 222
political messianism stream, of reli-
    gious Zionism, 199, 200
political sovereignty
    overview, 35, 36
    See also Israeli political sover-
        eignty; Jewish political
        sovereignty; sovereignty
political Zionism, 100
politics. *See* Israeli politics; religion
    and politics
"price tag" attacks, 152, 247n64
public leadership, *halacha* and,
    166
public spaces

Israeli women's exclusion from,
    203–5
See also religion in public spaces
public sphere
    halacha and, 181
    religion, secularism and, 30–31

rabbis
    courts of, 225
    IDF and, 236
    interpretations of non-Jews,
        214–17
    national-religious elite, 211–12
    settlements and, 208–10, 212–16,
        218–20
    sovereignty of, 227
    traditional rabbinical mold and
        Jewish Diaspora, 82
    See also religious Zionist rabbis
Rabin, Yitzhak, 68, 248n76
    assassination, 1, 94, 117, 160–61,
        182, 201, 208, 210, 211,
        212–13, 215
Rachel the Poetess, 205, 250n137
Ravitzky, Avi, 153, 173–74, 175,
    186–88, 199, 200
Rawls, John, 30–31
reactionary populism, 239
reason, common ground for faith
    and, 29–32
Rechnitz, Ido, 225–27
Reform Judaism, xv
Reines, Isaac Jacob, 185
religion
    IDF and, 137–39
    Israeli national identity and, 18,
        19, 85
    in Israeli particularistic identity, 18
    Israeli society and, x, 5, 17, 24
    Jewish history and, 92

religion (*continued*)
  Jewishness and, 116
  nationalism and, 88–89, 91–92
  public sphere, secularism and,
    30–31
  secularism and, 30–31, 84, 166,
    234–35, 238
  territorial nations and, 90
  US and, 87–88
religion and democracy, 162, 163
  secular foundations of democracy
    and, 166, 220, 221, 223, 237
  See also Israeli religion and
    democracy
religion and politics, 3, 159–60
  Christianity and, 163
  democracy states and, 164
  Islam and, 164, 165
  Judaism and, 164
  political hegemony in name of
    religion, 238
  questions about global develop-
    ments in, 240
  reciprocal connection between,
    163
  security and, 140
  See also Israeli religion and poli-
    tics; religion and democracy;
    specific topics
religion in public spaces
  Christian democracies and, 164
  Israel and, 165, 236
  Israeli democracy and, 235
  Israeli secularism and, 234
  Judaism and, 165
  Muslim countries and, 165
  religious counterrevolution and,
    235
  sacralization of, 234–37
religion-state relations, 176
  conflict in, 173–74

national-religious Jews' beliefs
  about, 180
religious counterrevolution, 67, 201
  democracy attitudes of Israeli
    religious groups and, 153
  dialectic process of, 19–20
  dilemma of obedience and, 150,
    151
  factors powering, 111–12
  growth in recent decades, 211,
    221
  halacha and, 172, 225–26
  Israeli democracy and, 153, 160,
    212, 229, 230, 235, 238, 239
  Israeli immigrants and, 75, 110,
    191, 195, 197
  Israeli political sovereignty and,
    230
  in Israeli religion and politics,
    163, 164
  Judaism, democracy and, 160, 238
  Kook and, 188, 189
  religion in public spaces and, 235
  religious Zionism and, 159, 182
  secular foundations of Israeli
    democracy and, 233
  secular Israelis and, 223
  secular Zionist revolution and,
    42, 53, 57, 65, 75, 76, 91, 152,
    153, 157, 170, 182, 186, 223,
    229
  Six-Day War and, 198
  stages, 185
  Zionist deficit and, 111, 170
  Zionist process and, 19–20, 152,
    172
religious education, 237
religious Israelis
  fallen Israeli soldiers and, 135–36
  Israeli democratic identity and,
    17

Israeli identity and, 6, 17
Israeli Jewish identity and, 17
Israeli military service and,
  135–39
on Israeli religion and politics, 152
secular Israelis and, 6, 17, 28,
  135–37, 144, 152
See also national-religious Jews
religious Jews, 170
  as chosen people, 88, 89
  different views of, 178–79
  in *halachic* community and addi-
    tional communities, 157–58
  Israeli secularism and, 74
  secular Jews and, 75–76, 159,
    189–90, 217, 250n138
  See also national-religious Jews
religious law
  enforcement outside state system,
    225–27
  See also halacha
religious Zionism, 17, 161, 205
  changes in recent decades, 201,
    212
  community of Israel, 152
  Declaration of Independence and,
    188
  democratic values and, 177–78
  descending continuum of believ-
    ers and, 228, 230
  different groups, views and
    approaches, 178–82
  dilemma of obedience in, 151
  early view of, 174
  ethnocentrism of extreme, 227
  foundation, 171
  halacha and, 159, 165, 173, 181,
    182
  halachic rulings, secular founda-
    tions of democracy and,
    168–69

on independence and messianic
  redemption, 153, 247n65
Israeli constitution and, 188, 189
Israeli women and, 208
on Judaism, 157
Kook and, 185–88
labor movement and, 151, 177
Land of Israel pillar of, 201,
  211
leadership and control of Israel,
  221–22
liberal, 182, 183
messianic redemption and, 153,
  185, 197, 198, 222–23,
  247n65
nation of Israel pillar of, 201, 211
national, 177
national-religious Jews and, 76,
  90–91, 177, 179
NRP and, 190–91, 228
Oz Veshalom movement, 199
political messianism stream of,
  199, 200
political restraint stream of,
  199–200
Protestant and Catholic
  approaches to, 178–79
rabbis of, 222
radicalization in 1990s, 203,
  204
religious counterrevolution and,
  159–82
sanctification of, 235
secular Israelis and, 159
secular Zionism and, 158–60,
  166, 169, 171, 173, 182,
  186–87, 198
secularism and, 173, 178, 179,
  182
sexual abuse and, 223–24, 225
Six-Day War and, 199, 200

religious Zionism (*continued*)
  on source of authority, 143
  Takana Forum, 223–25
  theological and ideological
    dimensions of, 165–66
  three pillars of religious national-
    ist concept of, 201, 211
  Torah of Israel pillar of, 201,
    211, 221
  Zionist religion and, 200
religious Zionist rabbis, 222,
    225–27
  Palestinian-Israeli conflict and
    leading, 208–10, 215–16
  Rabin's assassination and leading,
    208–11, 212–13, 215
  settlements and leading, 208–10
Rosenak, Avinoam, 178

Sabina (mother's sister), 33
sabras (native-born Israelis), xiii
sacralization of public spaces
  Israeli culture and, 237
  religionization of Israeli politics
    and, 235–37
Sagi, Avi, 157, 165, 166, 168, 173,
    187
Sarah (mother's sister), 33
Sasson, Hillel Ben, 221
Schiff, Ze'ev, 196
Scholem, Gershom, 79–80, 153
Schwartz, Dudi, 182
Schweid, Eliezer, 83–84
Scrolls of Fire, 70–72
secular foundations of democracy,
    137, 143
  halacha and, 152, 168–69, 177
  religion and, 166, 220, 221, 223,
    237

secular foundations of Israeli
    democracy, 74
  Israeli lack of constitution and,
    169
  religious counterrevolution and,
    233
  secular Zionist revolution and,
    170, 229
  vulnerabilities and weaknesses of,
    x, 4, 5, 6, 16, 20, 114, 169,
    189, 191
secular foundations of Zionism,
    126, 170, 171, 230–31
secular Israeli Jews, 29, 114,
    115–16
secular Israeli society, 22
  death narrative and, 143
secular Israelis, 170
  belief in God and, 82
  fallen Israeli soldiers and, 135–36
  Holocaust victims and, 78
  Israeli democratic identity and,
    17
  Israeli identity and, 6, 17, 81
  Israeli Jewish identity and, 17
  Israeli military service and,
    135–37
  on Israeli religion and politics,
    152
  Jewish, 29, 114, 115–16
  religious counterrevolution and,
    223
  religious Israelis and, 6, 17, 28,
    135–37, 144, 152
  religious Zionism and, 159, 166
secular Jewish identity, 65
  Zionist, 126, 127
secular Jewishness, national-ethnic,
    103

secular Jews, xvi, 22, 161
  Israeli, 29, 114, 115–16
  male Israeli, 29
  of north Jerusalem, 49, 50
  religious Jews and, 75–76, 159,
    189–90, 217, 250n138
secular Judaism
  culture of, 24–25
  secularization process, 81
secular law, *halacha* and, 161–62,
    167
secular sanctification, 235–36
secular sovereignty, 174
secular Zionism
  foundations, 126, 170, 171,
    230–31
  Kook and, 186–88
  messianic redemption and, 185,
    198
  religious Zionism and, 158–60,
    166, 169, 171, 173, 182,
    186–87, 198
  sanctification of, 235
secular Zionist revolution, 17, 19
  acculturation and, 46
  collective Israeli consciousness
    and, 44–47, 79
  Declaration of Independence and,
    112
  foundations, 230–31
  IDF and, 126
  Israeli democracy and, 81, 111,
    169, 229
  Israeli immigrants and, 74–75,
    191, 197
  Israeli political sovereignty and,
    44
  Jewish Diaspora and, 10, 47, 53,
    57, 59, 65

old Jews and, 170–71, 230
  overview, 41–42
  religious counterrevolution and,
    42, 53, 57, 65, 75, 76, 91, 152,
    153, 157, 170, 182, 186, 223,
    229
  traditional Judaism and, 76–77
  Zionist deficit of, 14, 41–42, 45,
    46–47, 75
secular Zionists
  halacha and, 182
  Israeli immigrants and elite, 74,
    75
secularism
  of democratic states, 166
  public sphere, religion and, 30–31
  religion and, 30–31, 84, 166,
    234–35, 238
  religious Zionism and, 173, 178,
    179, 182
secularization
  acculturation and, 45
  of Christian countries, 23, 42–43,
    45, 76, 81
  of Jewish collective, 23
  Jewish Diaspora and process of,
    43
  religion and, 234–35, 238
  of Western world, 42–43, 45
secularization process
  of Christianity, 81
  of Judaism, 81
security
  Hebrew language and, 142
  religion, politics and, 140
  survival struggle of Israel and,
    128
Sephardi (Jewish descendants in
    North Africa), xv

settlements, 199, 201
  halacha and, 209–10, 212–13
  IDI and, 217–21
  Israelis and conflict over, 145,
    217–21
  leading religious Zionist rabbis
    and, 208–10
  rabbis, 208–10, 212–16, 218–20
  withdrawal from Gaza, 175–76,
    210
  Yesha Council of Jewish Settle-
    ments, 217, 218
Shaked, Ayelet, 228–29
Shalev, Eran, 123–24, 175
Shalev, Gabi, 124, 133, 135
Shalev, Shaul, 122, 123–24,
  133–35
Shapira, Anita, 91
Shapira, Yehoshua, 218–19
Shapira, Yitzhak, 218
Sheleg, Yair, 214, 216
Short, William, 95
Shultz, George, 3
Simon, Ernst, 178
Simon, Uriel, 161–62
Sinai, 127
Six-Day War (1967), 122, 124, 127,
  129, 145, 190, 250n132
  religious counterrevolution and,
    198
  religious Zionism and, 199, 200
Smith, Anthony, 88–89
Smooha, Sami, 116
Sophocles (*Antigone*), 149–50
sovereignty
  establishment of, 99
  messianic redemption and, 198
  rabbinical, 227
  secular, 174

social imagination and, 99
territorial nations and, 99, 101
See also political sovereignty
sovereignty-in-the-making, Jewish
  sovereignty transition from,
  94, 101, 102
Sprinzak, Ehud, 200
state
  halacha involvement in affairs of,
    174, 176, 226–27
  religious law enforcement outside,
    225–27
  Torah laws and laws of, 226
  See also Jewish state; religion-
    state relations
State Education Law of 1953, 108–9
statism
  of Ben-Gurion, 107–8, 110–13
  Israeli national consciousness
    and, 110
  normalcy and Ben-Gurionist,
    110, 111
  Zionist, 171
  Zionist deficit and, 111, 113
Stern, Yedidia, 157, 166, 167, 174,
  176, 177, 223–24, 225–27
Strauss, Leo, 24, 94
survival struggle of Israel, 124
  ethos of survival, 125, 126, 127,
    128–29, 130, 139, 140
  Israeli political sovereignty and,
    125, 127
  occupied territories and, 127, 128
  repercussions on daily life, 125
  security agenda and, 128
  Zionism, 126, 129

Takana Forum, 223–25
Tal, Uriel, 198

Teitelbaum, Joel, 21, 22
Temple Mount, 223, 251n164
territorial nations
  acculturation in, 52–53
  religion and, 90
  sovereignty and, 99, 101
territorialization
  anomalous and organic, 127
  of national-cultural values and
    borders of Israel, 128
terrorist bombings, 131
  Ben Yehuda Street bombing
    (1948), 154, 156
  November 22, 1968, 156–57
terrorists, Jewish Underground,
  211
tikkun (repair), 1
"To the End of the Land"
  (Grossman), 134–35
Torah
  democracy and, 214
  Israeli law and law of, 226
  opinion, 203, 212, 213, 222
  See also halacha
Torah of Israel (pillar of religious
  Zionism), 201, 211, 221
traditional Jews, 170
  Israeli immigrant, 74–75, 109–10
traditional Judaism
  new Jews and, 76
  secular Zionist revolution and,
    76–77
  See also Conservative Judaism
Tzachor, Zeev, 97
Tzipori, Mordechai, 133–34

ultra-Orthodox Jews, 49
  anti-Zionist violent protests by,
    190

Committee for the Purity of the
  Camp, 225
Israeli man, 29
sexual abuse and, 225
Shas party, 203, 250n136
women, 206
ultra-Orthodox public, 174
United Nations (UN)
  Charter of, 114
  creation of Jewish State and Arab
    state (1947) by, 154–55
United States (US)
  Civil War, 18
  creation of Constitution of,
    95–96
  democracy of, 111
  founding fathers, 95–96, 111
  national consciousness of, 18
  otherness, ethnocentrism, white
    nationalism in, 227–28
  religiosity of, 87–88
University of Wisconsin, Madison,
  20–21
Unna, Moshe, 199, 250n133
US. *See* United States

Vider Cohen, Ayelet, 204–5
Volapük, 79–80, 244n31

Wallerstein, Pinchas, 217–18,
  220
Walzer, Michael, 77, 137, 170,
  231
War of Independence, 15, 54, 121,
  122, 156
Warhaftig, Zerach, 188, 189
Weinstein, Esti, 206, 207, 208
Welichker Wells, Leon, 61–62
West Bank, 127

West German constitution, 96, 98
Western world, secularization of,
    42–43, 45
Westphalia treaties, xv, 45, 163
Winter, Ofer, 137, 138, 139

Yehoshua, A. B., 90
Yesha Council of Jewish Settle-
    ments, 217, 218
yeshiva
    hesder, 211
    student exemptions from military
        service, 203
Yeshurun synagogue, 49–51
Yiddish, 65–67
Yiddishkeit (Jewishness), 15, 51, 54,
    78
yizkor memorial prayer, 72–73,
    74
Yom Kippur War (1973), 15,
    122, 133–35, 144, 145,
    250n132

Ze'ev (grandfather), 33
Zionism, xvi, 2, 6
    approaches to messianism and,
        174
    education and streams of,
        108–9
    Hebrew language revival and,
        64–65, 79, 170
    history, 200, 201
    Israeli political sovereignty and,
        44, 99, 100, 111, 117, 201–2
    Israeli religiosity and, 202–3
    Israeli society and, 19
    Israeli women and, 204, 205,
        208

Jewish Diaspora and, 10, 47, 53,
    57, 59, 65, 92, 100, 102
Jewish identity and, 27–28, 57
Jewish political sovereignty and,
    100
Judaism and, 76–77, 89, 90,
    169–70
Labor Stream, 109
Liberal Stream, 109
narratives of revival of, 16–17
negation of exile and, 10, 47, 57,
    59, 65, 73, 74, 76–78, 101,
    213–14
new Jews and, 27, 53, 74
pioneers of, 100
political, 100
Religious Stream, 109
secular Hebrew culture and,
    57–58, 64–65
survival struggle of Israel and,
    126, 129
See also religious Zionism;
    secular Zionism
Zionist deficit
    collective Israeli consciousness
        and, 46–47
    Israeli democracy and, 16, 46, 47,
        92, 111
    Israeli political sovereignty and,
        99, 100, 111, 117
    overcoming, 48
    religious counterrevolution and,
        111, 170
    of secular Zionist revolution, 14,
        41–42, 45, 46–47, 75
    statism and, 111, 113
Zionist ideology and, 127
Zionist process and, 41

Zionist identity, secular Jewish, 126,
127
Zionist ideology
survival struggle of Israel and, 126
Zionist deficit and, 127
Zionist movement, 1, 41, 42, 44,
46, 64–65, 90, 200
labor, 15, 106, 176–77
leaders of, 100, 101
Zionist process
craving for normalcy in, 101
Israeli democracy and, 20
religious counterrevolution and,
19–20, 152, 172

vulnerabilities and weaknesses of,
20
Zionist deficit and, 41
Zionist revolution, 9, 10, 27
Jewish history and, 7–8, 53
Jewish political passivity and, 44,
46
See also secular Zionist
revolution
Zionist statism, 171
Zionists
on Israeli collective identity,
108
See also secular Zionists